INSIDE A CLASS ACTION

this action is supported

by a grant from

JEWISH FEDERATION OF GREATER HARTFORD

INSIDE
A CLASS ACTION

THE HOLOCAUST AND
THE SWISS BANKS

JANE SCHAPIRO

TERRACE BOOKS
A trade imprint of the University of Wisconsin Press

Terrace Books, a division of the University of Wisconsin Press, takes its name from the Memorial Union Terrace, located at the University of Wisconsin–Madison. Since its inception in 1907, the Wisconsin Union has provided a venue for students, faculty, staff, and alumni to debate art, music, politics, and the issues of the day. It is a place where theater, music, drama, literature, dance, outdoor activities, and major speakers are made available to the campus and the community. To learn more about the Union, visit www.union.wisc.edu.

Terrace Books
A trade imprint of the University of Wisconsin Press
1930 Monroe Street, 3rd Floor
Madison, Wisconsin 53711-2059
uwpress.wisc.edu

3 Henrietta Street
London WC2E 8LU, England
eurospanbookstore.com

Printed in the United States of America

Library of Congress Cataloging-in-Publication Data

Schapiro, Jane.
Inside a class action : the Holocaust and the Swiss banks / Jane Schapiro.
p.   cm.
Includes bibliographical references and index.
ISBN 0-299-19330-6 (cloth: alk. paper)
1. Trials—New York (N.Y.).   2. Class actions—New York (N.Y.).
3. Unjust enrichment—United States.   4. Holocaust, Jewish (1939–1945).
5. Banks and banking, Swiss.   I. Title.
KF228.H65 S52   2003
347.73´53—dc21   2003005663

ISBN 978-0-299-19334-8 (pbk.: alk. paper)
ISBN 978-0-299-19333-1 (e-book)

For my father,
who believed in the value of this story,

For my mother,
who believed that I could write it,

and for Scott,
whose encouragement allowed me
to believe in both.

Here and there people wanted to know everything about all aspects of what we so poorly call the Holocaust. Yet, somehow its simple economic aspect seems to have been utterly neglected.

Why? Is it that we all felt the memory of the tragedy to be so sacred that we preferred not to talk about its concrete, financial, and material implications? Is it that the task of protecting the memory was so noble, so painful, and so urgent that we simply felt it undignified to think of anything else—and surely not of bank accounts? In truth, we feel reticent to talk about it even now.

—Elie Wiesel, Washington Conference on
Holocaust-Era Assets, November 30, 1998

Contents

Acknowledgments

The Swiss banks case is a mixture of stories that can be understood from many different vantage points. Each perspective offers truth as well as prejudice, and hence all are imperfect and incomplete. This book is based upon my observations, interviews, and research since 1996, when the first class action against the Swiss banks was filed. I attended court hearings, Senate and House Banking Committee hearings, press conferences, and meetings and spoke to sources on all sides of the case. I received broad access to information from Michael Hausfeld, one of the lead counsel for the plaintiffs. In addition to documents, notes, and my own personal observations, I have drawn upon more than thirty hours of privately taped interviews with Hausfeld, as well as our numerous phone calls and meetings. He never asked to read or censor my writing. Because I was allowed to shadow Hausfeld, I was privy to the myriad emotions that he experienced throughout this case, and thus this story reflects his own particular journey through this class action.

In an effort to get a fuller perspective, I interviewed more than forty other individuals, many of whom wished not to be named. They were enormously helpful and provided sources for meetings that took place. I also traveled to Switzerland and interviewed Swiss bankers, lawyers, and a Jewish leader who were intimately involved in the events. There were some individuals who did not wish to meet with me. Attempts to speak with several attorneys, officials, and Jewish leaders were rebuffed or ignored. To compensate, I took advantage of the continuing media coverage of the case. I followed the coverage in the *New York Times*, the *Washington Post*, the *Wall Street Journal*, and the multitude of Jewish journals. I also drew upon the transcripts from court and congressional hearings, as well as other books and articles related to the subject.

In addition to Michael Hausfeld, there are several other individuals who proved vital in my ability to grasp this story. Miriam Kleiman was always available to answer my questions or lead me to documents and sources that could provide me with the answers. I am deeply indebted to her. I thank Susan Bollen for her patience with me. I appeared in front of her desk daily, asking for documents and memos. I am appreciative of all of the people who granted me interviews and offered their particular perspectives. I am particularly indebted to one individual who asked to remain anonymous. He met with me many times in an effort to help me understand the nonplaintiffs' perspective. He also helped me reconstruct meetings in which negotiations took place. The archivist Greg Bradsher broadened my understanding of what was occurring at the National Archives and of how the story was literally unfolding through documents.

Aside from those who helped me to attain the story, there are numerous people who gave me encouragement in the writing of it. Ellen Oppenheim read the manuscript's many versions and critiqued and commented on each one. She was an essential part of the writing process. I am also fortunate to come from a family of writers and readers. My sisters, Barbara and Ellen Schapiro, both read and offered suggestions on the manuscript, as did my parents, Nancy and Ed. Barbara helped me through the marketing stage, as well. She was always positive and optimistic, both necessary ingredients in getting through the long haul of completing a book. I thank Al Lefcowitz, of the Writers' Center, for reminding me again and again to stay in the "active voice," Naomi Thiers for keeping my writing grounded, David Hendin for his experienced wisdom, Arial Goldberger for her editorial comments, and Raphael Kadushin, at the University of Wisconsin Press. I also want to thank my friends Debi Leekoff, whose company on walks gave me respite from the isolation of the computer, and Linda White, who provided me with a place to stay during my many trips to New York. And, last, I want to thank Scott, Naomi, Tamara, and Eliana for their unquestioning patience. They never once complained about the piles of papers covering the living room floor.

Thank you.

INSIDE A CLASS ACTION

Introduction

A light drizzle was falling outside as attorneys in the Swiss banks' case entered the gray concrete building of the U.S. Eastern District Courthouse in Brooklyn on November 29, 1999. Carrying their usual array of papers and leather briefcases, the defense and plaintiffs' lawyers talked among themselves as they waited for the elevator to take them to the second floor. The mood was more relaxed than in past gatherings. Nobody was huddled in a corner reviewing last-minute maneuvers or studying newly released documents. No one was whispering or arguing. The men exchanged handshakes and spoke in calm voices. They were on their way to Judge Edward Korman's courtroom to attend yet another hearing in the three-year-old case. Unlike at previous hearings, however, today they would not be debating or pleading a motion. This time they would all be sitting on the same side of the table, listening. Today, it would be the plaintiffs—survivors and heirs of the Holocaust—who would address the court.

"Good morning, ladies and gentlemen," Judge Korman began. "When I usually preside over proceedings in this courtroom, it's full of immigrants who are about to take the oath of citizenship, and I always begin by saying that it's an honor and privilege to be able to preside over such a ceremony.

"It is equally an honor and privilege for me to have participated in this case and to be here this morning to listen to you and to hear your views about the settlement of what has been known as the Swiss Banks' cases."

As Korman and the attorneys made opening remarks, several elderly men and women in the courtroom whispered to each other in Russian. Others sat in silence, their hands folded on their laps. Still others reread their notes, readying themselves for their turn at the microphone. The majority of the attendees were Holocaust survivors who had come to voice their opinions about a settlement that had been negotiated more than a year earlier between their lawyers and the Swiss banks. As class members in a class-action suit, they were there to pronounce whether, in their view, the settlement was fair and just.

"Fair, reasonable, and adequate?" one man's voice echoed through the courtroom. "And the Swiss lawyer was telling us complete closure. You want complete closure? Bring me back my father, bring me back my uncle, bring me back my whole family in Poland. It's not fair. Like someone said here, we are pragmatists; we have to accept what is offered; we know there is not much time. So we settle. This is a settlement, but, by all means, don't call it fair or adequate. It can never be complete closure."

One by one, survivors came to the front of the room. Some of the men were dressed in coats and ties. Others had on thick wool sweaters and rubber galoshes. Several of the survivors stumbled through their speeches with heavy accents or spoke with the help of Russian translators.

"My name is Naomi Nagel. I am a sole survivor from my parents. My parents were originally from Czechoslovakia and when the Nazis came in, they fled to—they wanted to flee to England, but they never made it. They went to south of France, where I was born. Then I was two-and-a-half and three years old. First my father was taken and then my mother to Auschwitz. . . ."

"Your Honor, my name is David Handwoho. I'm a Holocaust survivor. I also participated in the uprising in the Warsaw Ghetto. I was in various camps. For four and half years, I've been in camps, in and out, working camps as well as the concentration camps. . . ."

The plaintiffs had come to speak about the present settlement but found themselves returning to their pasts. Over and over they traveled back to those moments when their lives had shattered irrevocably.

"I'm a plaintiff in this action," one woman asserted. "Not only I experienced a material loss because of the damage of my properties, but also physical. During the evacuation from Odessa by ship, my ship was bombed by the Nazi planes. I was thrown out to sea. I was rescued, but because of the tremendous number of injuries, I lost my vision. . . ."

As they spoke, the long line of lawyers sat quietly. For the first time in this case, Korman was wearing his black robe and sitting on his bench. Fairness hearings are mandated in class-action settlements and are often the last detail in finalizing a settlement. For the survivors who had come to court, this hearing assumed more importance than a last-minute detail. This was their opportunity to tell their stories in an American courtroom. Their words and memories would be inscribed in the public record—a fact not lost on those who, in tearful reminiscence, referred to the silence of their deceased family members.

"My name is Alice Fisher. . . . This settlement is by no means sufficient or fair or reasonable . . . but we have no choice. . . . Anyhow, as you heard here, this is not just a material issue; this is a moral issue. . . . This puts the Holocaust on the map against all the denials. So with this, I am satisfied, at least that my parents' and brothers' memory will not be assaulted like they were."

"Your Honor, ladies and gentlemen," one man stated, "I'm sure today's hearing will be entered in the history of jurisprudence. I, as a Second World War veteran, listening to these speeches today, felt like I'm listening to the Nuremberg process all over again."

Not everyone who spoke believed that the settlement should be approved. The monetary sum wasn't enough. Nevertheless, the survivors had come to voice their opinions. Standing before the judge, they shouted, they cried, they argued. The class-action settlement forced the court to acknowledge the injustices that the plaintiffs, one by one, were listing. The survivors had come to participate in a democratic judicial process. This opportunity, more than any money or apology, might be as close as they were going to get to claiming justice.

On October 21, 1996, Michael Hausfeld, representing the plaintiffs, along with a team of lawyers, filed a class-action complaint against Union Bank of Switzerland, Swiss Bank Corporation, and Credit Suisse on behalf of Holocaust victims. The suit accused the banks of, among other things, acting as the chief financiers for Nazi Germany and thus of being accessories to the crime of genocide. Hausfeld wanted to use the suit to prove that the banks not only concealed and refused to return millions of dollars in dormant accounts but that they acted as a conduit for looted assets and slave labor profits. Such behavior, according to his suit, violated a code of ethics known as customary international law. This code is what gave the 1946 Nuremberg Tribunal its power to convict Nazi Party officials and private German bankers. It would also, Hausfeld hoped, give him and his team of lawyers the power to impose a civil liability on the Swiss banks. Clinging to that hope, Hausfeld worked pro bono on the case for more than two years.

While the class action was not the first or the only force that was exerted against the Swiss banks, it was, in the end, the mechanism that could bring about a final resolution. Nongovernmental organizations, government officials, politicians, and financial officers all played important roles, but the legal device of a class action could offer what the banks needed most—total peace.

Unlike political pressures and economic sanctions, a class action can both threaten and relieve. It is a legal forum through which thousands of individuals, united in interest and represented by one or more class members, can enforce their equitable rights. By using the power of a court-ordered discovery, the class of plaintiffs can force defendants to disclose documents and other materials in their possession. Such disclosure can be particularly threatening to insular institutions such as the Swiss banks. This threat can often be enough to move defendants to the negotiating table. The promise of relief can make them settle. Class actions can provide relief by offering legal releases that prohibit class members from pursuing similar suits against the same defendants. This ability to threaten and relieve empowers a class action and allows it to become the magnet toward which all other efforts eventually gravitate.

This book tells the story of one such class action as experienced by one of its lead attorneys.

1

Winds of Truth

Your Honor, Mr. Eduard Corman!

. . . I was boren in Bucovina, wich is the northeren part of Romania.

I had an UnKel, his name was Schye Heinrich. He has no children. My name was like his mothers name, and he loves me very much.

He taled me that he put aloth of mony in a bank in Switzerland. He said to me all the time: Bettyca! My dear child! you will be rich, verry rich. He died on his way to the Geto. He wanted to give me a smal suitcase with Documants, but a Soldier lift up his Revolver, and wanted to kill me. My mother pushed me away, so that I survived.

I have written to Swiss, but they answered me that they didn't find money. I am convinsed that it was money and papers, but someone distroied that.

I want your help. I came to Israel in APRIL 1944 direct from Geto and Concentration camps. It is a long story. I was biten fisicly and emotionaly. I have three Children. One son is ill, he served in the arme three years. I want to help him befor it's to late. I wayt for your answer, and your help. May God help all of us.

Letter to Judge Korman from Bracha Alon

On Thursday, June 29, 1995, Hans Baer was about to do something unheard of in the world of Swiss banking. As chairman of Bank Julius Baer, founded and owned by his family, he was going to break Swiss banking secrecy and issue a press release about an account at his Zurich bank. He wanted to clarify things. Eight days earlier, the *Wall Street Journal* had published an article about dormant Holocaust accounts in Swiss banks. Entitled "Secret Legacies," the article had focused on the family of the Holocaust victim Moses Blum. Blum's three daughters had searched for their father's funds in 1987. Their mother had mentioned Bank Julius Baer in her will, and the daughters had wanted to know whether their father had opened an account at the bank. The bank's response, according to the *Journal*, had been less than forthcoming.

"After first demanding a fee of 100 Swiss francs, about $86, for the administrative work, the Julius Baer Bank wrote back icily. Neither Mr. nor Mrs. Blum appeared to have been clients during the previous ten years, the letter said. 'Under Swiss law, banks are obliged to keep their records for a period of ten years only,'" it added, "'and therefore our search cannot go any further.'"[1]

This was the second article that had been published about dormant accounts in the past six months, and both had mentioned the Blum daughters and Bank Julius Baer. Baer was concerned. Were the accusations true? Did Moses Blum have an account in his bank, and had it never been claimed? Did his bank really respond in such a coldhearted manner? The more he dwelled on the June 21 article, the more he wanted to find out the facts. He was doubtful that he would find a Blum account. His bank had already searched in 1962 for Holocaust accounts and had found few. To him, the reason for this was obvious. His family was Jewish. How many European Jews would have wanted to put their money in a Jewish-owned bank? Even if the bank was in Switzerland, Germany could have invaded the small, neutral country at any time. The Baer bank would have been the first to go.

Baer's grandfather, Julius Baer, had founded the bank in 1890. Unlike many Swiss banks that had done a swift business during World War II, Bank Julius Baer's assets had declined. In fact, they had dipped below their 1920 level. Baer's grandfather and uncles had traded in securities to compensate for their losses, but in the end they had had to mortgage the building to cover their costs. The bank did survive, and after the war it regained its strength. The bank was now prospering under Hans Baer's chairmanship.

Baer was an anomaly among Swiss banks' CEOs. Not only was he Jewish but he also had a unique understanding of American culture. He had lived in the United States during the Nazi years. In 1940 his father had accepted a position at Princeton University as a physicist. Although his father died eleven days before the family was to depart, Baer's mother decided to take her children abroad, anyway. They settled in the Bronx, and Baer earned a degree in engineering at Lehigh University. He had not planned to go into banking, but, in 1947, a bank manager, who was not a family member, retired, and Baer decided to return to Zurich and enter the family business.

A large man with a long face, Baer sported big, oval-shaped glasses. His deep, serious voice belied the fact that he had a sharp sense of humor. He did not enjoy the irony that his bank, the only Jewish-owned bank in Switzerland during the war, had been accused of hoarding Jewish wartime accounts. He ordered bank officials to investigate the Blum account. When they presented him with their findings, he felt vindicated and issued a public statement:

> The result of the internal research by Bank Julius Baer was that the couple in question had opened an account with the bank a decade after the end of World War II, and that the surviving widow had subsequently closed this account, and disposed of the relatively small balance, in the early seventies. Besides the mere fact of the opening and the cancellation of the account, the bank had no further information left in 1987, as all the relevant documents and records had been destroyed after the statutory period of ten years had elapsed. Accordingly, the bank was not in a position to give the daughters any detailed information about the account relationship that their mother had terminated over one and a half decades before her death.[2]

With that statement, he had broken ranks. He had spoken about a specific account. Other bankers called him. What was he thinking? How could he have betrayed them? The issue of dormant accounts had risen to the surface before, and they had contained it without breaking secrecy. Why now?

He understood the other bankers' concerns, but, as a Jew, he also understood the emotional impact of this issue. This time the issue of Holocaust dormant accounts could spill over Swiss borders. The fact that the *Journal* had published an article on dormant accounts indicated that the issue had international interest. The Blum daughters were not the only heirs mentioned in the article. The reporter had found a survivor named Greta Beer who claimed that her mother had been treated rudely when she inquired at Swiss banks about her husband's account. Even though Baer had cleared up the misunderstanding about the Blum account, he was still bothered. There was no getting around the fact that the letter his bank had sent the Blum daughters in 1987 was indifferent. If nothing else, the Holocaust had taught the world that indifference carries its own burden of guilt.

Baer was surprised at the timing of the recently published articles.
Just a year earlier, he and other board members of the Swiss Bankers
Association (SBA) had begun to review their country's dormant account
laws. They were considering asking the Swiss Parliament to change
them. In countries such as the United States, an heirless account that
has been dormant for ten years automatically goes to the state. In Switzerland, a client's dormant account remains forever, although the
records can be destroyed after ten years. Claiming a Swiss account is
easy, unless: the client and heirs were dead, the account had been made
under a fictitious name, the account had been made by someone else,
the heirs had no records, the account was joined with others, the account had been emptied by others, or the account had been eroded by
bank fees. With Holocaust dormant accounts, the reasons were any and
all of the above.

When the bankers first began reviewing dormant account laws, they
were not thinking of Holocaust accounts. They believed that those accounts had already been identified and distributed years ago. The first
attempt to identify Holocaust accounts had halfheartedly occurred in
the 1950s, when the SBA declared that it would return all Holocaust-era
claims. The SBA had established three requirements: heirs needed to
possess official documents proving the death of the account's original
owner; they needed proof of their right of succession; and they needed
exact details about the banks in which the accounts existed. In addition,
the banks charged search fees. For claimants, these requirements posed
impossible hurdles.

In 1962 the Swiss government, recognizing the failure of the SBA's
previous attempt, passed a bill that required the Swiss banks to investigate all dormant accounts and return them to their rightful owners.
This attempt, too, was inadequate. The bankers were told to look for
dormant accounts belonging to any possible victims of the Nazis. One
of the clues that they believed would help them would be the appearance of Jewish names on the accounts. But banking officials had trouble
identifying Jewish names. Some names sounded more Jewish than
others; some did not sound Jewish at all. Many victims had deposited
money through companies and third parties. There were also questions
of enforcement. The banks controlled their own audits. As a result, only

a handful of banks in Switzerland in 1962 actually searched their records. They found approximately $2 million, belonging to close to one thousand claimants. Some seven thousand claimants were turned down.[3]

In the summer of 1995, Rolf Bloch, the head of the Federation of Swiss Jewish Communities, began meeting with SBA and government officials. He had heard that they were reviewing dormant account laws. Bloch, a small man whose bald head, round face, and large glasses conveyed an owlish look, believed that this was the Jewish community's chance to push for a final accounting of Holocaust dormant accounts. Switzerland's eighteen thousand Jews had always felt on the periphery of the nation's agenda. He wanted to force this issue to the center.

Bloch was busy talking with bankers and government officials about Holocaust accounts when Israel Singer, the general secretary of the World Jewish Congress (WJC), called him. Singer was calling on behalf of Edgar Bronfman, the wealthy U.S. businessman who was president of the WJC. Bronfman wanted to come to Switzerland to pursue the issue of heirless assets and unclaimed accounts. He had read the published articles and wanted to take advantage of the recent publicity. Singer asked whether Bloch could arrange a meeting for Bronfman with officials of the SBA. Bloch, who was the owner of a large chocolate factory in Bern, recognized the usefulness of having someone like Bronfman involved.[4]

Bronfman was chairman of the Seagram Company, his family's multibillion-dollar international conglomerate, and a major contributor to the U.S. Democratic Party. Although he had used his title as president of the WJC to pursue select Jewish causes, his power came more from his wealth than from his title at the WJC. The New York–based WJC was an organization with a small staff.

The WJC had not always been so small. Founded in 1936 by Stephen Wise and Nahum Goldmann, it attracted to its first meeting in Geneva 280 delegates from thirty-two countries. Its purpose was to combat Nazism. After the war, Goldmann took a prominent role in negotiating millions of dollars in compensation and restitution for Jewish victims of the Nazi regime. By the 1970s, the WJC, and its restitution mandate, had been supplanted by other organizations with other agendas; the

American Jewish community had turned to other nongovernmental organizations (NGOs) such as the Anti-Defamation League, the American Jewish Congress, and the Simon Wiesenthal Center. These organizations dealt with, among other issues, battling anti-Semitism and tracking former Nazis.

When Bronfman became president in 1981, he revived the WJC's flagging image. No longer would it be a quiet, behind-the-scenes negotiator. Anything became game—from publicizing the plight of Soviet Jews to researching the past of Kurt Waldheim, the former secretary-general of the United Nations and later president of Austria. Bronfman's in-your-face tactics propelled the small organization into the spotlight.

When Communist governments in Eastern Europe began falling in the early 1990s, Bronfman once again focused the organization on restitution issues. The plight of the double victims—Jewish survivors who had suffered under both the Nazi and the Communist regimes— became more visible. Archives that had once been sealed behind the Iron Curtain were now available to researchers. Historians were beginning to uncover old documents and to provide new information; they were finding that the trail of Nazi money consistently led to Switzerland.

Bloch asked Swiss president Kaspar Villiger and SBA chairman Georg Krayer to meet with Bronfman. Most Swiss were not acquainted with the multitude and diversity of Jewish organizations. These two were no exception. They took the title of the WJC literally. World must mean the world. Besides, the history of the organization led them to their own soil, to that first 1936 WJC meeting in Geneva. Even to Swiss non-Jews, the WJC had a familiar ring. The bankers felt compelled to pay attention. They arranged a date and time for the meeting.

Bronfman, realizing that this was his one opportunity to press the matter, took advantage of his role as president of both the WJC and the World Jewish Restitution Organization (an umbrella organization of Jewish organizations of which the Congress is a member). He asked the Israeli government to support him in his effort. Prime Minister Yitzhak Rabin of Israel gave him a letter of authority to represent Israel in restitution negotiations. Now Bronfman could say he was making the trip to Switzerland not only as the representative of a Jewish organization but as an envoy of the State of Israel.

On September 14, 1995, Baer waited with Krayer and other SBA members for Bronfman to arrive. The WJC leader was flying in on his private jet and was delayed. He was to meet first with Villiger in his office in the Federal Palace and then proceed to La Grande Société, a fancy club and restaurant close to the SBA headquarters in Bern. The press knew about the meeting, and a small entourage of reporters had gathered outside.

When Bronfman finally arrived, he carried himself like a foreign dignitary. He emerged from his black limousine, nodded to reporters, and entered the building. He was accompanied by Singer and Avraham Burg, a prominent Israeli who was the chair of the Jewish Agency. The three of them strode in like cowboys who had come to town to set things right. They represented a new brand of Jewish leaders. Unlike members of their parents' generation, who had felt vulnerable when discussing the Holocaust, these men were unapologetic in their demands. In the context of history, they could afford to be.

Bronfman's and Villiger's meeting went well. Villiger acknowledged the need for the banks to return all dormant Holocaust accounts. He emphasized that this problem belonged to the private banks and must be resolved by them, not by the government. When the meeting was over, the Jewish leaders headed to the restaurant to meet with the bankers. Baer and Krayer ushered them into a reception area, where they were served champagne and cocktails. Bloch had been invited, along with the banking ombudsman who had been investigating complaints, and several other officials. Everyone was standing. There were no chairs. Krayer had planned this out in advance. He would deliver his speech in this room and then host a luncheon in the restaurant. They and their guests could discuss the issue further around the luncheon table.

Krayer approached the podium and began reading his speech. He spoke for a long time and took the offensive. The banks, with the help of the banking ombudsman, had started to investigate their dormant accounts. So far, they had found $32 million in unclaimed assets. They wanted to match the accounts and distribute them as soon as possible. They were all eager to resolve this issue. Krayer then stepped aside.

Although Bronfman listened politely, he was not pleased. He did not like Krayer's emphasis on the $32 million. When it came his turn to

speak, he talked about justice and the need for a process and a final accounting. A number was not as important as establishing a process for
finding the number.[5]

Baer was tired. He had a bad hip, and all this standing was making
him uncomfortable. He also had a lecture to give and was worried that
he was going to be late. He didn't want to leave in the middle of the
speeches. He already knew he was going to miss the lunch. When the
champagne reception was over, he said goodbye and left, no longer worried that the dormant accounts issue would spin out of control. He was
happy that the other bankers were taking the issue seriously. The tone of
the speeches made it appear that things would get resolved very soon.

The other guests enjoyed an elegant lunch. Bronfman and Krayer
discussed details of the investigation. Bronfman challenged the $32 mil-
lion total. Besides the fact that the sum was meager, why had the banks
found any accounts at all after the 1962 audit? Every time the banks
were forced to investigate dormant accounts, they found more. Was this
because they never had conducted a comprehensive investigation?

Krayer listened to Bronfman's concerns and agreed to force the
banks to look once and for all into their dormant accounts. This time
the investigation would be comprehensive, definitive, and transparent.
The Jewish leaders would be informed every step of the way as to the
progress and process of the investigation. Nobody would announce any
findings until all the participants had consulted one another. Bronfman
agreed with those terms. Comprehensive. Definitive. Transparent.

Bronfman, Singer, and Burg finished their lunch, shook hands with
everyone, and left. They spoke briefly to reporters outside before duck-
ing into their limousine and being whisked off to their waiting plane.
Just as quickly as they had come, they were gone.

The bankers were taken aback. It was as if the "Great Oz" had appeared with a list of demands and then had disappeared in a puff of
smoke. Suddenly outsiders were telling them how to deal with a domestic
issue. Nevertheless, they felt that they had handled it well and were confident that the conflict would soon go away. Krayer told Baer not to worry.[6]

In the ensuing weeks, Singer flew back and forth to Switzerland to
meet with the bankers. He did not possess as formidable a reputation as
Bronfman, but what he lacked in wealth and prestige he made up in
emotion. An Orthodox Jew and ordained rabbi, he possessed a colorful

personality, full of contradictions. Calmly eloquent one minute, he could explode into a tirade the next. He had a sharp mind and could reel off historical facts spontaneously. Wearing a crocheted yarmulke off-center on his head, he was unmistakably Jewish to the bankers. His family had suffered under Nazi terror, and he was passionate when speaking about the Holocaust.

The bankers had hoped that their agreement with Bronfman would quiet the publicity surrounding the Holocaust dormant accounts. They were dismayed when new articles appeared on the subject. No matter how hard they tried, they could not close Pandora's box. In fact, the Swiss themselves had now begun rummaging through it, questioning their country's behavior during World War II.

Some Swiss pointed to the fiftieth anniversary of the end of World War II as providing the impetus for self-reflection. Though some members in the Swiss government did not want to commemorate the occasion since Switzerland had been neutral, there were many who did. One Swiss parliamentarian, Verena Grendelmeier, wanted not only to celebrate the armistice but also to honor it in a tangible way. In March 1995, she had proposed legislation to lift banking secrecy and return all remaining assets in dormant accounts. Even President Villiger had become swept up in a wave of contrition. Delivering the fiftieth anniversary commemorative address, he acknowledged Switzerland's guilt at turning away tens of thousands of Jewish refugees from the Swiss border. In his speech, he posed difficult questions to his country: "Was the boat really full? Would Switzerland have been threatened with extinction had it been more definitely receptive to victims of persecution more than it was? Was this question, too, affected by anti-Semitic sentiments in our country? Did we always do our utmost for the persecuted and disenfranchised?"[7]

Other Swiss ascribed their rising self-awareness to the passage of time. The two preceding generations had been too close to the war. The nation needed a new, younger generation that had no immediate connections to the Holocaust, that could approach the past with emotionless distance, that would not feel the primal shiver of a nation surrounded by war.

The interest in Switzerland's treatment of Jewish refugees, dormant accounts, and financial alliances with the Third Reich made Swiss Jews hopeful and afraid. They welcomed the examination of their country's behavior, yet they worried that it would provoke anti-Semitism. Even Swiss Jews as successful as Bloch and Baer admitted that Switzerland had a history of anti-Semitism. A Swiss banker had once told Baer that the banker would never promote a Jew in his bank, not because he was anti-Semitic but because it would be bad business.

By February 1996, Krayer was eager to get the spotlight off the private banks. He needed the dormant accounts issue behind him. The SBA was having its annual meeting, and he decided to call a press conference. It was time to bring the investigation to an end and announce the results. The banks' ombudsman had uncovered a total of seven hundred and seventy-five dormant accounts, amounting to $32 million. Krayer wanted to match and distribute the $32 million and be done.

Bronfman was furious when he heard that the bankers had gone public. What happened to the private discussion that they were supposed to have had? The proposed figure, $32 million, was the same number Krayer had mentioned to him back in September. He did not accept this amount, and he believed that the bankers had broken the cooperation agreement. In addition to this breach, Robert Studer, the chief executive of the Union Bank of Switzerland (UBS), announced the results of his bank's own internal investigation. According to Studer, the Union Bank had found $8.9 million in Holocaust dormant accounts.

"I think I can say in this case that the original amounts were peanuts," he pronounced smugly.[8]

Studer's comment enraged the Jewish leaders. Bronfman went on the attack. The Swiss bankers had been rude to him when he visited them in September. He told reporters how he had to stand in a room without chairs. He did not mention the champagne or the lunch. He talked instead about the $32 million figure and how bankers had hoped to buy him off.

"I realized what they really wanted us to do was to take the money and run," he later told *Time* magazine. He threw out $7 billion as being the more realistic total for heirless assets.[9]

What the bankers didn't know was that Bronfman and Singer had suspected that the SBA would break the secrecy agreement and had started plotting a course of action. Bronfman had met with the Republican senator Alfonse D'Amato of New York to discuss the Swiss banks affair. D'Amato was the chairman of the U.S. Senate Banking Committee and could wield a lot of power if he chose to get involved. Bronfman was well aware that this issue could help D'Amato politically, since the senator's 1998 reelection campaign would soon be swinging into force. A large percentage of D'Amato's New York state constituents were Jewish. The issue would also allow D'Amato a graceful exit from his effort to ensnare President Bill Clinton in a real estate scandal known as Whitewater. D'Amato had initiated hearings on the subject, but they had gone nowhere.

Aside from recognizing the political viability of pursuing the banks, D'Amato was enraged at the bankers' behavior. If the bankers broke their promise, he had assured Bronfman, then he would use his position as chairman of the Senate Banking Committee to take action.

After the bankers' public statement, D'Amato went to work. He appeared on the evening news along with Singer and Elan Steinberg, the WJC's executive director. He read from the U.S. National Archives documents and talked passionately about dormant accounts and Nazi gold. He railed against the postwar 1946 Washington Accord that had been signed between Switzerland and the United States, Britain, and France. Switzerland had gotten off way too easily. The U.S. negotiators had known from documents that the Swiss National Bank (SNB) had accepted more than $300 million in looted gold, and yet they had allowed Switzerland to return only $58.1 million worth of gold. Why? The time had come to turn over old stones.

It wasn't only from the United States that Switzerland was feeling the heat. In June 1996, Greville Janner, the vice president of the WJC in Britain and a Labour member of Parliament, wrote to the British foreign secretary and to the U.S. defense secretary and asked them to search for documents relating to the Swiss banks. He believed that much damning information would be found in their own archives. By summer's end, an all-out pursuit had begun.

The bankers didn't know what had hit them. Suddenly talk had spread from dormant accounts to looted gold to the Washington Accord. Documents were popping up right and left. Survivors were being interviewed. And Bronfman. Why had he portrayed them as being rude when they had tried to be gracious hosts? He had distorted the chairless cocktail reception. And why had he accused them of offering to pay

$32 million? They couldn't have paid him even if they had wanted to, since the money belonged to the account holders. The bankers admitted to themselves that they had erred. They should never have gone public without first discussing the number with Bronfman, and Robert Studer should never have used the word "peanuts" in reference to Holocaust accounts. And, yes, maybe the ombudsman's investigation had a few flaws. These mistakes would cost them dearly.

Krayer and Baer turned to Wilmer, Cutler & Pickering, a large defense firm in Washington, D.C., to guide them through the maze of American politics. Founded by Lloyd Cutler in 1962, the firm was one of the nation's highest-earning law firms. The Swiss Bankers Association had been a client of Wilmer, Cutler's since 1992. In 1994 SBA officials had asked the firm to help them review their dormant accounts laws. They had wanted to know how U.S. banks treat heirless accounts. The task had fallen on attorney Marc Cohen.

Cohen specialized in international banking. He was a bright thirty-six-year-old lawyer who could absorb lots of details. He had a sharp memory and could regurgitate facts and figures spontaneously. Having worked as a plaintiffs' lawyer before coming to Wilmer, Cutler, he liked to boast that he understood life from the other side. His sympathy did not often translate to other plaintiffs' lawyers. Many of them found his sarcasm more irritating than ingratiating. Nevertheless, Cohen knew everything there was to know about banking regulations. He visited Switzerland and wrote a memo comparing U.S. and Swiss laws regarding heirless assets. He thought that was the end of it. Then Bronfman had his September meeting in Bern.

Being Jewish, Cohen was well aware of the strong presence of Jewish organizations in America. He warned the bankers that the issue of Holocaust dormant accounts could become politically explosive in the United States. The WJC might not be influential in the States, but Bronfman was. His warnings came too late. Bronfman had already recruited D'Amato and had spoken to First Lady Hillary Clinton in an effort to enlist her husband's support.

Cohen believed that his client was being unfairly accused. From the media coverage, one would have thought that the Swiss banks had committed the Holocaust. It was true that the banks had not always handled unclaimed dormant accounts with sensitivity and thoroughness, but now the SBA officials were trying to rectify that. They were asking him to work on a solution with the help of Roger Witten, a senior partner at the firm.

Witten had served as an assistant special prosecutor in the Watergate Special Prosecution Force between 1973 and 1974. He was forty-nine and had just finished working on a high-profile case. He had been representing ABC News in a libel suit that Philip Morris had filed against it. The tobacco company had sued ABC over an ABC report that had claimed that the company had manipulated nicotine levels in cigarettes. In August 1995, ABC apologized to the tobacco company. The case had generated a lot of headlines and had spurred interest in Congress, repercussions that were becoming everyday events with the Swiss banks.

A slight man with a full head of silver hair, Witten exhibited a calm demeanor that was a rarity in a world of tense lawyers. His flat voice revealed a polite but cynical attitude. He was a smart attorney who had a knack for picking out technical inconsistencies. He also didn't fit the stereotype of a corporate defense attorney. He had a strong interest in campaign finance reform and had done a lot of pro bono work for the citizen's lobbying organization Common Cause. Like Cohen, Witten was Jewish and understood the danger of having Swiss dormant accounts turn into an international issue.

News that the firm had decided to represent the SBA, as well as Switzerland's three largest banks, Credit Suisse, UBS, and Swiss Bank Corporation, spread through Wilmer, Cutler's Washington office. Associates and paralegals began to talk about it in the cafeteria and around the coffee pot. No one was publicly objecting; after all, the SBA had always been an honest client. Its members seemed truly befuddled by the onslaught of accusations. The bankers appeared determined to resolve this issue.

The partners decided to call a meeting, nonetheless, to suppress any dissent before it manifested itself. Everyone should understand, the banks were not like cigarette makers who were killing people with their cigarettes and had no intention of stopping. The Swiss bankers wanted to correct the situation, and they had a specific proposal to prove it.

Krayer and Baer flew to Washington to meet with Witten and Cohen. They gathered in the lawyers' luxurious high-rise office near Georgetown and began to hammer out a solution. The only way to end questions about leftover Holocaust accounts would be to have independent auditors audit the banks. The WJC wanted this, as well. All they needed was a working structure. As both sides quickly discovered, every issue became fraught with controversy.

They finally decided on a committee and named it the Independent Committee of Eminent Persons (ICEP). Three members of the committee would be appointed by the World Jewish Restitution Organization (WJRO) and three by the SBA. The six members of the committee would appoint an additional member as chairperson. Then the committee as a whole would appoint an international audit company to investigate dormant accounts. The SBA would guarantee the auditors "unfettered access to all relevant files in banking institutions regarding dormant accounts and other assets and financial instruments deposited before, during and immediately after the Second World War."[10] The SBA agreed to fully fund the audit.

Baer finished the proposal with the lawyers, faxed it over to Singer, and waited for his approval. Baer wanted to sign it and return to Switzerland, as he had a lot of work waiting for him back home. He expected no problems. The audit was the solution for which everyone had been waiting. The American lawyers had suggested that the SBA include other Jewish groups in the committee, but Baer and other SBA officials had refused. They wanted to deal exclusively with the WJC, and the WJC wanted it that way.

The entire morning passed. Cohen finally called Singer late in the afternoon. What was the problem?

D'Amato had called for a hearing on April 23. Rather than signing the Memorandum of Understanding right away, some thought a better idea would be to have Baer come and present the ICEP plan at the hearing. That would be more dramatic and allow D'Amato to have his day.[11]

Baer, weary from American politics, agreed. At this point, he was still the best spokesman for the SBA. The fact that he was both Jewish and a Swiss banker allowed him to act as a liaison between the two groups. He and his colleagues were learning the game. Now, they were the ones who wanted assurances that the rules would not change.

On Tuesday, April 23, 1996, at ten o'clock in the morning, D'Amato pounded his gavel in the Dirksen Senate Office Building. With Senators Chris Dodd and Barbara Boxer at his side, and his aide Gregg Rickman holding a stack of documents behind him, D'Amato plunged in.

"This morning the committee meets to take up an important matter that has implications that go back to World War II, the Holocaust, and involves more than money, more than millions and tens of millions, maybe hundreds of millions and maybe more than that. But it involves the systematic victimization of people."[12]

D'Amato had assembled an impressive panel of speakers. He had Bronfman, Baer, and Undersecretary of Commerce Stuart Eizenstat. Eizenstat had served as the State Department's Special Envoy for Property Claims in Central and Eastern Europe. Rickman had also located Greta Beer, the survivor mentioned in the summer's *Wall Street Journal* article.

Beer lived in an apartment in a rundown neighborhood of Queens, New York. Divorced and childless, she had retired from her job as a tour guide. During the summer, she had enjoyed the attention the *Journal* article had given her. Reporters from all over the world had called her. They had asked her about her past. She never tired of repeating her story.

Born in Cernauti, Romania, in 1925, Beer had lived a very comfortable life. Her father owned Hercules S.A., one of the largest and wealthiest textile factories in Romania. He traveled extensively throughout Europe, collecting samples from other factories and buying new machinery for his own. The family often spent weekends hiking and skiing in the mountains of Italy. It was an existence filled with travel and culture, and Beer learned to speak several languages.

In 1939 her parents, fearful of war, sent her to a boarding school in Switzerland. She returned home a year later. Her father had been stricken with a kidney disease, and they needed to travel to Budapest to consult with doctors. In Budapest, her father's condition deteriorated. The family had only the possessions that they had brought with them from Romania, and she and her mother feared that they were running out of money. She remembered that her father had told her that he had a numbered account in Switzerland. After his many business trips, he would stop in Switzerland and deposit money. By the time she remembered this, her father had become too sick to respond. He died without giving her the number of his account or the name of the Swiss bank.

During the war years, Beer, her mother, and her brother sought refuge in the mountains and small towns of Romania and Hungary. At one point they lived in the house of a friend who was a Romanian colonel. They tried to stay one step ahead of the Germans and the Russians and managed to avoid the concentration camps. After the war, Romania fell to the Russians, and Communism's iron fist clamped down. With the help of a peasant, Beer crossed the border into Budapest and then made her way to Vienna, Austria. She joined up with her fiancé, Simon Beer, a man she had met in Romania after the war. They married in Italy.

In 1956 they received visas to America and settled in Jackson Heights, New York. Her mother followed them there, but after several years her health declined, and she went to live in Switzerland, hoping that the fresh mountain air would revitalize her. In 1962 she heard that the Swiss government was requiring banks to open their archives and search for Holocaust accounts.[13]

Beer was excited about the prospect of finding her father's account. She flew to Switzerland and accompanied her mother to the banks. Although she was not allowed inside, she waited at the entrances while her mother inquired. Bank after bank rejected her mother's requests to search for her money. Some demanded that her mother produce proof that she was a victim of persecution.

"Have you ever been hit over the head with a rifle butt?" she said one official had asked her mother in an attempt to establish credibility.[14]

Beer was more than happy to appear at D'Amato's hearing. She loved Washington, D.C., and had stood many times on the Capitol's steps. For her, it was an honor to testify. When she arrived in Washington, she panicked.

"I am completely unprepared," she cried to D'Amato. "I have no idea what to say." She later recounted how the senator had tried to humor her by speaking in broken Italian.

Beer closed her eyes and awaited her turn to speak. She was thin, and her shoulders bent forward. From a distance, she looked like a spindly fir. Her reddish brown hair was neatly coiffed, and she adorned herself with Native American jewelry. Silver bracelets with large colored stones hung from her wrists, and turquoise rings decorated each finger. The bright jewelry stood in stark contrast to her pallid skin. Alone and isolated, she welcomed the opportunity to talk. When D'Amato introduced her, she leaned toward the microphone and spoke in her thick Romanian accent.

> Ladies and gentlemen, members of the committee.
>
> My name is Greta Georgia Beer, born Deligdisch. My father, Ziegfreid Deligdisch, had studied pharmacy. I am a very, very proud American citizen since 1956.
>
> My father spread out, he built factories. The first one was a nail and metal company. The second one was Hercules S.A., which became the biggest textile mill in Romania. . . . My father used to travel in the fall and go from fair to fair. . . . At the end of his trips, he would invariably go to Switzerland and deposit money. Why? We looked towards Switzerland like a bastion, a citadel.
>
> Conflagrations, the sky over my city so close to the Russian border, Communism and the danger of the Nazis coming from the north, and this was the only safe haven. And my father used to open a so-called, we called it *chiffre* account, numbered account. And my father used to talk to us . . . and he used to say, don't worry, kids. You have nothing to worry. You are provided for. The money is safely deposited in Switzerland.[15]

Beer moved from thought to thought. Her story wasn't always chronological, nor was it always clear, but her yearning to reclaim her father's money was absolute.

"The only thing I can say, I do hope, Senator D'Amato, that the Swiss banks will see the light . . . to correct what has been done so wrong. I'm sorry, I don't read. I just speak from my heart, albeit, a very heavy heart."[16]

Reduced to tears, she left the room.

"I don't know what happened to me," she later pronounced. "It was as if a higher being was speaking. A completely different voice."

Hans Baer listened to Beer's story and had an idea. He could fly her to Switzerland and help her look for her father's account. When his turn came, he outlined the efforts the SBA had made in relation to dormant accounts and an independent audit. He was respectful of D'Amato and the WJC and tried to allay their concerns. He then concluded.

"I would like to say that I was very moved by the eloquent statement of Mrs. Greta Beer, and that it would be my honor and privilege to have her as my personal guest in Switzerland, to accompany her to wherever she would like to go in order to clear up her own unfortunate situation."[17]

Unbeknownst to Baer, Beer had left the room. She had not heard his invitation. After the hearing, he approached her as she was preparing to leave. He took her hand and once again extended his invitation.

Beer, whose heart was still pounding from the experience of testifying, did not recognize him.

"Who are you?" she inquired.

"I am Hans Baer."

She paused, then shook her head. "Oh, my God. You are on the other side."

She was flattered by his offer and was not going to refuse the chance to be personally escorted through his country.[18]

Baer flew back to Zurich only to return to the United States several days later to sign the Memorandum of Understanding with the WJC. D'Amato had been given his stage, and now they could move ahead with the audit. Baer believed that once the Memorandum was signed, the issue would be closed.

But people were talking. And not just among themselves. Singer and Bronfman had met with President Clinton, and he had expressed sympathy for their cause.[19] Clinton had assured them that he would put aside politics and work together with D'Amato. Rumors were also circulating that American attorneys were preparing class-action suits against the banks and that researchers were flocking to the U. S. National Archives at College Park, Maryland. People were investigating everything, from gold to looted artwork.

"Don't celebrate," one Jewish leader warned Baer as he prepared to leave. "There are people out there who mean to destroy you."

Three months later, Baer greeted Greta Beer in Switzerland. He tried to be the perfect host, arranging for her to go to concerts, museums, and operas. He knew that she was a fellow art lover, so he showed her around his estate, which was filled with paintings and sculptures from his art collection. He was surprised at her worldliness. She had traveled extensively.

He introduced Beer to Krayer and to the banks' ombudsman, whose task was to investigate Holocaust claims. He had people in his own bank research her father's account. They found a possible account in her father's name, but records indicated that her uncle, who had since died, had emptied it. There was no definite proof of this, and Greta denied that that could have happened. According to her, they had found her uncle's empty account, not her father's. They found no other account in her father's name, and she had no papers to prove otherwise. She returned home, disheartened. Several days later, Carlo Jagmetti, Switzerland's ambassador to Washington, stated publicly what he had heard—that the banks had found Beer's father's account but that it had been emptied by her uncle.

"I've been betrayed," she wailed.

As media attention grew, more and more stories came out about survivors who could not find their families' accounts. Accounts that had been liquidated would never be found, no matter how hard the bankers tried. By August 1996, the members of ICEP had been appointed and had agreed to have Paul A. Volcker, former chairman of the Board of Governors of the Federal Reserve System, serve as their chairman. The Swiss members had come up with Volcker, and everyone had accepted him. He was well known and was reputed to be a person of integrity.

The Swiss had put into place one more committee. In December 1996, the Swiss Federal Council established a committee whose mandate was to investigate the fate of assets moved to Switzerland before, during, and after World War II. The committee was called the Independent Commission of Experts and was composed of international historians and scholars. It was headed by Jean Francois Bergier, a professor of business administration and social history at the Zurich Polytechnic Institute. The commission's task was to examine not only the movement of assets but also the behavior of Swiss companies during the war and the

Swiss refugee policy. The Bergier Commission, as it came to be called, was given five years to conduct its research and produce a final report.

For the survivors, the Bergier Commission and the ICEP audit offered little consolation. Not only would it take several years to complete, but many feared that their families' accounts would never be found, no matter how hard the auditors searched. The accounts had disappeared long ago. Records had been destroyed. How would ICEP find what no longer existed? Many began to turn to American attorneys to help them in their efforts to reclaim their money.

Beer called attorney Martin Mendelsohn. She had heard that he and a Washington plaintiffs' attorney named Michael Hausfeld were preparing a class-action suit against the Swiss banks. Mendelsohn specialized in Russian affairs.

"He works with Yeltsin," she boasted.

If he could face the Great Russian Bear, then surely he could hold his own against the Gnomes of Switzerland.

Cohen and Witten doubted that a U.S. court would recognize jurisdiction in a case against the banks, yet they knew that they would have to fight it all the same. They warned Hans Baer and the other bankers about the class action.

The Swiss bankers were naively complacent. Class actions do not exist in the Swiss legal system, and the bankers had no idea how forceful a vehicle it can be. Powered by large numbers of claimants, a class action can roll toward its opponent like a tank. The noise it creates can often be enough to bring about a settlement. To the bankers, talk of a class action sounded like just some low rumbling in the distance.

2

Looking Back

Dear Mr. D. Gribetz:
Before June 22, 1941, I lived in the city of Mogilev, Belorussia, with my family.
From the first days of World War II, Hitler started to bomb our city. The Nazis
bombed Mogilev day and night. We couldn't stay in our own home. We hid in the
local forest starting June 23, 1941. As a result of a very rapid arrival of the Nazis,
our city was surrounded from north and south. . . . We were in a swamp forest with-
out any food or supplies. Our clothes were torn. Nazis surrounded us. Almost a whole
month, famished and weak, we walked westward. Moving, mostly only at nights due
to the knowledge that Nazis catch Jews and send them somewhere. We were terrified
of going into villages because Germans were there. . . . We only ate berries and mush-
rooms, and drank out of brooks. As a result, I got sick with typhus and had high fever
for several days, lying in the bushes. Then my mother and my younger brother got ty-
phus too. After a while, at the end of August, 1941, we were able to find a train sta-
tion that was "nazi-free." At night, we were able to get into one of the trains that were
heading West, where there were no Germans. The next morning, I was taken off the
train by the rail-men with high fever. Thanks to those people, I am still alive today. A
doctor cured me. By my mother soon died. All of our things were left behind. The
Nazis murdered my relatives, those who didn't leave with us when the bombing
started. Altogether, I lost twelve of my relatives; six of those were children. At the
present time, I am seventy-four years of age, and my health is very poor, my wife is
seventy-five. We are asking you for help for compensation from the Swiss Fund. . . .
We are waiting for your response.

Letter to the Court from Boris Berlin and Etya Mizikovskaya

The Hausfeld household traditionally has a party every year on the second day of Rosh Hashanah, the Jewish New Year. They never send out
invitations. That is too formal. Instead, they tell a few people, who then
tell a few more people, who tell a few more, until many in the Jewish

27

community of Northern Virginia have received word that the Hausfelds' open house is once again taking place.

In 1996 the Jewish New Year began at sundown on September 14.
Early in the afternoon of the sixteenth, the Hausfelds filled their last
cooler with ice and soda and opened their doors. As usual, people arrived and departed throughout the day, many of them coming straight
from synagogue services. Most guests knew exactly what to expect.
They knew that neither Michael nor his wife Marilyn would be waiting
to greet them. They would instead have to make their own way through
the crowd, snatching pastries and fruit tarts off the platters in the
various rooms. A wide assortment of people came: older community
members, parents with toddlers, teenagers who had come to visit the
Hausfelds' youngest daughter, neighbors, cousins, and actors who had
performed with Marilyn in local theater productions.

Marilyn was never hard to find. Mingling in the family room or
hallway, she liked to move from group to group. Always poised and
ready with a joke, she never had trouble working a crowd. Michael, on
the other hand, proved harder to locate. Reserved and less spontane-
ous than his wife, he preferred one-on-one conversations. Short and
trim, at fifty, he did not look like many of his colleagues in the law. He
had no double chin or expanding waistline. Only his newly renovated
suburban house with its country home decorations and his red Saab
convertible parked in the garage revealed the comfortable life that several successful cases had afforded him. His receding hairline and the
bird-like tuft of hair on top of his head were the only signs of middle
age. Behind his gold-rimmed glasses, his green eyes reflected an inner
intensity.

Late in the afternoon, he walked out onto the back deck. He had
wanted to enjoy the dry autumn air and spend a few minutes by himself. Leaning against the railing, he stood in the corner, immersed in his
own thoughts and oblivious to the surrounding noise. For the past four
months he had been researching and compiling documents pertaining
to the Holocaust. In a few weeks he planned to file a complaint against
three of Switzerland's biggest banks, and he was feeling anxious. The
complaint would accuse them of, among other things, complicity in
genocide. With every new fact revealed, it was becoming clear that this
case would present the greatest challenge in his career as a plaintiffs'

attorney. Never one to shy away from a difficult situation, he was surprised at his trepidation. It wasn't as much the enormity of the allegations that gave him pause as it was the responsibility of representing survivors and victims of the Holocaust. The Jewish New Year always made
him reflective, and on this particular afternoon he felt his past sweep
over him. He yearned for his father.

Walter Hausfeld had died sixteen years earlier, but Hausfeld thought
of him often. In some respects he wasn't sure how his father would have
viewed this case. Walter was a generous and forgiving man who loved to
be with people. Every Friday night, after reciting the blessings and eating his wife's Sabbath meal, he would push his chair back from the table
and begin telling a story that they had all heard dozens of times. No one
ever complained, neither his wife and children nor the guests who had
come to join them for the evening. They knew that the night would be
filled with stories, jokes, and songs and would last until the morning
hours.

Walter was a Polish immigrant who worked hard as a furrier in
Brooklyn. Many of the men and women who joined him on those Friday nights were members of the Tluste Society, an organization that he
had founded. They had tattooed numbers on their arms, and they often
found themselves slipping into the Yiddish that they had spoken as children growing up in Tluste, a small town in Poland. Walter was one of
the luckier members of the society.

When Germany invaded Poland in 1939, Walter had taken one look
at the ill-equipped Polish army circling the towns on horseback and had
decided to flee. He and his brother Meyer walked for days, arriving in
Stockholm, Sweden, where they made their way onto a ship headed for
America. Two other brothers were already living in New York. For years
these brothers had been urging the others to leave. Walter's fifth brother,
Michael David, decided to remain at home along with his parents and
aunts, uncles, and cousins. Shortly after Poland was invaded, the Nazis
rounded up the young men in the town and shot them in the woods. Michael David was one of those shot. The others died in concentration
camps.

In memory of his brother, Walter named one of his sons Michael
David. In memory of his father, Michael David now told himself beneath the browning leaves, he was suing the Swiss banks.

Although his parents had wanted him to be a doctor, Hausfeld decided when he was in high school that he wanted to go into law. He was introduced to the idea on the final night of the New York State Science Fair. The analog computer he had assembled had been selected for the fair. On the final night, his computer broke down. When his turn came to present his project to the judges, he gave a long explanation as to the computer's merits and why, even though it wasn't working, it deserved to win.

"The intention behind the machine is what's important here," he argued.

When he had finished his speech, one of the judges walked over to him.

"Son, if you don't go into science, go into law."

Hausfeld won second place.

After that night, he began to think about his career. Maybe he really would make a good lawyer. Having spent a summer working in his uncle's butcher shop, he knew he could never be a doctor. The sight of blood made him faint.

Spectacled and thin, he fit the high school stereotype of an egghead. A member of the debate team, a math and science whiz, and an honor student, he was a perfect candidate for a career in law. There was only one obstacle.

Ever since childhood, Hausfeld had scored poorly on standardized tests. No matter what answer he chose, he always picked the wrong one. He had trouble limiting himself. No one answer seemed totally correct. He could give a litany of reasons as to why his choice was the best, but there are no discussions on standardized tests. Even though he was the valedictorian of his high school class, his SATs were so low that the college counselor called him in.

"College will be difficult," she warned. "You will need to apply yourself."

In 1966 he graduated with honors from Brooklyn College. The prospect of law school, however, remained remote. His LSAT scores were so low that he was rejected by every law school. Only George Washington University took a chance and put him on its waiting list. This time the dean of admissions cautioned him.

"With your scores, law school will be very difficult."

In 1969 Hausfeld graduated from George Washington Law School in the top five percent of his class.

In school, he specialized in antitrust law. He liked being able to address himself to civil rights in the world of economics. Antitrust laws allowed for broad interpretations and required a creative and intellectual approach. When he graduated, a large and well-known law firm in Washington, D.C., recruited him. Although Hausfeld enjoyed antitrust law, he found himself becoming heavily involved with draft counseling and taking on less lucrative cases.

In 1972 Hausfeld met William Wilson, a young black police cadet who had been accused of cheating on his final exam and had been dismissed from the D.C. Police Academy. The more Hausfeld investigated, the more black cadets he found who had been accepted into the academy but were, for one reason or another, dismissed before graduation. It was obvious to him that there was discrimination occurring in the D.C. Metropolitan Police Department. That year, he took on, and eventually won, his first class-action suit. Midway through the case, one of the partners at his firm called him in. If he continued to take these kinds of cases and to work pro bono, they would have to part ways.

"There is no room for any of Nader's boys here," the partner snapped.

Crushed, Hausfeld went home. If he left the firm, he would have to admit that conventional law was not for him. He would continue to gamble on cases that were less lucrative. Married, with three young children, he was afraid that he would have to dip into the family's savings.

As he thought about whether to leave, he remembered a psychology class he had taken as a senior at Brooklyn College. He and four other students had been instructed to stand in front of the large lecture hall. They had been asked to give their opinions on the need for a curfew on campus. One by one they were called upon. Hausfeld was last. He had listened as the first four students had agreed with one another. They had all claimed a curfew could be useful. When it was his turn, he hesitated. He did not agree with them. Curfews infringe on students' individual rights. But they all sounded so certain.

"I agree with the others," he finally answered before returning to his seat.

The professor waited for everyone to sit down. "This was an experiment," she explained. "The first two students had been told how to answer. Most people, when confronted with large groups of people, do not stand by their convictions."

Embarrassed, Hausfeld slumped in his chair. "Never again," he vowed. "I will never again go along with the majority because I'm afraid to disagree."

It took him one day to decide to leave the law firm. Not long after, he heard that the Washington branch of the law offices of Harold Kohn had an opening for an associate. He went for an interview and immediately found a friend and mentor in Jerry Cohen, an attorney at the firm. Cohen had been chief counsel to the Senate Antitrust and Monopoly Subcommittee and had begun building a practice in class-action lawsuits. Hausfeld respected his innovative and compassionate approach to the law. He also admired Cohen's boldness in accepting risky cases. In 1986 Jerry Cohen split off from Harold Kohn and formed his own firm, Cohen, Milstein.

Cohen saw in Hausfeld a burning idealism. Here was a young lawyer who viewed the law as a forum for social change. Cohen believed that Hausfeld possessed a legal intelligence that would allow him to create that forum.

Cohen's style was different from Hausfeld's. Cohen did not like tense confrontations or ultimatums. Hausfeld thrived on them. Each understood the necessity of both styles and found that they were most successful when working together. The two of them complemented each other. They knew when to take center stage and when to recede. When it was time to get tough, Hausfeld emerged; when it was time to make peace, Cohen took over. Each case was beautifully choreographed. In 1986 Hausfeld became a full member of the firm.

When Cohen died of a heart attack in January 1996, Hausfeld grieved for months. Management of the firm fell largely to him and to his partner Herb Milstein, since their other partner, Stephen Toll, had moved out to the firm's Seattle branch. Alone and overwhelmed with new responsibilities, Hausfeld struggled with decisions. During moments of self-doubt, he found himself replaying Cohen's advice in his head.

"Trust your instincts," Cohen used to tell him. "Just step back from the noise and listen to yourself."

After all, Hausfeld's instincts had served him well. Over the years, he had established a reputation as a relentless litigator. After he settled for more than $60 million with Bristol-Myers Squibb and Abbott Laboratories for fixing prices on their infant formula, Judge Richard Ballinger, the judge who had presided over that trial, described him as a "bulldog." He had watched Hausfeld pause while questioning a witness, interject a joke, and then, without warning, tear into the witness again.[1]

Hausfeld enjoyed this image. He boasted when a newspaper article referred to him as a legal Bigfoot. When a client wrote that his intense demeanor reminded her of Buddha, he laughed.

"Bulldog. Bigfoot. Buddha. There's only one 'B' word left," he joked.

He liked to read from a poem that jurors in the Bristol-Myers trial had written after the trial. Based on the poem "Twas the Night Before Christmas" (their duty had lasted through Christmas), it was called "Twas Another Day of Jury Duty." He smiled as he read the middle stanzas:

> As dry leaves that before
> the wild hurricane fly;
> The witness' met with obstacles
> and looked to the sky.
>
> So up to the posters, and tripods,
> they flew,
> with a book full of pages,
> and additional charts . . . too!

That "hurricane," he bragged, was none other than himself.

With both the firm and the cases he took on, he enjoyed pushing the edge. When his firm joined the class action against Exxon after the *Exxon Valdez* oil spill, he requested to be the one in his firm to represent the Alaskan natives. They were a small group of plaintiffs compared to the commercial fishermen, but he was immediately drawn to them. He knew that their damages would be harder to prove as they could not claim, as the fishermen could, that they had lost income as a result of the spill. The Alaskan natives had no income. They lived off the land. He would have to argue, instead, that the natives had lost a way of life. This was shakier ground on which to stand. Exxon finally decided to settle at $20 million, though a jury imposed a sum of $5 billion for punitive damages. (Exxon later appealed this decision and the court lowered the punitive damages.)

Hausfeld's past was also littered with cases that had not succeeded. One case involved Martin Marietta, the Denver-based aerospace company. After finding evidence of water contamination, along with a dramatic increase in childhood leukemia, in a nearby Denver suburb, the plaintiffs had accused Marietta of dumping toxic rocket fuel into their drinking water. Though the judge conceded that there probably was a correlation, she threw the suit out on the basis that the plaintiffs could not quantify the amount of toxin present in the water. Hausfeld had become close with many of the families whose children were sick. He was devastated by the loss. He often referred to this case as one of his greatest disappointments.

Some cases hit closer to home, as when he represented the twin daughters of a family friend. The girls were observant Jews who were valedictorians of their high school class in Hausfeld's hometown of Fairfax, Virginia. As valedictorians, they were prepared to lead their class through commencement exercises. When they realized that graduation was scheduled for a Saturday, the Jewish Sabbath, they notified the school board that they would be unable to attend. They petitioned the board to change the date. The board turned them down. Hausfeld took it to court, arguing that having graduation on a Saturday was a violation of the girls' First Amendment rights. Although he failed to convince the judge, the school board never scheduled graduation on a Saturday again.

After the case, the twins told Hausfeld how difficult it had been for them. Nobody at their school had understood why they had chosen to pursue this issue in court. They had been taunted and physically harassed. He had been free to come and go while they had remained inside the thicket of the controversy.

Hausfeld faulted the school administrators for not publicly defending the girls' right to be heard. He also faulted himself. He had not used this opportunity to educate the students at the school. This could have been a learning experience. He had been so intent on winning that he had lost sight of what the girls were experiencing.

"What is the most important aspect to being a successful lawyer?" he later asked his law students in a class he was teaching at George

Washington University Law School. Remembering this case, he answered in the same breath: "To understand the people one is representing." As an extra reminder, he hung a framed article with a photo of the girls on the wall of his office.

With the Exxon case behind him, his life had become less frenzied. He no longer had to fly back and forth to Alaska every few weeks. As much as he appreciated being home, he missed the intensity of the case. It had become a self-contained world. Every waking thought and even his dreams had absorbed the details of that world.

Marilyn had grown accustomed to his absorption and knew immediately when he had entered such a case. He missed exits while driving on the Beltway. He wrote notes to himself on restaurant napkins or on popcorn containers at movie theaters. At three in the morning, she'd find him at the dining room table with legal pads spread out before him. For the most part, she accepted his obsessiveness. She was busy pursuing her own interest in theater. There were times, though, when she felt he had become a prisoner of his own convictions. He would suffer migraine headaches that nothing seemed to alleviate. He would lose his appetite and have trouble sleeping. At these times, she would load the car and drive them to their country home in Berkeley Springs, West Virginia. On their front porch, they'd watch the sun set behind the hills and listen to the geese overhead. Off in the Allegheny Mountains, he would become captive to a different set of laws, and gradually, she hoped, they would help him escape.

But Hausfeld was fiercely competitive. He set up each case like a board game. Every one had to have well-defined rules, distinct boundaries, and, most important, a clear set of opponents. He thrived on order and neatness in his personal life, and this was the only way he could play in a profession that brought a messy array of personalities and agendas. Those who shared his vision were good, and those who differed were bad. For those who fell somewhere in between, well, they would have to choose.

One of the guests at the New Year party was Hausfeld's longtime friend Marty Mendelsohn. He worked around the corner from Hausfeld in a plush office building in Washington, D.C. A partner at Verner, Liipfert, Bernhard, McPherson & Hand, a large law firm whose directory boasts names such as former Senate majority leader George Mitchell, former senator Robert Dole, and former ambassador Robert Strauss, Mendelsohn had carved a niche for himself in international trade and business.

His and Hausfeld's friendship went back years and extended beyond their professional lives. They had taken trips together with their wives, and they included each other at their family events. Mendelsohn, like Hausfeld, was Jewish and had grown up in Brooklyn. He was a big hulking man with a deep baritone voice and dark circles ringing his eyes.

In early June, he had telephoned Hausfeld. "We're looking for the best son of a bitch available, and your name came up."

"Is this a personal or professional judgment?" Hausfeld asked.

"Professional, of course," laughed Mendelsohn.

The "we" Mendelsohn had referred to was the Simon Wiesenthal Center, in Los Angeles. Established under the name of the legendary Nazi hunter, the Wiesenthal Center had become a strong voice among Jewish organizations. As an international center for Holocaust remembrance and social action, it had, among other accomplishments, won an Oscar for its documentary on the Holocaust.

Mendelsohn was the center's chief counsel and had solicited Hausfeld's help once before in a case that the center had initiated. In 1985 it had filed charges against Andrija Artukovic, a Nazi war criminal under Croatia's cruel Ustashe regime. Artukovic had earned the title "butcher of Croatia." The Wiesenthal Center had discovered that Artukovic was living in California. Mendelsohn and Hausfeld sought damages against him for his involvement in the murder and suffering of Jews in Yugoslavia during World War II. This was the first time lawyers had attempted to bring civil charges against a Nazi war criminal. The case was thrown out, but Artukovic was deported several years later.

Mendelsohn described the suit against the Swiss banks. It would be filed on behalf of survivors, heirs, and the deceased, and not the Wiesenthal Center. The center could provide them with names of survivors and heirs who might have had money deposited in a Swiss bank. The suit must represent all entities: survivors, heirs, and the deceased.

Mendelsohn, who had done some prior legal work for Senator D'Amato, had watched and encouraged the senator's growing involvement with the issue. He had attended D'Amato's first Senate hearing and had listened to Hans Baer's attempt to "quiet" things by proposing a voluntary independent audit and an all-expense-paid trip to Switzerland for Greta Beer.

He couldn't help feeling cynical. The banks were using a dam made of twigs to try and stop a torrent of allegations. They were building it on ground that was already eroded by broken promises. Either the bankers didn't care, he thought, or they truly believed that neither D'Amato nor the WJC was powerful enough to change the landscape. Maybe they were right. Maybe there needed to be something more. If a legal case could be brought against the banks, then a court would force the banks to open their books.

Because of his connections to D'Amato and the Wiesenthal Center, Mendelsohn had too many competing interests to be the lead attorney. He knew the job would require someone who was creative and incredibly persistent. The banks had a history of denial and obstinacy. Hausfeld would have the staying power to see it through.

For Hausfeld, Mendelsohn's call came at a good time. None of his active cases required large amounts of energy. One of them, a race discrimination suit against Texaco, had been lingering in the courts for two years. Things were quiet at home, as well. His son, Ayal, was studying art at the Rhode Island School of Design, and his older daughter, Ari, was a teacher, living on her own in Virginia. Only his daughter Wendi was at home, finishing high school.

When Hausfeld presented the other attorneys in his firm with the possibility of taking on the Swiss banks, it was obvious to them that he had already made up his mind. It was also obvious that this would be one of those cases that would completely envelop him. What made this case different from past cases, however, was his announcement that they would be doing it pro bono. No one would collect legal fees. Their time would come free. He would approach only firms that would agree to work pro bono.

"Jewish leaders and journalists have already begun calling the money 'blood money,'" he explained "and lawyers' fees will only taint the final settlement. This is a rare opportunity to make history."

Hausfeld approached two attorneys at the firm, Rich Lewis and Paul Gallagher. Lewis had been named a partner in February 1996. Tall, with curly hair and a high forehead, he bore a striking resemblance to the singer Art Garfunkel. He specialized in environmental health law. For ten years he had been representing communities and individuals that had been exposed to toxins released by corporations, and he was becoming worn down. The courts had become less and less sympathetic, and industry-funded science had become more and more difficult to combat. Lewis viewed the Swiss banks case as something different and as an interesting legal challenge. He was Jewish, but he had no immediate relatives who had been affected by the Holocaust, and he had not read much about it while growing up. Nevertheless, he agreed with his senior partner that this case was an historical opportunity worth pursuing. All he needed to do was find the time.

Gallagher was thirty-four and had just joined the firm that July. He had been working for the past four years at a large firm doing insurance coverage defense. It was boring and unfulfilling, and every night he would go home dissatisfied. He had begun to question whether law was right for him. With a wife and a young son, he did not like spending long hours away from home. When he heard that Cohen, Milstein, Hausfeld and Toll was looking for an attorney, he immediately applied. He knew that the firm took on interesting and diverse cases, and he was hungry to find some meaning in law. Clean cut, with short-cropped black hair and striking blue eyes, Gallagher still had his little-boy looks. As a Republican, he knew that he would be in the minority at the firm. Still, he wanted a job where he would feel that he was serving others, and the firm looked to be able to provide that opportunity. He was offered a position, and he accepted. If he was unhappy there, he told himself, then law wasn't for him. The next few years would be his trial.

When Hausfeld approached him about the Swiss banks case, Gallagher hesitated. He was already swamped with work and was unsure of how the case would fit in with his other assignments. Although he was not Jewish, he believed that not being Jewish could be an advantage in this case. He would have more emotional distance than Hausfeld. He also believed that the case would be over in a matter of months. The banks were already making concessions due to political pressure. The lawsuit would be the last straw. The threat of a U.S. court would surely make the banks come to the table and talk seriously. He could handle a few months of extra work. After all, wasn't this the kind of case for which he had been searching?

The three lawyers had to decide where to file their complaint. Many of the claimants they were investigating lived in New York. In addition, all three Swiss banks had branches in Manhattan and conducted business in New York. They could argue that, because the banks had a strong presence in the United States, they could be tried there. This condition for personal jurisdiction they believed they would have no trouble meeting.

Hausfeld also had to decide which outside attorneys he would ask to help him. He knew that Mendelsohn would be beside him the whole way, but he needed someone else who would be strong enough to stay the course, no matter how politically explosive the issue became. That person would also need to have the resources to support the case pro bono. When he decided that he would file the complaint against the banks in Brooklyn's Eastern District Federal Courthouse, he immediately called a heavy-hitting class-action attorney named Mel Weiss.

Weiss was sixty-two and the senior partner at the Manhattan firm Milberg, Weiss, Bershad, Hynes & Lerach LLP. He was one of the nation's best-known class-action attorneys. His firm led the market in suits filed on behalf of defrauded shareholders and investors. He alone had made millions.

Weiss had worked on several cases with Jerry Cohen, but he had worked on only one case, the *Exxon Valdez* case, with Hausfeld. The two of them had served on the Plaintiffs' Executive Committee, and it was there that Hausfeld had witnessed what he had always heard described by others as Weiss's intimidating and sometimes abrupt negotiating style. He had watched Weiss bang his fists against the table in defiance while the defense stared at him in amazement. He had listened as Weiss aimed his wrath at members of his own team when they began showing signs of weakness or shortsightedness. But Hausfeld had also observed something else.

Beneath his rage, Weiss possessed an uncanny ability to view the world from his opponents' frame of reference. He could determine, to the smallest detail, what it was the other side wanted, needed, and most feared. He then shaped the negotiations around the answers to those needs and fears. For Weiss, negotiating was an art. Every gesture, every word, every pause became a sign. Those who could read the signs correctly were successful.

Weiss did not take his own success for granted. Growing up in a poor neighborhood in the Bronx, he had worked for years before reaching the fiftieth floor of his spacious Manhattan office building. After graduating from New York University Law School, he went to work at a Wall Street law firm. It was there that he recognized the tremendous power large corporations had and the need for an equally forceful power to counterbalance it.

In 1966 Congress passed legislation that broadened the power of class-action suits. These suits make it possible for an individual with claims to sue on behalf of a large group of individuals who share those claims. Weiss was provided with just the tool he was looking for.

Complex litigation had become more and more expensive, and class actions were a way of leveling the playing field. Weiss seized upon the opportunity and founded a firm whose primary focus was securities cases. It was full of risk, yet filled with potential. Since class-action lawyers cannot collect a penny until a case has been won or settled, and since a case can take years to be resolved, a class-action attorney operates on faith and hope. In the event of a settlement or courtroom victory, a class action can bring in millions. In one of Weiss's sweetest victories, he recovered nearly $1 billion for investors against Drexel Burnham Lambert, the junk bond firm, and its leading purveyor of the bonds, Michael Milken.[2]

Many defense attorneys and businessmen began to view class-action lawyers with disdain. To them, these lawyers were parasites who fed at the bottom of the food chain. As Weiss took on one corporation after another, lawyers and businessmen came to fear as well as detest him. Milberg, Weiss grew to one hundred and thirty lawyers and took the lead in securities litigation. Suddenly the firm was no small parasite. It had become, as one attorney described it, an "800-pound gorilla."[3]

Over time, class actions extended to personal injury and product liability cases, prompting suits against companies such as those responsible for asbestos contamination and for illnesses resulting from silicone breast implants. Huge punitive damages were awarded by juries sympathetic to individuals' stories. Class actions became even more lucrative and powerful.

The fear that one can spend years on a case and never recover a cent looms over every class-action attorney. That risk creates a shared understanding and camaraderie among those who have chosen this area of law. The world of class-action attorneys is small and resembles an extended family with different branches dispersed all over the country. Many firms are spin-offs from other firms. After more than thirty years in the profession, the successful Weiss had become one of the "family's" grand patriarchs.

He had come to enjoy the good life. Married, with three grown children, he no longer had the constraints of raising a family. He chartered a private jet and spent his time traveling around the world. The stocky and always nicely dressed Weiss, with his closely cropped salt-and-pepper beard, was often seen frequenting fine restaurants and smoking expensive cigars. Attuned to details, his eyes often darted back and forth beneath his black bushy eyebrows and steel-rimmed spectacles. They took in everyone and everything.

He worked constantly. On the sidewalk, inside a restaurant, onboard a yacht, his gruff voice and heavy New York accent could be heard barking into his cell phone.

His spacious office overlooking Manhattan displayed evidence of his well-networked life. Framed articles about himself and his firm, as well as photos of him shaking hands with President Clinton and assorted New York politicians, hung on his walls. He was considered one of the Democratic Party's most significant donors.

In 1995 the Republican-dominated Congress passed a law to limit shareholders' "frivolous" class-action suits. Plaintiffs' lawyers knew that they would have a better chance of fighting the bill's passage if the Democrats had control of the Congress. In 1994, however, the Republicans had gained control of both the House and the Senate. President Clinton vetoed the bill, but the veto was overridden.

Unlike Hausfeld, Weiss had no immediate family members who had died in the Holocaust. Nevertheless, he felt a personal sense of injustice when reading or talking about it. When Hausfeld called to ask him whether he would join the suit against the banks, he immediately remembered a high school assignment in which he had been instructed to write an essay impugning a person or an event using emotion over facts. He had chosen to do his on acts committed during the Holocaust. He had expressed such strong feelings that his teacher had read his piece aloud. More than forty years later, he still remembered that piece.[4]

Although he was working on a large class action against the insurance giant Prudential, he would find time for this suit.

Hausfeld knew that Weiss's seniority would bring credibility to the case. Weiss would not be afraid of an opponent as strong as the Swiss banks. In fact, he would relish the challenge. He saw in Weiss the same boldness that he had admired in Jerry Cohen. He needed him in this case, where the stakes were so high. From the documents his researcher, Miriam Kleiman, was bringing him, he knew that it wasn't just the banks he and Weiss would be challenging. It would also be Swiss history.

In February 1996, Miriam Kleiman found herself out of a job. She had been working for a Jewish organization and had been let go. She blamed herself. If she hadn't asked for an evaluation of her job, they might not have eliminated it. She could have continued without anyone questioning her performance. But two years had passed, and she had become restless. She had wanted increased responsibilities, as well as more money. She had asked for a title change. Shortly after, her job was eliminated, and she was dismissed. Two weeks after leaving, she went on unemployment.

Kleiman was twenty-eight and single. Originally from Cleveland, she had been drawn to Washington. She believed in the power of politics and the "rightness" of certain causes. Washington was the political vortex, and she had wanted to be swept into it.

When she first arrived in Washington, she had gotten a job with the American Israel Public Affairs Committee as a research analyst. The idea of combining Jewish issues and politics had excited her. After six years of working with that combination she had become disillusioned with the politics, and she promised herself that her next job would involve "nothing Jewish" and "nothing with Capitol Hill." Other than those two conditions, she was open to anything.

Although she had told herself that she was done with Capitol Hill, she couldn't rid herself of it in her personal life. She had been dating a legislative aide for several months, and the relationship was becoming more serious. While she wanted to stay in Washington, she was confused as to what she would do.

Extremely friendly, she was an attractive brunette with a sarcastic wit. Packed with nervous energy, she talked incessantly, flitting from one story to another in rapid succession. People were entertained by her humor and enthusiasm, as well as by her idealism. Unlike many young arrivals to Washington, she had not yet lost her sense of mission. She just didn't know what her next one would be.

In March, just one month after leaving her job, she received a call from Doug Bloomfield, another former Clevelander. Bloomfield was a Washington consultant to the WJC. He had heard that she was looking for a job and thought that he might be able to offer her something very temporary. Was she aware of the Swiss banks and the Holocaust dormant accounts? Senator D'Amato wanted to try to find more documentation on the topic and had written to the U.S. National Archives in College Park, Maryland. The WJC was also interested in researching the topic. The organization could hire her as a researcher for two days. He suggested that she meet with D'Amato's legislative director, Gregg Rickman. He was the one in charge of D'Amato's Swiss bank inquiry.

Although she was skeptical about reentering the world of Capitol Hill, she went to Rickman's office. She immediately felt at home with the senator's young assistant. Not only was he Jewish, he was a former Clevelander.

During the past few months, Rickman had been listening to survivors' stories. His own father-in-law was a survivor. He had come to believe that the Swiss bankers were criminals who must be brought to justice. D'Amato and the WJC could make that happen. All they needed were the proper weapons.

He showed her a letter that he had received from Dr. Michael Kurtz, assistant archivist at the U.S. National Archives. Kurtz was responding to Rickman's inquiry as to whether the archives might have information about Swiss Holocaust dormant accounts. The U.S. National Archives and Records Administration preserves records created by organizations of the executive, legislative, and judicial branches of the federal government and happened to have a substantial quantity of records relating to World War II. Kurtz wasn't sure what there was exactly, but he offered one suggestion: Rickman should begin by researching Operation Safehaven.

An Allied intelligence effort begun near the end of World War II, Operation Safehaven had as its primary purpose preventing a defeated Germany from placing its assets in "safe havens" that they could later use for a future war. In 1944, when the war appeared to be turning against Hitler, the Foreign Economic Administration, a department of the U.S. Treasury Department, proposed a plan to gather data on German hidden assets. Its goal was to uncover and prevent the sale and disappearance of Nazi assets, looted and otherwise, after the war and to prevent neutral countries, such as Switzerland, from becoming "safe havens" for Nazis' spoils. By the war's end, the Safehaven operation involved many U.S. agencies, including the Treasury, State, War, and Justice Departments, as well as the Office of Strategic Services (OSS), the forerunner of the CIA.

From the beginning, Safehaven was plagued with conflicts. Rivalries existed within and between departments as well as between the United States and Great Britain. The mission of Safehaven was strengthened, however, during the United Nations Monetary and Financial Conference in Bretton Woods, New Hampshire, in 1944. Neutral countries were called upon to take action to prevent the transfer, disposition, or concealment of assets belonging to governments, individuals, or institutions in occupied countries. This included looted gold.[5]

On March 8, 1945, Lauchlin Currie, an assistant to President Roosevelt, persuaded the Swiss Federal Council to agree to take active measures to advance the Safehaven objectives. Two months later, the Americans discovered that the Swiss had purchased several thousand kilograms of looted gold from Germany.[6] After the war, the OSS and the Foreign Funds Control of the Treasury Department continued to track the flight of German capital and to investigate linkages with the neutral countries. As the Western world turned its attention toward rebuilding Europe and fending off the threat of Communism and the Soviet Union, Operation Safehaven lost momentum. Its intelligence, however, helped shed light on the underbelly of Nazi Germany's economic relationships with other countries, most notably the neutrals.

Kurtz believed that the Safehaven documents could provide the first evidential crumbs for Rickman. Of course, locating them would not be easy. U.S. archival records are organized according to who created them. To try to find the important U.S. Safehaven documents, one would need to research the files of all of the departments and agencies involved with that program: State, Treasury, the military, Justice, OSS. To make things even more difficult, files within each department are stored in the order in which they were made, and thus many files relevant to Safehaven are sandwiched between thousands of irrelevant ones. Nevertheless, Kurtz told Rickman that researching Operation Safehaven would take only a few days. To Rickman, a few days seemed a small price to pay for a smoking gun.

Kleiman could not resist Rickman's idealistic enthusiasm. This wasn't a job but an historic opportunity. Two days later, they entered the tall, windowed foyer in the U.S. National Archives facility at College Park. Although Rickman was researching for Senator D'Amato, and Kleiman for the WJC, they both believed that they were working toward the same objective: to find evidence of Holocaust-era dormant accounts held by Swiss banks.

The U.S. National Archives facility at College Park is a large modern building. It contains six floors of record storage and research rooms. Unlike at a library, one cannot walk in, locate a source on a computer, and pull the desired item off the shelf. A researcher at the archives must follow a litany of rules, from carrying only a pencil to having to request the desired file or files.

Kleiman learned the system quickly. On her first day at the archives, she requested to look through nine cartons of files that contained Safehaven papers. A lot of the papers she was handling were yellow from age. Some were nothing more than memos written on brittle, tissue-thin paper. Kleiman felt as if she were sorting through people's desk drawers. Sifting through them was tedious. Sitting hunch-shouldered over bureaucratic paperwork, reading letter after banal letter, hardly felt historic to her.

On her second day at the archives, she was culling through a carton of files when she pulled out a Safehaven intelligence report dated July 12, 1945. It listed one hundred and eighty-two financial accounts held by the Société Général de Surveillance, a notary and trust company in Geneva. According to the intelligence report, these Holocaust-era accounts had never been reclaimed by the depositors. The accounts were in different currencies, and Kleiman could not decipher their total value. She copied the list and gave it to Rickman who quickly faxed it to the Congressional Research Service. After converting the numbers and adjusting for inflation, the agency found that the document referred to $2 million in accounts, which were worth over $20 million in present day values.

They thought they had struck gold. Here was a list of dormant accounts worth $20 million that the banks had never included in any of their previous audits. The news was leaked to the press, and D'Amato used it to bolster his accusations against the banks.

"Adjusted for inflation, these accounts today would be worth in the area of $20 million, two-thirds of the amount which was found by the Swiss after their search in 1995. It just doesn't add up," D'Amato declared during his first Senate Banking Committee hearing.[7]

No one spoke of the fact that the Société Général de Surveillance was not a bank. In fact, it was a firm that had been founded by a Jew and had provided Jews and others a place to protect their money. It was meant to be a safe haven for Jewish assets. Société Général later investigated and found postwar account activity for all but four of the accounts.[8] This was hardly the smoking gun. Nevertheless, the revelation that there were documents such as the Société Général in the National Archives awakened everyone.

Kleiman began arriving early at the archives and spending entire days sifting through different cartons. She and Rickman were joined by two other researchers from D'Amato's office. As she continued to find documents, she received mixed messages from the WJC. Yes, the WJC leaders wanted her to find documents, and, yes, they wanted to use them against the banks, but did she need to share every one of them with Rickman? They were the ones who had brought the issue to the public. Why should D'Amato ride in on his white horse?[9]

Despite what Kleiman felt were territorial scrimmages between the WJC and D'Amato, she and Rickman continued to work closely together. They moved through the archives at a frenzied pace, requesting carton after carton. They came upon an OSS intelligence report dated May 9, 1945, that detailed the extraction and smelting of dental gold fillings from deceased concentration camp prisoners. The prospect that victims' dental gold, known as nonmonetary gold, might have entered the pool of Nazi monetary gold made headlines. A 1946 document was found that described the well-known Merkers Mine site, a salt mine in southern Germany where American troops had found a huge cache of gold, jewelry, and art that had been stored there by the Germans. There were bags of victims' gold rings and dental fillings. The Allies

had inventoried the Merkers assets and had sent the gold, both monetary and nonmonetary, to the Tripartite Gold Commission.

The Tripartite Gold Commission was established by the Allies in
1946 to oversee the distribution of looted gold that had been found in
Germany or that had been transferred from Germany to another country. The Allies believed that the looted gold had come from countries'
national monetary reserves. The commission, whose members include
the United States, France, and Great Britain, still had, in 1996, $68 mil-
lion worth of gold to distribute. Some of it was stored in the U.S Federal
Reserve. Could that store also be tainted with victims' dental gold?

Kleiman and Rickman found a document referring to an account
held by Mussolini at a Credit Suisse branch in New York and another
document listing Swiss firms that might have been concealing German
interests. In a matter of weeks, the question of Switzerland's dormant
accounts had become overshadowed by larger questions of Swiss financial collaboration with the Nazi regime and of Switzerland's economic
behavior during and after the war. It was this sudden expansion of the
debate, more than any one document, that put the Swiss government on
the defensive.

D'Amato and the WJC leaders were media savvy and knew the importance of sensational sound bites. These documents provided the perfect material. Rickman and Kleiman watched as D'Amato and the Jewish leaders spoke to reporters and waved their documents in the air.
Each would dramatically claim that they were in possession of a recently declassified document. In truth, the vast majority of the documents that Rickman and Kleiman were finding had been public for
years.

When a researcher copies a document at the U.S. National Archives,
he or she must place the copy's date in the corner. This date can be easily mistaken for the date of declassification. The researchers told
D'Amato and the others of the error, but the "confusion" conveniently
persisted.

Kleiman and Rickman couldn't help feeling important. Hunkered
down in a research room at the National Archives, they were comrades-
in-arms embarked on a noble mission. They were, as one of D'Amato's young researchers put it, "standing on the precipice of history."

Watching the Swiss ambassador dodge questions about documents that she herself had unearthed gave Kleiman a sense of power. She thought of Harriet Beecher Stowe, the author of *Uncle Tom's Cabin,* and remembered reading how Lincoln once introduced Stowe as the "little lady who wrote the book that started this great war." This version of herself as Stowe was a far cry from how she had felt just a few weeks earlier.[10]

As the issue heated up, the researchers came under increased pressure to find more information. Several freelance researchers came to College Park to assist the two. By summer, the research force had more than doubled in size. Rickman and Kleiman were considered the leaders, but, in reality, no single supervisor oversaw the effort. The person who carried the brunt of having so many researchers pursuing the same topic in such an uncoordinated manner was an archivist at the U.S. National Archives at College Park named Greg Bradsher.

Bradsher, a warm affable man, had been at the archives for more than twenty years. Although he was not an expert on Safehaven, early in his career he had been responsible for property records related to the occupation of Germany. In 1983 Bradsher had been going through the records of the Treasury Department, particularly the Foreign Funds Control records. As an archivist, he had to decide which records to keep permanently and which to throw out. He went through one carton, dated 1944, and saw records labeled Safehaven. He then grabbed another carton, dated 1948. He found the same thing. By the time he had finished, he had gone through twenty boxes, all of them containing Safehaven papers.

"This stuff must be important," he thought, and, with the power that only an archivist can wield, he permitted those boxes of "stuff" to remain.

In April 1996 one of Bradsher's staff asked where the Foreign Fund Control records were. A researcher was requesting them. Bradsher became curious. Who was asking for them? And why? He was led to Kleiman.

Bradsher, a fast talker himself, met his match with Kleiman. She explained what she was doing and how this was going to be a big issue because she had found a document that she had let D'Amato know about and that he was going to have hearings and the press was very interested and Bradsher had better get prepared for an onslaught of researchers.

They would be investigating Nazi gold and slave labor and Argentina and . . .

By late summer her predictions had come true. Researchers from the Swiss banks, the Swiss government, Wilmer, Cutler, historians, journalists, survivors, and scholars were at the National Archives. Tired of answering the same questions, Bradsher printed a ten-page guide to the most relevant documents. Little did he know that this guide would grow to more than three hundred pages and that he would find himself a year later addressing an international conference on the topic at Monte Verita (Mountain of Truth), in the foothills of Ascona, Switzerland.

By September 1996 Kleiman was a nervous wreck. She was working day and night and was still getting paid only hourly. She loved what she was doing, but she wanted more stability. What she thought would be a day or two of research had turned into six months' work. With little money and no job security, she found herself in the same position she had been in six months earlier.[11]

"I can't keep going," she confided to Rickman. "I have to leave."

Rickman returned to his office.

The next morning, she found a message from him at the archives. "Hold firm."

He knew that Mendelsohn was preparing a lawsuit against the banks. Maybe he needed a researcher.

A week later, Kleiman was sitting in Hausfeld's office. She told him what she had found at the archives and then listened as he described the complaint that he, Lewis, and Gallagher were busy preparing against the banks.

Hausfeld spoke in a hushed voice.

"These are not ordinary claims we're asserting, and this is not just about money." He paused after each thought. "In this case, we will be invoking moral and legal principles in an attempt to achieve justice." He explained that they would be accusing the banks of profiting from slave labor, Nazi plunder, and deposited accounts. They needed someone to coordinate the evidence.

Kleiman felt herself being drawn in. It wasn't as much his lofty language that resonated as it was his pauses, the stilled spaces he placed between words.

She took a deep breath. She was determined not to make the same mistakes that she had made in her previous jobs. This time she would ask her questions first.

"How often will I get reviewed?"

"Never," replied Hausfeld.

"How will I know if I'm not doing my job well?"

"I'll yell," he answered.

"Could I talk to someone about the firm?"

"Why?"

"So I can find out about the corporate culture."

"We have no culture."

Back and forth they went until, baffled and frustrated, she said good-bye. On her way out, she stopped at the desk of Hausfeld's secretary.

"What is it like to work for him?" she whispered.

His secretary smiled. "He sucks you up like a vacuum cleaner. You have no choice. He makes you want to work for him."

She took the job.

The next week, a team of paralegals went over to Rickman's office to copy all of the documents. No sooner had they brought them to Kleiman's new office than Lewis and Hausfeld called her in.

They had some bad news. Ed Fagan, a lawyer in New York, had filed a class-action suit against the banks in the Eastern District of New York, the same district in which they were planning on filing.

The bad news was not so much that some lawyer unknown to Hausfeld had filed but, as Hausfeld saw it, that this lawyer's complaint did not begin to address the multitude of issues that Hausfeld wanted to pursue. It did not mention slave labor or refugees, and it did not try to link the allegations with any legal theory. Hausfeld was afraid Fagan's complaint would dilute his own effort. For this reason, he wanted to hurry and file. But first he needed to write an accurate story. At present, all they had were piles of documents. They needed to translate the raw intelligence into a cohesive narrative. And that narrative would need to stand up in a court of law.

"It's one thing to accuse someone of tax evasion and fraud," Lewis reminded Kleiman, "but it's quite another thing to accuse them of complicity in genocide."

Kleiman had written reports in her other jobs, but nothing compared to this task. She wasn't a lawyer, but she knew enough to know that this was not the usual procedure. In most cases there is a story, and one collects documents to support it. In this case, there were documents, and one needed to find the story. She sequestered herself in her office. She and her boyfriend had just become engaged, and for the moment she seemed to be living in two worlds; between reading documents and writing a story about the Holocaust, she was constantly telephoning caterers and hotels. Nevertheless, she worked on the report nonstop. She knew that Hausfeld had a vision of what he wanted, and she was determined not to disappoint him.

In a matter of weeks, they had put together a rough draft of more than one hundred pages, with an appendix of several hundred more. Hausfeld tried to bolster his claims with a broad historical review. He used documents and communiqués found at the National Archives, in history books, in experts' reports, and in transcripts from the Nuremberg decisions to examine everything from Swiss neutrality to the use of the Swiss-based Red Cross to transfer looted assets. The research and writing had taken his firm eight months to complete. Although its sources were limited to National Archives documents and previously published reports and books, his complaint was an attempt at exposing the economic crimes of the Holocaust and at melding history and law. In that respect, no matter the date on which anyone else filed, he believed his would be the first true complaint.

3

Plaintiffs Speak

Highly respected Judge Korman.

My name is Chya Hoffman born Weiss. I am a Romanian Satu-mare. My parents we was ten children. The Germans come in they sent everybody in the Ghetto. My father was very rich. He had a big store: furs, coats, materials . . . we was very rich, big house, three employees. . . . My mother and father traveled a lot, put a lot of money in Swiss bank. The Germans come in, they took them away to the Gestapo. They bleed them . . . how do I say this . . . they beat them to bleeding. She tell where she put the money, where she put everything. We was hiding in the basement, three big rooms. Everything was there from the store. . . . They was beating them, she was telling the truth where she hid everything. In the meantime, when they come home to tell us, bleeding very bad . . . my father made a bunker in the room under the couch with my brothers. . . . We have a big house, we have two streets, the garden is there.

When the Germans come to take to the Ghetto my parents, we run out in the other side. We were hiding with Christians. My parents were taken away. From there we went to Budapest, hiding with Christian papers. My mother put us on buttons and the buttons were diamonds and this was covered. In Budapest we can sell this. We had what to eat. After that . . . we had to go. We was hiding . . . two days, by the Swiss Consulate. It was so many people we can't be there. I ran to the street. They catch me. They took me to the police. They take from there. They take me to camp concentration, near Vienna. . . . I was there till the end. I was a young girl. My sister hiding in Budapest. . . . My brother was in Romania. . . . I noticed, my father put a lot of money in the Swiss bank. Send it every Friday come the broker who took the money in the bank. . . . I don't know who, I don't know where this is.

I'm working in a nursing home. I'm a seventy-four-year-old. I have four children. Many grandchildren, thank God. My husband is eighty-two, sitting here. He's retired already. Just I support the house. I'm working like a horse . . . the housework, dishes, cooking, baking, cleaning. . . . I would like very much to try to retrieve the money from the Swiss bank. I went there a few times. No answer. I ask Judge Korman. Please

52

take into consideration. I need it very badly this money, our money. I don't be charity. I never used to be charity. I'm working for the money.

November 20, 2000, Swiss Banks' Fairness Hearing

On an afternoon in late September 1996, the attorney Ed Fagan sat at a table in his small Manhattan office and examined several crumpled pieces of paper. Seated next to him was Gizella Weisshaus, a client of several years whom he was representing in a convoluted real estate dispute involving her deceased cousin's house. The two of them were huddled over the table. They were trying to piece together the scattered papers. She was a Holocaust survivor, and these scraps were the only remaining evidence she had of her past—these and the fragments of her memories.

This one, she explained, is my Displaced Persons Identity Card. This one was issued from the International Refugee Organization. Here is my Romanian birth certificate, my parents' marriage certificate, a photo of my family. She continued until she turned to the *New York Times* article sitting on the table. Suddenly her melancholy turned to anger. Thirty years ago, she had tried to retrieve her father's money from the Swiss Union Bank (its name was later changed to the Union Bank of Switzerland), but, without her father's account number, she had returned empty-handed. This was the reason that Weisshaus and Fagan had gotten together. It was this issue that would change both of their lives forever.

Until that afternoon, Fagan had not given much thought to the Holocaust. He had grown up in a religious Jewish family in San Antonio, Texas. To him, the Holocaust was history, and, though significant, it did not define him as a Jew or as a lawyer. He knew of no relatives who had perished under the Nazis, and he had felt no need to focus on its details.[1]

After graduating from Yeshiva University's Cardozo Law School in New York City, he remained in the east. He worked for a firm in New Jersey and Philadelphia before setting up his own private practice in 1988. He was living with his wife and two children in New Jersey.

Fagan had concentrated his practice on personal-injury cases and was having trouble making ends meet. A virtual unknown among the big-name plaintiffs' attorneys, he seemed to be always on the lookout for that one lucrative case that would send him into the plush and dramatic world of high-powered stakes. While he waited for his break, he struggled to support his small firm, Fagan & Associates. He placed ads in the New York yellow pages, seeking clients for personal-injury lawsuits.[2]

Curly-haired and thin, the aggressive Fagan was constantly moving, his body perpetually fueled by caffeine. With angular features and deep-set eyes, he looked younger than his forty-four years. Bearing a trace of a Texan accent, he spoke loudly and without inhibition.

In 1996 he faced a serious accusation—that of soliciting clients at the scene of an accident. In the plaintiffs' business this is called "ambulance chasing," and its stigma can follow an attorney for a lifetime.

On December 20, 1995, an American Airlines jet had crashed into a Colombian mountainside, killing one hundred and sixty people. Less than two weeks later, American lawyers were seen in the halls of the Intercontinental Hotel in Cali, Colombia, where many of the victims' relatives were staying. According to a January 22, 1996, *New Jersey Law Journal* article, Fagan was one of those lawyers sighted. The article claimed that he had made two trips to Colombia and had obtained retainer agreements from the relatives of two of the victims. A week later, an article in that journal talked about a proposed New Jersey bill that, if passed, would prohibit the solicitation of victims by lawyers for thirty-one days after a disaster. Fagan, who had been admitted to the New Jersey bar, was mentioned.

"I did not go down there talking about a lawsuit," he told the journal. "If, after I helped, someone said it might be nice to represent us, that would be fine." Unlike the other lawyers, he claimed he was only asking, "What can I do to help?"[3]

He was busy tending to his practice when his mother-in-law called to tell him to read a *New York Times* article entitled "Hard Calculus: Nazi Gold vs. Swiss Banks' Secrets." The article outlined the rash of accusations that were being leveled against the Swiss banks. It mentioned the Swiss National Bank's purchase of Nazi gold, a possible account in Hitler's name at UBS, jewels looted by the Nazis, the morals of neutrality, and dormant accounts.

He immediately recognized the tremendous legal potential. Why hadn't some other attorney jumped on it? Never one to waste a minute, he began thinking about constructing a suit. The issue of dormant accounts would be one of the safest routes to follow. But he needed a plaintiff. When Weisshaus walked into his office and began talking about the article and her father's missing account, he could hardly contain himself. This was it. He had his plaintiff. How much luckier could he get?[4]

He was intent on being the first one out of the gate and on securing a position as class counsel. On October 1, 1996, less than two weeks from the time that he had read the article, he signed his name to an eighteen-page complaint and filed it with the U.S. district court for the Eastern District of New York. It was still unclear what other plaintiffs besides Weisshaus were out there, but for the moment that didn't matter. Fagan sued on behalf of her and all other victims and survivors of the Holocaust. As for the defendants, he named the Union Bank of Switzerland, the Swiss Bank Corporation, and the Swiss National Bank. In his haste, he erred and listed the Swiss Bank Corporation a/k/a the Swiss National Bank. In fact, they were two separate entities. He was asking for $20 billion in damages and had every intention of collecting legal fees when the case was over.[5]

Gizella Weisshaus's spirits were renewed. She finally had something besides her own voice to raise against UBS. She had an American lawyer whose zest and commitment appeared to be boundless. More important, she had the U.S. legal system. She immediately threw herself into the case, showing up at Fagan's office and volunteering to stuff envelopes and answer phone calls from inquiring survivors. She and Fagan were determined to get as many survivors signed onto the suit as they could.

Weisshaus turned to her own community for support. She lived in the Williamsburg section of Brooklyn and belonged to a sect of Hasidic Jews called the Satmars. The name derives from Satu-Mare, a Romanian city that Romania was forced to cede Hungary during World War II. The Satmars established their American community under the leadership of Rebbe Joel Teitelbaum.

Williamsburg looks like a modern-day version of an eastern European shtetl. Yiddish is spoken everywhere: on the streets, in the kosher butcher shops, around the dinner table. Men wear traditional black hats, dark coats, and trousers. When they walk briskly down the sidewalks, their long, coiled sideburns (*payot*) dangle like toy Slinkys. The women dress in long sleeves, dark stockings, and below-the-knee skirts or dresses. Married women wear wigs *(shaytl)* to cover their heads. To anyone unfamiliar with Hasidim, Williamsburg appears like a time warp where present and past converge.

Many of the older members of the Satmar community were Holocaust survivors whose world had collapsed long ago. As survivors, they were stuck in the anomaly of their own survival, and they had only their lifestyle, their religion, their memories, and, as Weisshaus would soon convince them, their assets to help them reclaim their past.

For some survivors outside the Satmar community, especially those who were not religious, Weisshaus was not a charismatic spokesperson. Dressed in mothball-scented polyester dresses, black corrective shoes, and hats with large ersatz flowers, she was, to them, a walking billboard for the "old country." She appeared the antithesis of Elie Wiesel, the handsome and eloquent survivor who had attained international stature. Nevertheless, the media flocked to her. She was the first plaintiff in a case that was just beginning.

Weisshaus was not shy with the press. She granted interviews for magazines in the United States and Europe. A photo of her sitting on her bed appeared in *People* magazine. With every article, there was a recap of her past, a few lines describing her last moments with her father. As alienating as her personality was to some survivors, her story was all too familiar to them.

During the war, her father had gathered his family of nine together to tell them that he had hidden money in the house and that he had a bank account in the Swiss Union Bank. The day after his talk, the family was stuffed into boxcars and transported to Auschwitz. Weisshaus's mother and six brothers and sisters were sent immediately to the gas chambers. Her father followed later. Weisshaus was pushed into a separate line and sent to work as a slave laborer at an oil refinery and then at an ammunitions plant. Later, she endured a forced death march and was liberated near the Czechoslovakian border. She eventually returned to her home in Shiget, Romania, and recovered some of her father's hidden assets in the dark crevices behind the walls and ceiling. Among the possessions that she found was her father's gold watch. While she used most of what she recovered to buy herself, her husband, and her two children passage to the United States, she kept the gold watch. Its frozen hour was one of her few souvenirs of her past.[6]

Six children and twenty-eight grandchildren later, Weisshaus, at sixty-six, was still searching for the rest of her father's money. She had approached the Swiss banks during the 1960s, had even paid their search fee, but, without her father's account number, nobody would help her. Although she still lacked the proper documents, she believed that this time would be different. Attention was surging like a wave on this side of the ocean, and she planned, with her lawyer, to ride the crest to the other shore.

As energized as Hausfeld was by the Swiss banks case, he had become distracted by the sudden movement of another, older case. In 1994 he and a colleague had filed a class-action race discrimination suit against Texaco. Although they had conducted scores of depositions and obtained declarations and expert witness reports to support their allegations of race discrimination in the corporate offices of Texaco's headquarters, the suit had remained bogged down in a federal courtroom. Prospects for a decent settlement looked grim until October 1996, when a former Texaco official produced a taped conversation that he had secretly recorded at a Texaco business meeting.

On the tape the executives were discussing the race discrimination suit. After having the tape enhanced and transcribed, Hausfeld and his colleague determined that the executives had referred to black employees as "black jelly beans" and "niggers." The *New York Times* got hold of a copy of the tape. Hausfeld watched as news of it dominated the headlines. Although Texaco later asserted that their executive had said "poor St. Nicholas" and not "niggers" and that "black jelly beans" was a term used in a diversity training class, it was too late. The Reverend Jesse Jackson had joined forces with Hausfeld, and Jackson was talking of a Texaco boycott. On November 15, a confident Hausfeld stood before the press and announced a $176.1 million settlement with Texaco.

While Hausfeld was consumed by the Texaco suit, Lewis, Gallagher, and Kleiman were devoting enormous amounts of their time to the completion of the Swiss banks complaint. Not only did it have to be legally precise, but every day Hausfeld would insist that a new document be added to the fact section. Gallagher did the legal rewriting of the complaint, Kleiman dealt with the historical narrative, and Lewis had the task of finding those few qualified individuals who would consent to being class representatives. These individuals would have their names listed on the complaint and represent the larger class of unnamed claimants. Since a class action is often referred to by the first name that appears on the complaint, a plaintiff's name can be irrevocably branded on a class action.

Lewis knew from his experience with environmental health cases that being a class representative in a class action can be emotionally and psychologically draining. Large defense firms can be intrusive and harassing in their efforts to discredit individual plaintiffs. Lewis had watched defense attorneys in cases involving chemical exposure subpoena medical, school, and library records of class representatives.

Some class representatives view their roles as a form of service, not unlike jury duty, while others see their job in more noble terms, as their opportunity to redress a deep-seated injustice. While there is no legal obligation to talk to the press, the class representatives are often the first to be approached in a high-profile case.

In the Swiss banks case, journalists did not have to wait for the assignment of class representatives. They already had the personal stories of survivors who were testifying at D'Amato's hearings. Some of the survivors would go on to become class representatives, while others would fade into the anonymity of the larger class.

On October 18, 1996, two days after the Holocaust survivor Lewis Salton had testified at D'Amato's second Senate Banking Committee hearing, Rich Lewis went to pay him a visit at his Manhattan apartment. Spacious and nicely decorated, the apartment was Salton's second residence. His other home was in Connecticut. Of all the survivors whom Lewis had interviewed, Salton, at eighty-five, was the most lively and energetic. He was well dressed and had a full head of white hair. He looked more like an elder statesman than a frail and aging survivor. He had a contagious smile and a playful sense of humor. He had shed his old-country habits long ago and appeared every bit the wealthy businessman that he had become.

Salton could have been the poster child for the American dream. He had arrived in New York as a young refugee with nothing but a rare stamp from his father's stamp collection. After several unsuccessful business ventures, he invented an electric hot tray that could keep food warm for hours. The Salton Hotray, as it came to be called, was a huge success. Popular in the suburbs with housewives who used it for entertaining, it also made a hit on college campuses, where it allowed students to warm food in their dorm rooms. He reaped the benefits of American capitalism and enjoyed the luxuries that his newly earned money provided. He bought a country home, began traveling around the world, and outfitted himself in nice suits. In his appearance, he looked like any other successful American professional, but when he opened his mouth and spoke in his thick accent, it was obvious that he carried a very different history.

Salton was born in 1911, in Krakow, Poland.[7] His father, Bernard Salamon, worked as a lawyer. He was also an avid stamp collector who traveled throughout Europe, buying and selling stamps. Many times Salton overheard his father on the telephone with a Zurich stamp dealer named Luder Edelman. His father made several trips to Switzerland to visit Edelman, and Salton was certain that his father had opened a bank account in Zurich. Since it was illegal at the time for Poles to send money out of Poland, his father was always concerned about his transactions becoming known. He kept to himself and conducted his business in silence. His quiet life was shattered when the war broke out.

In 1939 Salton was twenty-eight and living in Warsaw. As soon as he heard that the Germans had invaded Poland, he fled to Russian-occupied Poland, where he arrived just two hours ahead of the German army. From Poland, he trekked for a year and a half, making his way to Panama and finally to New York. Throughout his journey, he managed to hold onto a rare first-edition Austrian stamp his father had given him before the war. If he was ever in trouble, his father had instructed him, he should sell the stamp. When he finally reached New York, he went directly to a dealer in New York City. He sold the stamp for $500. With the sale of this stamp he began to remake his life. Over the years, he couldn't help looking back, retracing the steps of his father, his stepmother, and his stepsister, all of whom he had left behind.

In the fall of 1942 Salton's stepmother and sister had been shipped by cattle car to the Belzec concentration camp, where they had been stripped and gassed. Salton's father, who had become separated from his wife and daughter, had been transported by truck to the Polish National Forest of Niepolomice, where he and other Poles had been ordered to dig large trenches. On September 26, 1942, the SS had lined up ten people at a time, made them stand naked on the ground in front of the trenches, and shot them to death. Six hundred and twelve Jews, including Salton's father, were murdered that day. The Saltons' home and possessions had been looted.

In 1947, for the first time after the war, Salton returned to Europe. He wanted to find his father's money. He went to Zurich and looked up the Luder Edelman Company. He identified himself. Before he could say why he had come, the stamp dealer wanted to know where his father's stamp collection was.

"It's gone," Salton responded. "It disappeared long ago." Salton then asked about his father's transactions. "Did he pay you here from a Swiss bank?"

"Of course he paid," the dealer answered. "We wouldn't have given him anything for free."

"Which bank was it?"

The dealer shrugged and disappeared. A few moments later he returned empty-handed. He had no records relating to Bernard Salamon.

From there Salton went to several of the large Swiss banks, including Credit Suisse and Swiss Bank Corporation. Although the officials were cordial, when it came to locating his father's account, they too shrugged and shook their heads. At every bank, he received the same response. Without any documents and with only secondhand knowledge that his father had paid in Swiss francs to the Luder Edelman Company, he was powerless. After fifty years, he was still asking the same question: did anyone have a record of his father's account?

After hearing his testimony, Lewis believed that Salton qualified as a class representative. His failed efforts at retrieving his father's Swiss bank account were representative of the experiences of many members of the class who had similar dormant account claims. In addition, Salton could represent those whose possessions had been looted by the Nazis. Much of this loot had been deposited in Swiss banks.

Salton agreed to become a class representative on the complaint. He had an emotional need to retrieve his father's money.

"I am not bitter," he explained, "but I want the Swiss to stop denying the role that they played in the Holocaust."

Lewis enjoyed his visit with Salton. They talked, they joked, and they discussed the lawsuit.

Salton liked to reminisce about his first experiences as a new immigrant in New York City. "I was walking from downtown Manhattan to Brooklyn when I saw a large crowd of people hovering together. They were standing shoulder to shoulder, peering intensely in the same direction. I assumed that they were looking at a fire or a terrible accident, so I stopped. What I saw surprised me. Two men were pouring water on the ice rink in front of Rockefeller Plaza. My father had always told me that time was money, but here were three hundred people watching men pour water on an ice rink." He laughed. "Later, I stopped in a drugstore to order a soda. I saw the waitress put something called a straw into my drink so that I wouldn't have to lift the glass. I knew then that I would have no trouble making a new life for myself here."[8]

For Rich Lewis, who had had no prior contact with Holocaust survivors, his interviews were eye-openers. He was learning details about a chapter in history that he had only read about in books, and he was discovering the diversity of survivors' experiences and personalities. Although there was no prototypical survivor, he had to decide on individuals who could best represent the single identity of the class.

He had talked to many survivors and heirs who, like Salton, had knocked on the doors of Swiss banks in a futile effort to recover their families' accounts. He had heard tales from those who had been forced to perform slave labor, who had had their family businesses Aryanized and their homes looted. Some were wary about becoming involved in the lawsuit, while others yearned for the involvement and recognition of being a class representative. Most figured they had nothing to lose. They signed their names onto the suit and hoped that the American legal system could finally break the silence of the Swiss banks. What did it matter which lawyer led the fight? To them, what was important was that the banks return their money.

Early in the morning of October 21, 1996, Hausfeld dropped off the last riders in his neighborhood carpool, parked the minibus, and walked to his office on New York Avenue. Ever since his neighborhood had lost a subsidy that had provided them with a commercial driver, he and another neighbor had been taking turns driving a bus of fellow commuters to the city and back. Most of the time he enjoyed this role. It gave him a chance to be with his neighbors and helped frame his day. Lately, though, this responsibility had become intrusive. He was moving too fast to be bound by such a rigid schedule. In a few hours, he would be filing charges against Switzerland's three largest commercial banks. By evening, missing his carpool would be the least of his problems.

Hausfeld's fifth-floor office was built on top of what had once been Washington's Greyhound bus station on 12th and New York Avenue. He had been there only a few years and was enjoying the new space. The majestically designed Greyhound building was just a short distance from his prior office on 14th and New York, but when he walked into its elegant lobby, he felt as if he had crossed a major boundary. Suddenly, he not only had room to store boxes of files, but he had a comfortable reception area that he adorned weekly with fresh flowers, spacious offices for his twenty-five attorneys, and two furnished conference rooms. The office still paled beneath the shadow of D.C.'s powerhouse defense firms down the block, but for a small plaintiffs' firm, Cohen, Milstein, Hausfeld and Toll had established a presence.

He liked arriving before everyone else and starting the day in silence. He picked up the Swiss banks complaint on his desk and flipped through the pages. Although he and Gallagher had gone through the complaint page by page, he had made several notes to himself during the night and now wanted to make a few changes. After these revisions, that was it. They needed to file.

He had researched Fagan's past and believed that the New York lawyer couldn't match him in experience or status, yet he also knew not to underestimate the power of the media. Fagan had been announcing that he had large numbers of survivors signing onto his suit, and, with each of his public appearances, he collected more signatures. Hausfeld was surprised at how much time Fagan was spending on recruiting plaintiffs. In a class action, lawyers don't need numbers. A class action represents a class of individuals, and thus individual signatures become irrelevant. To Hausfeld, Fagan's interviews sounded more like infomercials.

Hausfeld knew that there was no way Fagan could match the number and breadth of law firms he had recruited. Hausfeld had assembled a list of fifteen law firms, each of which had pledged to contribute $20,000 to the case.

Headed by Hausfeld and Weiss, this "Dream Team," as some would later call it, consisted of firms well known in the plaintiffs' world. Some of the attorneys were active in the ever-growing antitobacco suits, while others had worked on the *Exxon Valdez* class action. Most of them had belonged to a controversial consortium of plaintiffs' firms called the Complex Litigation Committee. Members of this group believed that if they could recruit medium and large firms across the country to work together on complex cases, it would give plaintiffs' attorneys more power against the large defense firms.

"It's a cartel of elite lawyers whose sole goal is to drum up business," one attorney who was not a member of the committee charged. Another critic claimed that the committee was exclusive and unethical.

In spite of such dissent, the committee continued to meet and work together. One of the cases Hausfeld had brought to the committee involved defective polybutylene pipes. Used primarily in trailer homes, these pipes had leaked water and damaged homes across the United States. When he first introduced this case, many members were reluctant to participate. They didn't think that the suit had potential. Convinced that the case was worthwhile, Hausfeld pleaded with the members until they finally agreed to sign on. The case settled for $950 million.

After the polybutylene case, he asked committee members to participate in the Swiss banks suit. How could they say no? Even if he was asking them to do it pro bono.

His list of attorneys spanned the country, from Weiss in New York to the seasoned plaintiffs' lawyer Robert Lieff, of Lieff Cabraser Heimann & Bernstein, in San Francisco. He recruited firms from one coast to the other, drawing from Alabama, Louisiana, Mississippi, Tennessee, North Carolina, Philadelphia, Minnesota, and Washington state.

"We have an army of lawyers," Weiss would later declare to the court.

They were prepared to fight the Swiss banks. First, though, they needed to win the battle raging in their own backyard, with an opponent who was proving to be as stubborn as the banks.

Since his filing, Fagan had been inundated with calls from survivors who had heard about his suit. The issue of Switzerland and the Holocaust had become a hot item in the news. He welcomed interviews and began initiating what would later become his trademark: the Fagan press release. He also began getting calls from other attorneys who were interested in his suit. He had aligned himself with an attorney in Germany named Michael Witti, but it was obvious that if this case continued to grow, he would need more help in the United States. Without much money and with little experience leading large class actions, he might have trouble convincing a judge that he could be lead counsel for such a major suit. It was good timing, then, when he received a phone call from Robert Swift, a Philadelphia attorney who was a partner in a well-respected firm.

Swift was fifty years old and the managing attorney for the Philadelphia firm of Kohn, Swift & Graf P.C. (This was the original firm from which Hausfeld and Jerry Cohen had broken.) He had been at the firm twenty-three years, working with its senior partner, Harold Kohn. Kohn was considered to be one of the best antitrust lawyers in the country. In much the same way that Jerry Cohen had served as a mentor for Hausfeld, Harold Kohn played that role for Swift.

Clean shaven, with tortoise-shell glasses and thinning hair, the serious Swift often came across as formal. Always polite and courteous, he spoke in a monotone and deliberated quietly before responding to a question. His temperament struck some of his colleagues as more befitting a diplomat than a high-stakes attorney. Nevertheless, he had proved himself to be a successful litigator and had racked up a string of victories over the years. He was especially proud of one case, which was still lingering in the courts. It was this case that prompted his call to Fagan.

In 1986 Swift had filed a complaint on behalf of Filipino human rights victims against the former president of the Philippines, Ferdinand E. Marcos. Marcos and his family had fled to Hawaii after having imposed fourteen years of martial law and terror on his country. He was charged with the torture, execution, and disappearance of ten thousand Filipinos.

Swift was the chief trial counsel. In 1992 a jury found the Marcos estate liable. Three years later, it awarded Swift's Filipino plaintiffs $1.9 billion in damages. This was the largest personal injury verdict in human rights history.

There was one problem. Marcos had died, and most of his money was stashed away in Swiss banks. To get to it, Swift would need to shift directions. Anticipating this, he had already begun flying across the Atlantic.

The Marcos case dragged on. In an effort to prevent the release of her husband's money from the Swiss banks, Marcos's wife, Imelda, appealed to one court after another. Swift claimed that Swiss Bank Corporation and Credit Suisse were sitting on a huge fortune amassed by Marcos. Whether it was as large as Swift claimed became a question. However, whatever the sum was, the bankers did not want to let go of it easily.[9]

Ten years had passed since the opening of the court case against Marcos, and Swift and his plaintiffs had yet to receive a penny. Paid or not, he was continuing the fight. The $1.9 billion verdict had established him as a trailblazer in the area of human rights litigation. The case became a touchstone of his career. He talked about it constantly. Anyone who came in contact with him and had not yet heard of the class action could expect a lecture.

His office, with its broad view of the city of Philadelphia, looked like a Marcos museum. It was filled with photographs, articles, and mementos from the case. On the largest wall, framed in glass, hung the chart he had used during the trial to demonstrate damages. On another wall was one of Marcos's signed orders of execution, and on yet another wall was a framed cartoon of Marcos breaking through a glass coffin with the verdict amount of $1.9 billion written underneath. (Marcos's wife had put Marcos in a glass case in Hawaii, hoping eventually to be able to bury him in the Philippines.) Stacked in a corner were Philippine newspapers, all bearing headlines about the case, and a photo of Swift with the current Filipino president.

In addition to understanding the plight of the Filipino victims, Swift believed that he understood the stubbornness of Swiss bankers. He understood the methodical and literal-minded Swiss, how they took their time and analyzed everything. He understood the nuances of their culture. Their value of money. No one would be better than he to lead the survivors in their fight against those banks.

He decided that he would work with Fagan, but he made it clear that, while Fagan would have an important role, Swift would be lead counsel.

Swift had read Hausfeld's complaint and was less than impressed. He did not like Hausfeld's heavy reliance on books and the pages and pages of extraneous historical information. To him, Hausfeld's pleadings concerning slave labor and the looting of assets seemed weak. Was this Hausfeld's attempt at showmanship? Whatever it was, it was obvious that Hausfeld was vying to lead the case.

If Swift was going to join this case, he was going to be one of the drivers. So what if Hausfeld had enlisted an impressive list of attorneys? Swift possessed the road map to the Swiss banks. Of course, he might need someone in addition to Fagan to help him navigate. When a colleague suggested Burt Neuborne, Swift encouraged his colleague to call the New York University professor.

It was just two months into the fall semester, and Neuborne was exhausted. Alone in his small office, he leaned back in his chair and closed his eyes. He had been teaching law for more than twenty years, and usually he had no problem adapting to the rhythm of academic life. There were other colleagues who withered at the sudden onslaught of classes and students, but not he. He became energized. He loved the mixture of nervousness and excitement that stirred in him moments before entering a classroom. It was the same adrenaline rush that he experienced before walking into a courtroom. Born a talker, he found that nothing pleased him more than spending a day before a captive audience talking about the law.

This semester was different. No matter how hard he tried, nothing— no legal argument, no student question, no creative theorizing—could rescue him from the grief he was feeling. Just two months earlier, on September 1, his daughter Lauren had died unexpectedly in her sleep. Having had a heart attack when she was sixteen, she had learned to live with a pacemaker. On the night that she died, scar tissue had blocked the pacemaker's impulse, causing a massive arrhythmia.

Newly married and completing her fifth year of rabbinical school, Lauren had been impassioned by social causes. She had wanted to follow the same path that she had watched her parents journey down during her childhood. Both had been active in the civil rights movement, and Neuborne had served as national legal director for the American Civil Liberties Union.

The loss of Lauren bore down on him like an oppressive weight. He kept thinking that if he could find some adequate way to honor her, then the pain might lift just a little.

In early November he received a phone call from a former colleague who had a proposition. Swift had recruited him to work on the Swiss banks case, but he was feeling overwhelmed by the seriousness of the allegations. He knew that Neuborne had been successful in setting up mechanisms for distributing assets in discrimination cases. Maybe he would consider devising a distribution plan for the survivors and heirs in the Swiss banks case.

Neuborne hesitated. Why even think about distribution at this stage of the game? Besides, the odds of winning such a case seemed impossible. Why would a U.S. court recognize jurisdiction? What legal theories could they use? As these questions swirled around, the memory of Lauren remained a still life in the background. What better way to honor her than to secure a sliver of justice for the victims of the Holocaust? Even if the case were to fail, it would raise questions about neutrality, human rights, and the burden of responsibility—questions she would have believed worth asking. He was awestruck by the timing of the call. Whether it was a sign or just one of life's synchronicities, he came to believe that he had received that phone call for a reason. He agreed to serve as a consultant to the case and vowed, as a gesture to Lauren, not to ask for any payment. This would be his personal tribute to her.

When he attended his first strategy meeting with Swift and Fagan, he realized the real reason that he had been invited. It certainly wasn't because of his status or wealth. One glance at his office, with its secondhand furniture and peeling paint, made that all too apparent. And never mind his work with distribution.

No, he had something none of the others had. He had something the other lawyers wanted. He had a recent victory with Judge Edward Korman, the judge assigned to the Swiss banks case.

Neuborne had successfully argued before the judge that the New York ballot access rules were too restrictive and prohibitive. The rules were subsequently declared unconstitutional. This victory had enabled the Republican presidential candidate Steve Forbes to be placed on the New York primary ballot.

A Democrat at heart, Neuborne was not ashamed of representing those who opposed his liberal biases. Over the years, he had represented people and organizations he did not support. To him, nothing took precedence over defending First Amendment freedoms. If that meant defending the Nazis' right to demonstrate in Skokie, Illinois, a community with a large concentration of Holocaust survivors, then so be it.

After graduating from Harvard Law School in 1964, Neuborne had gone to work on Wall Street as a tax lawyer. He was paid well and was on his way to becoming a partner at the firm. Everything was great except for the fact that it was the 1960s. The streets had become rife with civil disobedience. He felt like a voyeur to the unrest happening outside his office window. After three years, he asked the firm for a leave of absence so that he could defend antiwar demonstrators. He never returned.

Before Lauren died, Neuborne, who was fifty-seven, had been content with his lot in life. He had loved the combination of teaching at NYU and defending civil liberty cases. He had appeared on Court TV as a commentator for the O. J. Simpson trial, and he had even had a short fling with Hollywood. Two writers for the movie *The People versus Larry Flynt* had seen the excitable and animated Neuborne on Court TV and had asked him whether he would play the role of the lawyer for the right-wing advocate Jerry Falwell. Neuborne enjoyed the irony of playing Falwell's attorney, since Neuborne had helped write the real-life brief for Flynt's *Hustler* magazine.

"The stage directions for the script said Falwell's pompous and obnoxious lawyer approaches and I'm thinking I've got to do something about my TV persona," he joked.[10] The balding and round-faced Neuborne never missed a chance to mock himself.

When he accepted the Swiss banks case, he was confronted with another irony. He was suddenly allied with a former adversary. More than two decades earlier, he had confronted D'Amato in a New York courtroom. The Republican Party had been accused of requiring employees on Long Island to kick back one percent of their salaries each year as a "voluntary" contribution to the party. Neuborne, as opposing counsel, had questioned D'Amato, who was then the presiding supervisor of the Town of Hempstead, mercilessly. The Republican Committee was forced to return millions of dollars.[11]

Neuborne had another memory of D'Amato that transcended the courtroom. Lauren's first heart attack had occurred during that Republican Party trial. She had been taken to Central Brooklyn Hospital but needed to be transported to Mount Sinai Hospital for surgery. The trip was risky. She was connected to a temporary pacemaker that was operated by a battery attached to her leg. If the ambulance were to go over a bump and the wires were to get tangled, the pacemaker could stop.

D'Amato called Neuborne. Politics were politics, but babies were babies. Was there anything he could do? Neuborne explained the situation. Several hours later, D'Amato called back. He had arranged for the Brooklyn Battery Tunnel to be closed and for a police escort and a helicopter to shadow the ambulance. Lauren arrived at Mount Sinai Hospital in seven minutes.

Compassion was not the adjective everyone associated with D'Amato. He could be a political animal who went after people and issues with a vengeance. By December, he had directed all of his antipathy toward the Swiss banks. President Clinton's administration, pleased that the New York senator had turned his attention away from the Whitewater scandal, did not object. For the class-action attorneys, not to mention the WJC leaders, having D'Amato as an ally was a tremendous boost. He had already held two hearings on the subject and was making life very uncomfortable for the Swiss bankers and government officials.

He had begun his October 16 hearing in New York with a complicated accusation against the Swiss government, relating to the Swiss-Polish Agreement of June 25, 1949. The Swiss had signed a treaty with the Communist government of Poland to transfer dormant assets of Polish Holocaust victims held in Swiss banks to the Swiss National Bank. Switzerland had made no effort to locate the heirs or publish their names. What made this agreement so intolerable to D'Amato was that these Polish assets were put in the SNB in an account under the control of the Polish National Bank. These assets were then used to pay Swiss claims against Poland. In other words, the assets compensated Swiss citizens who had had their properties confiscated by the Communists. In a series of clever maneuverings, the money had come full circle, ending right back in the hands of the Swiss.

"Imagine that," D'Amato exclaimed. "Polish Jews had their assets taken over and paid over to the Swiss. The agreement was denounced at the time by the American Government, which filed a diplomatic demarche with the Polish Government. However, it was consummated. We're very concerned that Swiss citizens and corporations blatantly benefited from the Holocaust while the interests of the survivors were totally ignored. . . . Just unconscionable."[12]

He delivered his final punches through the testimony of six survivors. As articulate as Lewis Salton was during that hearing, another survivor, Estelle Sapir, provided the raw emotion. Leaning into the microphone, she did not bother with formalities.

"Two times I went to the Swiss banks. Two times they asked me for a death certificate for my father. The second time I went to Basel and when they asked me, I know I saw it [her father's account papers], a young man come out from behind, and the first thing he asked me, 'show me the death certificate for your father.'

"And I answer him, how can I have a death certificate? I have to go find Himmler, Hitler, Eichmann, and Mengele, and I start to cry and I run out from the bank, running in the street."[13]

Sapir was the daughter of Jozef Sapir, a wealthy Jewish businessman from Poland who had deposited much of his fortune in Credit Suisse. The last time Sapir saw her father, she was fourteen, and he was imprisoned in a detention camp in southern France. She remembered him telling her through the barbed wires, "Try to survive. You have money in Switzerland, plenty of money, don't worry. Don't go to Switzerland, the Swiss will send you back to the Germans."[14]

Sapir possessed a few pieces of paper with her father's name on them; one of these she believed was a deposit slip from Credit Suisse. She was the only survivor testifying who had papers and a ledger book with her father's name on it. She claimed to have had more proof, but it had been stolen from her niece when her niece's purse was snatched on her way to getting them photocopied for the hearing: a stroke of bad luck some skeptics found incredible.[15]

Sapir lived in a tiny apartment in Queens, New York, and suffered from a stomach ailment that made her painfully thin. Standing less than five feet tall, she spoke with a strained and accented voice. Her frailty and poor health generated a sense of urgency that caught everyone's attention. Profiled in a documentary about Nazi gold and the Swiss banks affair, she quickly became a symbol of the survivors. Her cause was adopted by D'Amato, and she signed on as a class representative for Fagan and Swift.

Greta Beer watched as these other survivors catapulted into the limelight. Here was Weisshaus, standing beside Fagan at press conference after press conference, and Lewis Salton, being interviewed as the class representative for Hausfeld, and now Estelle Sapir, smiling under D'Amato's protective wing. Where did that leave her? Didn't she deserve a little more recognition? As she would later find out, she was just one of many survivors who were beginning to feel forgotten, lost between the whoosh of politics and the sluggish pace of a lawsuit.

4

The Devil's Bridge

Dear Ms. Trescott:

In regard to your article in the Dec. 19, 1996, edition of the Washington Post. I was liberated by the American Army from a concentration camp on April 30, 1945. . . .

I was born in Hungary and we were deported to Auschwitz-Birkenau in May 1944. From Birkenau we were transported to Germany, where we worked 12–14 hours a day for the Wurtembergische Metalwaren Fabric. While there our camp was adjacent to a French prisoner of war camp, they received packages from home and the International Red Cross, but we, the Jews, received nothing.

The factory received payment for each slave laborers work, but we did not receive any compensation, not even to this day did we receive any wages!!! We received meager food and almost no clothes. My two sisters and I were in our early to mid-teens and worked as welders.

Isn't that a nice job for pre-teen and teen age girls?

Until today I wonder how we survived in the bitter cold German winter.

Sincerely,

Lilly Levinson

December 22, 1996, a copy of this letter was sent to Judge Korman

As soon as Hausfeld filed his complaint against UBS, Credit Suisse, and the Swiss Bank Corporation, he began amending it. There were new documents to add. Rich Lewis had begun talking to Swift about the possibility of consolidating their complaints, but Hausfeld was hesitant. He believed that Fagan's complaint was too narrow. In addition, Fagan had put the Swiss National Bank as a defendant, a move with which Hausfeld disagreed.

It wasn't that he didn't believe that the SNB was guilty of accepting Nazi gold looted from occupied countries' central banks. Several studies and books had already established that fact. Exactly how much, and whether the SNB knew that some of the gold it had accepted had come from concentration camp victims, was at this point still unclear. These questions would later become the focus of a major investigation. He was reluctant to add the SNB because of a legal concern. Since the SNB is the central bank of Switzerland, it could be protected by governmental immunity. While the private commercial banks may have taken in far less gold than the SNB, they would not be able to seek legal cover under government sovereignty. He believed that naming the SNB as a defendant could jeopardize the lawsuit. Fagan later eliminated the SNB from his complaint, as well. This, however, would not resolve the issue of whether to go after the SNB.

Swift and Fagan had made it clear that they were unenthusiastic about Hausfeld's broad sweeping complaint and that they were downright opposed to his slave labor claims. When it came down to it, they weren't the only ones who questioned the validity of the slave labor claims. Even attorneys in Hausfeld's own camp wondered whether this claim wasn't a stretch.

Hausfeld was trying to use the Nuremberg Judgment and several books to establish the Swiss banks' liability. He wanted to show the link between the use of slave labor in Germany by German companies and cloaked accounts in Swiss banks. Several German companies doing business between 1933 and 1946 had set up accounts in Swiss banks under disguised names. They used those disguised or cloaked accounts to deposit assets that included profits from the use of slave labor.

One of the companies that provided an example of such a link was the German corporation IG Farben. Farben used slave laborers from Auschwitz to work in its factories. Concentration camp victims labored in the Buna-Werke synthetic rubber and fuel plant, which later became a part of the camp Auschwitz III. Along with Buna, a synthetic rubber that the German air force and army had attempted to use, IG Farben had also manufactured Zyklon B, the poison gas used for mass murder at the camps.

Hausfeld cited Safehaven documents that named IG Chemie in Switzerland as a cloaked subsidiary of IG Farben and listed the president of IG Chemie in Basel, Switzerland, as a director of the Swiss

Bank Corporation. Although IG Farben was forced to pay 27 million Deutsche marks to the Claims Conference in 1957, and the company was broken up, no one had ever claimed the assets of IG Chemie.[1]

Hausfeld was determined to keep the slave labor claims, even though they faced legal challenges. Not only would he have to prove that certain bank accounts reflected cloaked assets, but also he would have to identify what portion of those assets were directly attributable to slave labor. It would involve estimation, since those accounts had long since been liquidated.

Using the Nuremberg Judgment as a precedent would require a leap of faith. Only two German bankers had been indicted at Nuremberg. The plaintiffs would have their work cut out for them trying to prove that what the Swiss bankers had done was analogous to what the Germans had done. While some attorneys viewed the slave labor claims as an attempt at sensationalism, others considered them futile but harmless. One attorney for the banks called them "goofy." Despite the response, Hausfeld was stubborn. Slave labor would stay.

He had only to turn to Capitol Hill to find the name of a former slave laborer who could serve as a class representative. Rickman's father-in-law, David Boruchowicz, provided the perfect match.

Born in Warsaw, Poland, in 1925, Boruchowicz was the youngest of six children. After the Germans entered his city, his father sent him to a trade school. Boruchowicz had an aptitude for mechanics, and his father thought machinist training might serve him well. A year later, the German company Transvania took over the school and turned it into an airplane parts factory. Boruchowicz was forced to eat, sleep, and work in that factory. Each day, he watched as the Nazis added another row of bricks to the wall around his city, sealing him and his family off from the rest of the world. Determined not to watch helplessly, he joined the underground resistance and went into hiding. He was found soon after the Warsaw uprising and transported to the Majdanek labor camp. As a registered machinist, he was sent to Auschwitz's Buna factory. Working twelve-hour night shifts, he was put to work with ten thousand other slave laborers repairing giant hydraulic presses.

In the fall of 1944 news arrived that the Russians were within kilometers of the camp, and the Buna factory was closed. That December

Boruchowicz and the other prisoners, dressed in nothing but their thin uniforms, were forced to march in the snow and bitter cold. Arriving at Buchenwald, he was transported to Theresienstadt, where he managed to escape three weeks before the liberation of the camp. Weighing eighty-one pounds, Boruchowicz began the slow process of returning to life. Of his family, he found only two sisters alive. Everyone else had died in the camps. He emigrated to Toronto, Canada, where he married and had a family. For Boruchowicz, whose daughter was now married to D'Amato's young aide, the personal had become political.[2]

The more Hausfeld read, the more he was convinced that the Swiss banks had allowed themselves to become partners in a Faustian pact. By cloaking assets derived from slave labor, and by receiving and then converting looted goods into usable currency for the Nazis, they had provided a necessary link to the chain of Nazi power. But just how necessary? And what did the Swiss get in return? Self-preservation, as the Swiss were claiming, or profit, as the WJC, D'Amato, and the plaintiffs were claiming? Either way, in Hausfeld's black-and-white world, those who cavort with the devil are no different from the devil. Time and again he quoted from the Nuremberg conviction of Emil Puhl, the vice president of the German Reichsbank: "Without doubt all such acts are crimes against humanity and he who participates or plays a consenting part therein is guilty of a crime against humanity."[3]

How could one prove that the Swiss had knowingly participated? Hausfeld kept poring over the different documents Kleiman was bringing him from the U.S. National Archives. Without direct access to the banks' archives and records, he was severely limited. Safehaven documents, historical studies, and expert analyses could present only a blurry reflection of what had happened. Court-ordered discovery would be the only way to get closer to the truth, and that wouldn't happen until a U.S. court decided that it had jurisdiction. First, the court would need to make a decision on a number of issues that sought to defeat the claims. Hausfeld and the others would need to convince the court that they had real allegations based on real proof. It was a vicious circle that left him mulling over reports of conversations and comments that had been uttered more than fifty years earlier.

Trying to reconstruct past events by piecing together old memos,

letters, and communiqués can be like attempting to rebuild a lost city.
Dusty stones are often all one has. Every day Hausfeld asked Kleiman
for more documents, and every day she would sift through the papers
the researchers at the National Archives had found, highlighting passages she thought might be relevant to the case, and leave them on his
desk. He would read the highlighted passages; then he would read the
other lines; then he would reread the passages. Maybe Kleiman had
missed something; maybe there was some word, some skipped-over in-
nuendo that could shed some light. Many of these papers were communiqués from U.S. officials. Written thoughts, observations, reconstructed
conversations. How much context was lost in not being able to see the
arching of an eyebrow or the corners of a smirk? He kept searching for
those few remnants of proof buried beneath the banality of jargon.
Every once in a while, he found a shard.

In 1942 the U.S. Treasury Department had recorded "isolated transactions" it believed reflected on the "business habits and ethics" of the
Swiss Bank Corporation. One of those transactions had involved written correspondence between a New York agent of the Swiss Bank Corporation named Mr. Lichtensteiger and his colleague in the London
office. Lichtensteiger was describing to his London colleague a conversation he had had with the vice president of the New York Federal Reserve Bank. The conversation had centered on six shipments of gold the
Swiss Bank Corporation had sold to the New York Federal Reserve for
$19,454,017.

According to Lichtensteiger, the vice president was curious as to the
origin of the gold. Lichtensteiger said that he had replied by telling him
that "we really could not tell and that we had seen assay and weight certificates from the Rand Refinery, LeLocle, Johnson Matthey, etc. so that,
in fact, we were completely ignorant of the origin of the gold." The vice
president had responded by stating that "he would appreciate it if we
could provide him with some data should an opportunity occur." The
London branch manager then responded to Lichtensteiger's letter with
his own questions. Addressing the gold one last time, Lichtensteiger
wrote back to his London colleague: "What the origin of the 'stuff' is, I
can only surmise, preferring not to ask although I have spoken many
times on the telephone with Mr. von Arx. On opening boxes over here
we have sometimes found Rand refinery certificates, also Rothschilds

and others, including LeLocle's, but somehow, I have an uneasy suspicion, which makes me think, at times, of the monument below the Devil's Bridge in the Reuss Valley."[4]

Hausfeld read and reread this document, trying to understand that last reference. The footnote added by the Treasury Department back in 1942 said that the Devil's Bridge reference related to a Russian battle that had taken place in 1799, a fact the department had picked up in a guide book to Switzerland. But why would that be used in reference to gold?

Hausfeld called Kleiman and told her to telephone a Swiss historian whom they knew. Maybe he could lead them to the source. Several hours later, she ran into his office, waving the document.

"It's great. It's absolutely great!" she exclaimed.

Devil's Bridge was an ancient Swiss folk tale. It took place in the Reuss Valley, a very rocky, treacherous area between two mountains in the Alps. According to the tale, the townspeople who lived on one mountain wanted to build a bridge to the other mountain so that they could cross at the top as well as at the bottom. The devil appeared and offered them his assistance in building the bridge. In exchange, he said he wanted the soul of the first person who crossed. The townspeople agreed to this, and the devil built the bridge. Thinking that they could outsmart him, the townspeople sent a goat as their first soul. The devil became infuriated. He destroyed the bridge and turned the goat into a boulder at the bottom of the valley. The boulder in the Reuss Valley came to be known as the Devil's Bridge Monument.

Hausfeld loved this document. A Swiss legend involving a pact with the devil fit so perfectly. He took the reference and ran with it, retelling the fable to a reporter and to an audience at a local synagogue.

"You see," he told his listeners, "deal with the devil and you suffer the consequences."

Some Swiss interpreted the fable differently. In their reading, the Devil's Bridge was a reminder of how exceptional the Swiss were, that they could do business with the devil and still survive. Hausfeld preferred his reading. He repeated it as if it were a mantra.

"Deal with the devil and suffer the consequences."

As for the lawsuit, what was important was that a Swiss banker mentioned gold and the devil in the same breath. Who the devil was, no one doubted.

For a while Hausfeld was on a roll, finding subtleties and meanings in almost every document he examined. Some of them, like the Devil's Bridge, he added to the complaint, and others he used during interviews to make a point. One letter that he liked to share was from the wife of a Swiss officer, dated October 24, 1943:

> We are over-run with children, mostly Jews, that are pushed across our frontier and whose identity it is in many cases impossible to find out. This is a serious problem because we have to house them, clothe them and feed them and what shall we do with them after the war if there is nobody to claim them? Many are babies and one of the men in charge of this new department told me that he went to the Grand Passage to buy fifty bassinets! The number of refugees in Switzerland has now reached the very high figure of 62,000 and many of them are not worth a damn![5]

Hausfeld didn't use this letter to illustrate the Swiss attitude during the war. Instead, he quoted from it to reveal what he believed was the Swiss assumption—that Jews would not be returning after the war.

"After all," he reminded his audience, "if the assumption back in 1943 was that parents would not be returning for their most precious assets, their children, then why would bankers have ever believed that these same parents would be returning for their material assets?" After a dramatic pause, he added: "And if they believed that they wouldn't be returning, then where are those assets today?"

> Your Honor, ladies and gentlemen,
> I was born in Israel. I am the son of Holocaust survivor, representing my sister, my brother and my mother. However, I think that I speak for a lot of other people my age and generation. We grew up without any relatives from my father's side of the family. . . . There is one thing common to all of us here; we are all tired, very tired. You're looking at the face here; people are tired. They're tired to hear about it, they're tired to speak about it, but that's not an excuse to accept it. We should wash our face and get back to the battle. . . .

Switzerland ambassador to Washington urged his government to wage war against allegations that Swiss banks have failed to account for missing funds. In 1961, nearly forty years ago, my father visited in person the Swiss National Bank in Zurich, asking to be allowed to look into available numeral lists of deposits, where the depositors did not come forward since the end of Second World War, and/or to allow him to submit a family list for inspection, checking, search and so on. The application was rejected; he was simply thrown out. He was not the only one. We heard about many of them today, too. The neutrals asked for war and they should get war. I urge this Court to move to trial. . . . I'm claiming my lost childhood given to . . . an emotional unavailable father. The deep impact of such painful childhood memories shape the adult life and characters of my sister, brother and myself. We are second generation Holocaust survivors and we're still paying the price. . . . (November 29, 1999, Swiss Banks Fairness Hearing)

On Wednesday, January 8, 1997, at four thirty in the afternoon, Christoph Meili, a twenty-nine-year-old Swiss night watchman, began his rounds in the main building of UBS at 45 Bahnhofstrasse, Zurich. He was employed by a security company named Wache AG and had been assigned to guard the construction site of UBS's rebuilding project.

He went to check an adjacent building where the bank's shredding room was located. As he entered the room, he saw two carts filled with old documents and books. A green book with the title "Management Minutes" lay on top of one of the piles. The years 1916 and 1917 were inscribed on its cover. He was surprised to see so many documents destined for the shredder. The Swiss Parliament had just passed a law forbidding the banks to destroy documents relevant to the Holocaust.

The years 1916 and 1917 hardly seemed relevant, so he left the documents and continued his rounds. After several minutes, his curiosity got the best of him. He returned. He picked up two black-bound books and laid them on the conveyor belt. The years 1945–1965 were inscribed on the covers. He opened the books and found entries beginning with February 1945. The entries were divided into categories of bonds, stocks, and real estate. He ripped out the real estate entries and replaced the books so that no one would notice that they had been handled. He brought the ripped pages to his locker, along with another book dated 1920–1926. He then continued his shift. When he finished his job, he took the pages home.

Meili studied the entries. Some of the documents listed auctions of property in Berlin. He knew that the Swiss banks had been accused of profiting from the forced sale of Jewish property and assets. These documents should never have been removed from the bank's archives. Before deciding what to do, he wanted to make sure that the documents were indeed going to be shredded.

He returned to the shredding room the next day. The two carts were still there, only this time they were empty. He found two more books strewn under garbage bags in a metal container. He stuck these books in his locker and later took them home.

Now he was sure. UBS was destroying documents. His certainty led to confusion and fear. Had he violated banking secrecy laws by removing the documents? Could he be brought to court?

Meili, who was Christian, had a wife and two young children. He was working as a security guard to support his family while he finished school. Unsure of what to do, he called the Israeli Embassy. An official instructed him to put the books in the mail. Thinking this was too risky, he called the office of the Jewish community in Zurich. The next day officials met him at his house. They took the material to the police.[6]

Once his discovery was made public, UBS faced harsh criticism. The *New York Times* ran a front-page article about Meili's unearthing. D'Amato called the discovery outrageous. The lawyers cried foul. The shredding violated the document preservation order that they had filed with the court. The Swiss public was appalled.

CEO Robert Studer and his staff at UBS were dismissive. What was all the ruckus about? The documents were from a small bank that UBS had acquired after the war. The information had little historical importance. Some of the material cited minutes from meetings dating back more than a century. Besides, the material was now in the hands of a Zurich prosecutor, who would determine whether the bank's archivist had violated the government ban on the destruction of documents.

Meili was thrust into the spotlight. People wanted to know just what had possessed him to take action. He did not look rebellious. He had a youthful face, with a thin nose and high cheekbones. His gold-rimmed spectacles and short-cropped hair gave him a conservative appearance.

In broken English, he explained his reasons, citing different ones at different times. He said that Steven Spielberg's film *Schindler's List* had inspired him. Then he said that he had received a message from God. As he spoke, he worried about the sudden rush of attention. He had received death threats with anti-Semitic messages and had begun sleeping with a rifle under his bed. His life was unraveling. The security company had fired him, and the Zurich prosecutor had announced that he was investigating whether Meili had violated banking secrecy by removing the documents.

Fagan moved in on the situation. He sent his German colleague to take Meili's sworn declaration. He invited Meili to Washington, D.C., then escorted him around and stood by his side along with D'Amato.

As he grew closer to Fagan and D'Amato, Meili became estranged from his own country. Swiss citizens had applauded him when they had thought that he was fighting a lone battle against a mighty bank. Now, as they watched him stand side by side with an American lawyer and a politician—especially a lawyer and a politician who were demonizing their country—they lost all sympathy.

UBS officials did not apologize. Some Swiss bankers began hinting that there might be more to this affair than met the eye. Questions arose. Meili might have had ulterior motives. Why was he in the shredding room? The room was not in the main building where he was assigned. UBS employees had seen him coming out of the shredding room in December. Why? Was his discovery purely chance? UBS made it clear that the prosecutor was asking these questions. UBS had nothing to do with Meili's firing or the prosecution's investigation of him or the fact that the documents were in the shredding room to begin with.

Roger Witten watched as the affair spun out of control. No one seemed to care whether or not the documents were Holocaust-related. That fact had yet to be determined. Momentum was building against the banks. The SBA officials were not taking command, and UBS's reputation was crumbling fast. Every misstatement ignited a new controversy. In fact, one such conflagration had occurred just a few weeks earlier.

On December 31, 1996, Jean-Pascal Delamuraz, the outgoing Swiss president, gave an end-of-term interview with the French-language newspaper *Tribune de Genève*. He told the newspaper that the WJC's insistence on the establishment of a Humanitarian Fund was "nothing less than extortion and blackmail."

"If we agreed now to a compensation fund, this would be taken as an admission of guilt." The fund "would make it much more difficult to establish the truth."[7]

Delamuraz's comments were a response to a leaked cable that had been written by Thomas Borer, a Swiss diplomat. Borer had been appointed by the Swiss government to lead a task force dealing with Switzerland's role during World War II. He had become Switzerland's official spokesman on the issue.

Many Swiss considered Borer a good choice. He was handsome and poised before the camera. They assumed that he would be able to relate to Americans. After all, his fiancée was a blond and glamorous former Miss Texas. As time passed, and the controversy grew instead of waned, some of the Swiss involved with the issue started to question Borer's effectiveness. Maybe his traditional good looks were a deterrent. His perfectly sculpted cheekbones and deep-set eyes were perhaps, well, a bit too Aryan looking.

The cable that Borer had written to his aides summarized a meeting that he had had with Bronfman and Singer. Borer claimed that the WJC leaders were threatening to organize a boycott of Swiss banks by Jewish business leaders and organizations if the Swiss did not establish a $250 million compensation fund to help Holocaust victims and their heirs.

Elan Steinberg, the executive director of the WJC, denied that the Jewish leaders had made any such threats. According to him, it was the Swiss who had proposed the $250 million figure. He latched onto Delamuraz's blackmail comment with its anti-Semitic connotation and demanded an apology. Delamuraz hesitated. The Swiss consul general in New York, Alfred Defago, intervened.[8]

Defago was on good terms with Singer and had expressed sympathy for the survivors. Some Swiss bankers and lawyers were becoming wary of him. They had heard that he had taken Greta Beer out to lunch and was quite friendly with Singer. Nevertheless, they allowed him to act as a liaison and construct an apology that both sides would accept.

Delamuraz wrote Bronfman a letter. He was sorry that he had offended Bronfman's feelings, "as well as those of many other people concerned, particularly those of the Jewish community at large." Bronfman accepted his apology. The Humanitarian Fund remained unresolved.[9]

Witten and his team at Wilmer, Cutler were helpless. The Swiss government was not their client. They could not control what government officials did or said. Delamuraz should never have labeled the WJC's demand for a fund as blackmail. Never mind that many of the bankers and lawyers believed that the boycott threat was exactly that. Hadn't they all learned by now not to say what was on their minds?

Before Witten could catch his breath from Delmuraz's comment and Meili's discovery, another Swiss official fell prey to his own words.

The Swiss ambassador to the United States, Carlo Jagmetti, was sixty-four years old and had been a diplomat for more than three decades. He had served as an ambassador to Paris before arriving in Washington in 1993. He was a military man who was adept at politics. He was well respected and was looking forward to retiring in a few months. He had every reason to be proud of his career.

In December he had written a cable to Borer and several officials in his government, outlining a strategy for dealing with the controversy. He urged everyone to work toward the solution of a global payment. The ongoing investigations must be completed, and Switzerland should try to solve the Holocaust matter by following a legal strategy. He asked that his country maintain its dignity in the process. In conclusion, he wrote: "This is a war that Switzerland must wage and win on the foreign and domestic front. You cannot trust most of our adversaries."[10]

The cable was leaked. The last two sentences got excerpted and printed in newspapers. If he just hadn't used military jargon to get his message across. The WJC leaders and D'Amato accused Jagmetti of anti-Semitism. On January 27, 1997, he resigned.

"It was never my intention to want to gloss over events that occurred in the years before, during, and after World War II or to question the necessity of openly coming to terms with the past. Regrettably, sometimes harsh language is needed to get results. My words were, and are, a call for the Swiss to get our act together."[11]

This was the second time somebody had leaked a communiqué. Some of the Swiss bankers and lawyers began to question Defago's close relationship with Singer. They had even joked about that friendship, calling Defago "Definger" behind closed doors. Now, some began to wonder whether Defago had leaked the communiqués. The bankers really didn't know. They were sure of only one thing. They needed a change of strategy.[12]

For two years, the CEOs of the three banks had been content to let the SBA officials take charge of the Holocaust matter. Baer had been successful in creating the Volcker Commission. The Swiss government had initiated the Bergier Commission. Everyone had agreed that the safest bet was to stay quiet and let the SBA do the talking. But that was before Delamuraz had made his comment and Meili had come on the scene and Jagmetti had misspoken. Suddenly the SBA seemed ill equipped to deal with the crises. Something needed to be done, and someone needed to initiate the new action.

Ranier Gut, the chairman of Credit Suisse, had been the first of the Swiss bankers to entertain the idea of a Humanitarian Fund. Credit Suisse was the second largest Swiss bank and had the most subsidiaries in the United States. Gut understood the danger of having the Holocaust question continue to chip away at his bank's reputation. He feared that if the boycott proposal were carried out, Credit Suisse would lose a valuable share of its global business. A proud Swiss, he was also an international statesman who was less xenophobic than the hard-line executives at UBS. After the Meili incident he became convinced that he needed to take the lead. He appealed to his government to heed the WJC's call for an interim Humanitarian Fund. He urged banks, insurance companies, and the government to contribute to the fund.

On January 23, 1997, Gut announced that the three banks were contributing $71 million to the fund. Although they used words such as "humanitarian" and "goodwill" to describe their contribution, the bankers' participation was also an attempt to redeem their reputations in the business world.

The Swiss government endorsed the idea of the fund but would not commit to contributing to it until after Bergier's nine-member historical commission had published its conclusions about the scope of Switzerland's wartime relationship with Nazi Germany.

The government might not have agreed to give money to the fund, but the Swiss Federal Council wanted to control its administration. It would set up a board of seven directors—four of them Swiss, to be named by the government, and three to be named by the WJC or the World Jewish Restitution Organization. The Federal Council named the Swiss Jewish leader Rolf Bloch as one of the members.

Wilmer, Cutler lawyers warned the Swiss against putting the WJC in charge of distributing the fund. The Jewish organization had already been given a big role. This new responsibility could exaggerate its sense of entitlement. Allowing other international Jewish organizations to participate could dilute its influence.

Distribution of the fund was going to be an enormous task. The fund's board would need to identify survivors throughout the world and assess which ones were needy. The Humanitarian Fund was to support persons in need who had been victims of Nazi persecution. This included both Jews and non-Jews, many living in Eastern Europe. Was the WJC up to the task? Could its small staff and high-profile leaders sustain such an effort? Those questions fell on deaf ears. The Swiss government, in an effort to create peace, placed the WJC in a central role.

In the light of the cooperation between the Swiss and the WJC, the lawsuit lingered like a dark sky. Was the storm coming or going? Gut was realistic. He knew that the fund was not the final answer. Only an out-of-court settlement would bring closure. Once again, he broke from the pack. He hired the attorney Frederick Schwarz of the New York firm Cravath, Swaine & Moore to help his bank in settlement talks. He hoped that Cutler's closely allied firm in New York could break the deadlock that had developed between the banks and the plaintiffs, and between Hausfeld and Witten.

Witten was still angry at Hausfeld for having sent a letter to the president of the Federal Reserve Bank of New York, asking him to suspend the charters of the three Swiss banks. Hausfeld had promised to withdraw the letter but never had. On top of that, Hausfeld was now interfering with the Humanitarian Fund. Hausfeld wanted the fund to be put under the supervision of a U.S. court. Hausfeld would soon learn that Witten wasn't the only one angered by that demand.

5

An Uneasy Alliance

Hello everybody.

My English is not so perfect but I want to ask a few questions. I am a survivor of the Holocaust. I was a young girl. I come from a wealthy family. My father has insurance in Switzerland and my husband, he died a few years ago, he didn't get nothing. . . . I was two times homeless, one time '44 and the second time '56 because we came after the revolution. We can't come from Hungary because they don't let us come over. I had to leave the children. My husband was four years in . . . a very bad concentration camp. He got sick with the kidney and he suffered his whole life. I was working alone. I don't have time to go to school because I have to work. We don't have food stamps. I'm ashamed to go ask. We suffered and we hungered. We, you know, the Germans take everything from my family, everything, we don't have, only one dress and we don't have what to eat. I was four times survived from Mengele. . . . Like a dog I was sick and I am still, my head is shaking from when I came back from the concentration camp and I have every month $400 medication. . . . So please Judge Korman take care of this case because, we getting older . . . people dying, we not young anymore and we need the money. . . . I don't got nothing. Only once I got $650 dollars. Thank you very much for listening and excuse me for my bad English.

November 20, 2000, Swiss Banks Fairness Hearing

Marilyn Hausfeld watched as her husband became more and more preoccupied with the case. She'd hear him at night shouting on the phone to Mendelsohn. The same names kept cropping up. Fagan. Witten. Swift. She knew that they were people involved with the case, but she did not question him. Over the years, she had learned not to become absorbed in his cases. There were too many, and every one seemed fraught with personality conflicts. How often had she heard him yelling about somebody?

She was amused by his double personality. He behaved so differently at home. If their kids wanted something, they knew to go to him. He never said no. He was such a pushover that they called him marshmallow. She had trouble believing that this was the same guy whose reputation in the legal world had earned him the name "pit bull." She supported his work but had little patience for legal banter. To her, nothing seemed to destroy a story more than a bunch of lawyers haggling over technicalities. She preferred theater. As an actress, she liked being able to step inside a story. Law and theater might both deal with the human condition, but she found theater much more absorbing.

She had donated money to start a theater company at the Jewish Community Center of Northern Virginia. She wanted to bring Jewish theater to her suburban community. The Center Company was her baby. She could pick a play and choose a director. She always kept her eye out for an interesting opportunity.

In late fall of 1996 she met the Washington author Richard Rashke. Rashke had written *Escape from Sobibor*, a nonfiction account of the escape of three hundred inmates from the Sobibor death camp. His book had been turned into a movie starring Alan Arkin. Now he was writing a play based on his interviews with Esther Raab, a survivor of that escape. The play revolves around the conflict between Esther's memory, personified by a young Esther, and Esther's postwar existence, personified by an older Esther.

Rashke was almost finished with the play when he met Marilyn. He was anxious to have a staged reading. Maybe she would be interested in acting the role of the older Esther.

Marilyn fell in love with the play and began searching for a local stage. The Jewish Community Center was in the middle of another production, so she found a small warehouse in Reston, Virginia, which had been converted to a theater. She and Rashke assembled a cast and set a date in March for the informal performance. They invited only local friends and family, with one exception. Esther Raab, the survivor, wanted to see the play and meet Marilyn. She and her husband were going to travel from their home in New Jersey.

Marilyn did not give much thought to the fact that she was performing *Dear Esther* at the same time that her husband was involved with a

Holocaust-related case. She knew she liked the story, and she liked how
Rashke had handled it. She was more concerned about Esther's arrival.
She didn't want to disappoint her.

Michael Hausfeld was inspired by the play and believed that anyone
working on the case would be, too. "Looting." "Slave labor." The play
gave visual meaning to the words he had been using. He invited Kleiman and researchers at the National Archives to the reading. When the
performance was over, Esther came on stage and hugged Marilyn. The
audience broke into applause. Hausfeld looked back at his researchers.
For a brief moment, his personal and professional lives had coalesced.

"I want a news blackout," Hausfeld announced. "No more talking to reporters. No more interviews. I'm tired of spending my time answering
their questions and watching them get the story wrong."

He sat at the head of the conference table. It was nine in the morning on Wednesday, February 19, 1997, and he was having his weekly
strategy meeting with Gallagher, Lewis, and Kleiman. The others knew
why he was calling for a blackout. The *Newsweek* reporter Michael Hirsh
had just published an article about the case. The first two sentences
alone had upset him.

"It once seemed so clear: Hitler's victims vs. greedy Swiss bankers.
Then the lawyers got into the act."[1]

"I spent a long time on the phone with this guy," he grumbled to
Kleiman.

Hirsh had questioned him about his objections to the banks' Humanitarian Fund. The gesture from the Swiss banks was intended to get
money to needy survivors right away. Why was Hausfeld demanding
that the fund be put under control of the U.S. District Court? Wouldn't
this prolong the distribution?

"I'm not objecting to a Humanitarian Fund," he had explained. "I
just want to make sure that the money will be used for humanitarian
needs and not to pay off any legal claims."

He didn't trust the banks. What was to stop them from paying out
the money slowly and using whatever was left to pay off the settlement
in a legal case? He had heard a rumor that the banks wanted to issue
checks from the fund in exchange for legal releases. A U.S. court could
distribute the money faster.

Hirsh labeled Hausfeld a "spoiler" and wrote "that this legalistic squabbling may just defeat the fund's original purpose—to get money quickly to aging survivors." He reported that Hausfeld's demand had taken the WJC by surprise.[2]

Hausfeld's demand had also surprised Fagan, who had told Hirsh that the motion was "going to unnecessarily complicate things when it took such a long time beating the hell out of the Swiss banks to get them to this point." Fagan had said that he feared Hausfeld's preemptive strike would confuse things by "lumping the fund together with separate legal claims."[3]

Hausfeld was tired of Fagan's comments. No matter what happened, he was not going to work with him. He didn't care that in December he had considered combining their cases and co-leading with Swift. He hadn't realized then just how far apart they were. Now, he had no intention of joining forces. Besides, he had other things on his mind.

"Let me tell you about our meeting yesterday at Mel's office." Hausfeld's mood suddenly lightened.[4]

"The major NGOs were there. Rabbi Cooper from the Wiesenthal Center, two lawyers for the World Council, someone from B'nai B'rith, the Anti-Defamation League, The Gathering. . . ."

"Don't forget Elan Steinberg," Gallagher interrupted. He had accompanied him to New York.

"I'm getting to him."

Hausfeld then stood and folded his arms.

"Okay, so here was Steinberg, standing in the corner with his arms folded. Whenever we proposed something, he objected. It was obvious he didn't want to be there. In fact, he told Mel that the only reason he had showed up was out of respect for him."

Hausfeld and Weiss had been trying for months to get the WJC to join their suit. If they could get the major NGOs behind them, the banks would be forced to settle all the claims at once—something the banks wanted, as well. They also knew that uniting with the NGOs would marginalize Fagan and Swift.

In spite of his and Weiss's efforts, the WJC leaders would not budge. Hausfeld began to suspect them of having forged a secret alliance with Fagan. Maybe they were referring survivors to Fagan in exchange for Fagan's assurance that money from heirless assets would go to them. In his paranoid moments, anything became possible. Hausfeld's paranoia might have been dispelled had he known Singer and how he liked to operate. In an interview after the case, Singer described his own idiosyncratic style of negotiating, a style he had learned in President Lyndon Johnson's era.

"You can either be outside the tent or you can be inside the tent. I found a third place, and that was outside, as well as inside the tent, urinating on the president's shoe."[5]

Hausfeld knew only one thing. Relations with the WJC were going from bad to worse.

"Lawyers are scum," a Swiss journalist once heard Bronfman mutter after an interview.[6] Although Bronfman had intended for his comment to remain private, his sentiment had become obvious to others long before. Why should he trust lawyers, especially class-action lawyers? They get in the way. They place demands and try to stick their fingers in the money pot. Hausfeld's attempt to enjoin the Humanitarian Fund was an example of such intrusion. Bronfman wanted to remain the leader of this issue. He had done a fine job. Why should he relinquish control now?

Many leaders of the smaller Jewish organizations agreed. They had no desire to challenge him, and, besides, they had to work together on other issues.

Hausfeld was frustrated. He felt he was being unfairly stereotyped by the WJC. Wasn't it obvious to the Jewish leaders that he was trying to get more money from the banks for them? How could they accuse him of being greedy when he was working pro bono?

He and Weiss would just have to work around the WJC and get other NGOs to join them. He called Stanley Wolfe, one of the attorneys for the World Council for Orthodox Jewish Communities. (Wolfe later took a sabbatical and was replaced by Steve Whinston.)

The World Council had filed its own suit in January. The suit alleged that the banks had profited from the looting of synagogues and other community-owned property. It based its arguments on many of the same legal theories Hausfeld had used in his complaint. Wolfe agreed that consolidating their complaints made sense.

Weiss used his friendship and his good relations with Jewish leaders to win support.

"We have assurances from the Wiesenthal Center, ADL, and the World Council that they are in our tent. On Monday we're meeting with the gypsy organization. They should be ours." Hausfeld then shifted his attention.

"Credit Suisse has billions in pension funds in New York. I want to take discovery on their investors and depose Neil Levin, of the New York Banking Department. The way I figure it, if Witten loses jurisdiction, he'll fight it, but we'll already be into discovery, so they'll lose either way."

"I don't think we'll do a good job of discovery," Lewis sighed.

Hausfeld could always count on Lewis to present the practical side of a situation. Lewis had been assigning tasks to the participating firms. He had been less than impressed with their responses.

"With pro bono, there's not a lot of will."

"I gave them a case worth lots of money," Hausfeld said, thinking back to the polybutylene pipes case. "They'll do it pro bono. Or let me put it another way. This case will not *not* get done due to lack of will. Let's decide what we have to do and do it. We need to put on blinders and go after what we want."

The time had come. He had given Witten a list of demands back in November, and the banks had not agreed to any of them. He wanted to move the case to court.

He had not yet designated a sum of money. Instead, he was calling for an audit committee to identify all looted, cloaked, and deposited assets. The committee would arrive at a dollar amount. The Volcker Committee would continue to investigate dormant accounts but would be a working subgroup of the audit committee. He also wanted to expand the scope of the Bergier Commission. Hausfeld wanted the commission to be placed under the supervision of the U.S. District Court.

"We offered a proposal for a global resolution. It's been three months, and nothing's happened. Why should we wait any longer? The Historical Commission has been set up for months, and there's no meeting planned until June. The Swiss government says they won't contribute to any fund until it reads the commission's report. Where's that report coming from? And the commission's not looking at the accounts of Nazi war criminals. All those accounts are still there. Witten says those accounts are legitimate and protected under secrecy.

"Let's give Witten forty-five days to respond. That allows us to move forward with third-party discovery. The Swiss are going to focus on subject matter jurisdiction. They know they've lost personal. But we could lose on subject matter. The deposits happened long ago and in a foreign country. We need to show that many of those deposited assets were transferred to banks here." Hausfeld then turned to Kleiman.

"What's the attitude of the researchers these days?"

"In the beginning, they felt that the Swiss were being beat up on unfairly," she answered. "Gregg had come in and said that they were going to topple the government. But now they see that their documents are being presented in a thoughtful way."

"Everyone is clamoring for justice," he responded, half-listening. "What is justice here? Just dormant accounts? All of the facts, all of the activities have to be unfolded."

He turned to Lewis and Gallagher.

"Our complaint is our focus. We pled it well, it's what we want, it addresses the Swiss role. We have nothing to be ashamed of in filing this complaint. Let's move this case into the judicial phase and talk in a forum where we know the rules."

His mind was racing. He thought about the report that Stuart Eizenstat had been commissioned by President Clinton to write. Eizenstat had been assigned the task of describing the Allied efforts to recover assets that had been stolen by Germany during World War II. His report was due out in March.

"I've been told that Eizenstat's report excoriates Swiss collaboration. I want to subpoena all of the individual agencies that Eizenstat's using. We need their original research reports, before they get synthesized." Then he added, as if to justify his move to court, "But we can't serve third-party subpoenas if we're in a standstill."

He knew that ending the standstill would upset both sides. Witten could accuse him of walking away from settlement talks, and Swift could accuse him of trying to take control. By sending a letter to the court, he would be putting everybody on alert. He and Weiss would be staking out their territory. They wanted to raise their complaint like a flag; have it fly above everyone else's.

Hausfeld's complaint was called the Friedman complaint, after Jacob Friedman, one of his class representatives. Friedman was seventy-six.

Born in Czechoslovakia, he had grown up in Romania. He was the only surviving heir of his parents, both of whom were gassed to death at Auschwitz in the spring of 1944. Jacob Friedman was very sick. His son was concerned that the lawsuit would put undue stress on his father, but he went ahead and consented to having his father become a class representative. Lewis had convinced him that his father's story was too important to ignore.

Friedman's story differed from many of the other survivors' stories. Friedman had, himself, physically deposited money for his father in three Swiss banks. During the years 1937 and 1938 he had made seven trips to Switzerland to deposit money in his father's Swiss accounts. Friedman, who was seven years old at the time, had traveled by train to Zurich and had stayed with an acquaintance of his father. Each time he went, his father had told him which bank to go to and had given him an envelope that contained an account number. He remembered on one occasion bringing two kilograms of gold into Switzerland and being sent to the town of Le Locle to have the gold melted down to assess its purity. He was then given 10,000 Swiss francs to deposit. The banks he had visited belonged to UBS and the Swiss Bank Corporation.

In 1971 an acquaintance of Friedman's met with officials from UBS in Switzerland to try to find the family's account. He was told that it could not be identified without an account number. In July 1996 D'Amato wrote letters to UBS and the Swiss Bank Corporation inquiring about Friedman's father's accounts. Representatives from the banks said that they could not identify the accounts. They did add, though, almost as an afterthought, that they were aware that Friedman had sent an inquiry to more than one bank.[7]

This comment caught Hausfeld's attention. How did the bankers know that Friedman had written to more than one bank? The only way they could have known was if they had communicated with one another about personal and confidential information regarding Friedman's father's accounts. To Hausfeld, this provided proof that the banks conspired to conceal accounts. It was one more accusation he would bring to court.

On the plane to New York, Hausfeld leaned across the aisle to Gallagher and read aloud from an article in that morning's *Washington Post*. "Over the heated objections of many of its lawyers, the high-priced

New York law firm of Cravath, Swaine & Moore is representing a Swiss bank that wartime U.S. officials described as the 'most frequent violator' of rules against laundering Nazi gold."[8]

Twelve attorneys at the New York law firm had written a memo objecting to their firm's decision to represent Credit Suisse in Holocaust settlement talks. To them it "was a matter of great moral consequence." The leaked memo was a rare breach of corporate loyalty and would soon spark op-ed pieces and make for good gossip in the legal world. For Hausfeld, the question of the firm's obligation to represent the bank was of little interest. He had decided long ago that as an attorney he had a right to refuse certain clients. What he was focused on now were the descriptions of the large defense firms.

"Cravath stands among a handful of firms at the pinnacle of the American legal profession." "The blue-chip Washington firm of Wilmer, Cutler & Pickering . . ."

"'Pinnacle,' 'blue chip,' it's always the defense firms who are portrayed as the strength and power, never the plaintiffs' lawyers," Hausfeld lectured Gallagher.

"Plaintiffs never get the tremendous firms behind them, yet they have the burden of proof. The Swiss looted money in spite of the legal system, and now they get the power and comfort of the legal system to protect them. It's up to the survivors to prove the banks' misconduct. The defendant just gets to sit there and fend off accusations."

Gallagher nodded.

"And so many of the plaintiffs do not have the money to pursue the case on their own." He was becoming more and more angry.

Gallagher had grown accustomed to Hausfeld's lectures. He was sure that any minute Hausfeld would start talking about his plans to establish an institute within a university that would combine law, business, and ethics. The idea had sprung from a course Hausfeld had initiated at George Washington University entitled Law and Matters of Social Conscience. Talk of his dream institute usually followed one of these outbursts. This morning was different. Hausfeld could not be distracted. It was Friday, February 28, and that afternoon they were meeting Judge Korman.

By the time they arrived at Weiss's office, Hausfeld was fired up.

"Here's the situation," he immediately started in to the circle of lawyers assembled in the conference room. "Things look good now that we have the World Council. Stanley Wolfe is ready to speak to the court on behalf of NGOs and their relationship to the Friedman lawyers."[9]

He went down the list of items on the agenda. As he spoke, his knee bounced frenetically under the table. The case was fluid again, and the thought of litigation made his adrenaline surge.

Weiss was at the head of the table, leaning back in his chair, squeezing a rubber ball in his hand. Bronfman had promised him he would meet but never followed through. If the WJC didn't want to join the litigation, too bad.

The more agitated Weiss got, the harder he squeezed the ball. They could succeed without the WJC. They had fifteen law firms and the World Council on their side. They were powerful. They just needed to convince the court. He would present the judge their proposal for who should lead this case.

They would suggest that ten attorneys be appointed to the Plaintiffs' Executive Committee: six from the Friedman complaint, three from the Weisshaus complaint, and one from the World Council. Hausfeld would be lead counsel. Weiss would make sure the judge knew that they had the most firms, had done the most research, and were working pro bono. When they were done with that issue, Hausfeld would ask the judge to set a date for the oral argument. It was time to get the process moving.

As prepared as they were, there was still one mystery: Judge Edward Korman. Unlike Neuborne, no one among the Friedman lawyers had recently come before him. All they really knew about him was that he was quiet and unpredictable.

"He wants to move up to the second circuit," one attorney threw out.

"He wants this case badly," another one added. "This case is to him what Agent Orange was to Judge Weinstein."

Only Mendelsohn had something tangible to present. He and Korman had been childhood friends. He told the others that Korman had been born to Jewish parents who had immigrated to the United States before the war. He was a private person who did not come close to the outspokenness of Judge Jack Weinstein.

When they arrived at the Federal Courthouse, Swift and Neuborne were already waiting in the corridor on the fourth floor. Fagan was directing Weisshaus and her group of survivors to seats in the first row of the courtroom. Most of them were elderly women who looked ill at ease in a courtroom. Every now and then, one of them would turn to Weisshaus and whisper in Yiddish. The assertive Weisshaus would then tap Fagan on the shoulder and present a new demand or question.

Hausfeld scanned the scene. Witten was standing with his New York colleague off in a corner. Several other attorneys, all of them men, were huddled together. As the hour approached, more and more dark suits clustered like iron filings around last-minute strategies. There were no flashy characters: no suspenders, no bow ties, no fedoras. In fact, Hausfeld's tie, with its rich pastiche of pinks and blues, provided the only splash of color. He viewed men's ties as one of the few expressions of individuality remaining in the corporate world. Shopping for ties in duty-free shops was one of the few indulgences he allowed himself on business trips. He not only chose his ties carefully but noticed the ties of others. There were none that day that caught his eye.

When the judge entered, everyone stopped talking and gathered around the large conference table in the front of the room. Korman was a lanky man whose gray hair stood in tight coils on top of his head. He was tall and large boned, but his constant slouch made him appear shorter. His posture gave him a perpetual look of weariness. Instead of his judge's robe, he was dressed in a coat and tie. He walked past his high bench and headed toward the table, where he quickly signaled everyone to sit down. He seated himself at the head.

"Who's going to start?" he asked.[10]

Weiss introduced the agenda. In a brusque though polite voice, he suggested that the discussion could get ugly. "There may be things that one or more of us want to say that are quite candid and need not be aired in a public way, if it can be avoided."

Swift concurred and suggested that they take the discussion into Korman's chambers. Korman agreed and led Weiss, Swift, Hausfeld, Neuborne, Wolfe, Fagan, and Witten into his chambers. After ten minutes, they reemerged. Such secrecy, the judge had decided, was unnecessary.

"Your Honor," Weiss began, "I speak for a large group of law firms in the Friedman case, who have gathered together to work together on a pro bono basis. . . . My concern is that this case has to be organized on the plaintiffs' side as quickly as possible, so that we can act as a team and try to get all of our thoughts filtered through an executive committee, so that when we deal with the defendants, we can speak with one voice." He then presented the Friedman proposal.

Swift spoke calmly.

"This is a case of epic proportions. It's a case that has been waiting for some fifty years for resolution. It's a case that we think we have been, in terms of the Weisshaus attorneys, capable to manage. . . . At present, we represent twelve thousand class members individually . . . one of the difficulties has been the presence of NGOs, nongovernmental organizations, which some of the parties are very closely tied to. I shouldn't say the parties—some of the lawyers are very closely tied to. For example, Mr. Wolfe purports to represent a nongovernmental organization that seeks to be the class representative of all nongovernmental organizations. In the Weisshaus case, we purport to represent individuals, because it was individuals who were harmed, individuals who have a damage cause of action."

Swift's antipathy toward NGOs was rooted in past experience. He had been battling Amnesty International and other human rights organizations in the Marcos case. Those confrontations were fresh in his mind.

Hausfeld felt his pulse race. He thought of a memo Fagan had distributed in January, outlining everyone's responsibilities if the two camps were to combine. Along with public relations, Fagan had assigned himself the task of coordinating all of the NGOs' interests. He couldn't believe that Fagan and Swift were now claiming that these organizations were at odds with the class action and that lawyers who dealt with such organizations were betraying the survivors.

Korman was bewildered. Where was the conflict? What were the organizations seeking that was different from what the individuals were hoping to gain?

"I think the organizations have an interest in seeking some solution for themselves," Swift explained.

"Your Honor," Wolfe could not hold his silence, "I do represent an organization, an organization that has its roots in Eastern Europe, whose refugees are here, who has communal interests that were destroyed in Europe. They have a legitimate place."

"The question is not whether it's valid. I just want to know what the conflict is," Korman repeated.

"Your Honor, I don't think there is a conflict," Weiss responded, "but what you just heard from Mr. Swift is an indication that the people involved in his litigation do think there's a conflict, and that's wherein lies the problem."

Swift let Neuborne talk before resuming his argument. "We represent so many individual class members that we could file multiple suits and contend that therefore we should have control. But I don't think from the standpoint of our group that having Mr. Hausfeld in an administrative head setting is particularly appropriate. There have been some difficulties with that, in that as much as they mention Mr. Fagan in some of their allusions in chambers, we could mention the same thing. . . . The important thing is that to go ahead, there must be at least parity. We were the first filed case."

Hausfeld stared directly at Swift. Stay calm, he reminded himself as his foot began tapping the floor.

After several more exchanges with Weiss, Swift returned to the issue of organizations. "There's an NGO, the Wiesenthal Center, that has a web page that says the Friedman case is their case and they're raising money for it."

"So what?" Korman shot back.

"As your Honor will come to learn more about this case, that will play a significant role," explained Swift.

"I don't understand. If you want me to follow your arguments, you're going to have to say what you mean," Korman responded in a low voice. His words had a weighted, tired tone.

"Let me be more fulsome then," replied Swift. "I think there is a tension here between NGOs that would like to recover money for their own interests versus those of class members who are entitled to the money."

Back and forth they went until Neuborne, whom the Weisshaus lawyers had purposely seated next to the judge, tried to inject a more conciliatory perspective.

"I don't consider myself bound to one set of lawyers or another set of lawyers. I consider myself committed to making this case go forward. If there's any way that some justice can come out of this, I want to do everything I can to make that happen. It seems to me the best way to organize it would be to organize this so that both sets of lawyers feel that they are roughly equally represented in an organizational structure."

"Your Honor, the words 'roughly equal' doesn't seem to make any sense here," Wolfe contended.

Korman turned to Weiss. "Why do you need six?"

"We have a large troupe of lawyers. I don't want to lose the ability to call upon those lawyers. This is a big matter. It's going to take a lot of personnel to pull it home."

"We could go out and we could add any number of other firms to the group. But without parity, I think we're going to have a significant problem from the plaintiffs' side," Swift interjected.

After several more exchanges, Neuborne could not contain himself.

"Judge, this is embarrassing." Leaning forward in his chair, he shook his head vigorously. "Could I suggest something? Can you give us a couple of days to come up with a governing structure? This is the first time I saw Mr. Weiss's list. Maybe I should have seen it before, but it is the first time that this has been presented to me. I can't believe that people of good will sitting down can't come up with a governing structure that we're all comfortable with. If we can't at that point, then impose one on us."

Swift seconded his suggestion, although he couldn't resist putting in one more pitch for the Weisshaus lawyers. "I would also note our seriousness in this case is in part indicative of the fact that our clients are present in the courtroom."

Korman glanced over at the spectators. Weisshaus and her friends were leaning forward, straining to hear what was going on. Every so often they would look at Fagan. Why was there so much arguing? What did this have to do with the banks in Switzerland?

"I don't know if that matters, either," he answered. Turning to Swift, he addressed the issue of pro bono.

"Mr. Weiss says he's doing it pro bono. Are you doing this pro bono?"

"I don't intend to, nor does my group, nor should that matter."

"Does that create a conflict?"

"I'm doing it pro bono," Neuborne interrupted.

"But no one has applied to the court for a fee at this point. Are they doing it for their costs, as well? In the Marcos case, I've run up over half a million dollars in costs," Swift added.

"I don't know," Korman shook his head. "I'm just asking the question, whether the fact that you're interested in getting paid and they're doing it for nothing creates some sort of a conflict in the way the case ought to be pursued."

Swift had expressed his opinion before. Lawyers fighting for human rights not only deserved to be paid, they should be paid. Human rights would never develop into a solid body of law unless smart, aggressive, professional litigators were attracted by large recoveries. Hausfeld's pro bono commitment was a public relations ploy that did not help further human rights.

"I don't see that as a conflict," he answered politely.

Korman wanted to move on. "What's next?"

Hausfeld explained that the defense had until May 15 to respond to all of the plaintiffs' discovery motions. The banks planned to file a motion to dismiss the entire case for lack of jurisdiction and would most likely request the court to delay a decision on the other motions until jurisdiction had been decided.

"We would prefer if . . . we might be able to set a schedule for the response to all motions."

He was pushing to set a hearing date and keep the litigation moving. Just as he expected, Witten objected, suggesting that they reconvene on May 2 before setting any hearing date. This would allow more time for settlement talks.

Korman agreed with Witten. No hearing date would be scheduled until May 2.

Eager to wrap up matters, Korman returned to the Plaintiffs' Executive Committee. It was Friday. If by the following Thursday afternoon the attorneys had not agreed upon a structure, he would impose one. But he had one suggestion. What if Neuborne assumed a neutral role as counsel to everyone?

"Perhaps, given that you seem to have a reasonably pleasant personal relationship with Mr. Weiss."

"He gives my school a lot of money," Neuborne laughed. "If it's possible, for the record, it's essentially an accident that I'm sitting with the Weisshaus plaintiffs. They're just the first people who asked me. I would have helped on this, anyway. Secondly, my role thus far has been essentially one of an adviser on class-action strategy and tactics. I have not been intimately involved with the group at all, so I hope it's possible to play a role as a resource for everyone, but we'll see."

Neuborne's reply provided the Weisshaus lawyers with their first hint of disloyalty from one of their key players. Maybe he could not be trusted.

The judge departed, and the plaintiffs' attorneys lingered in the hall. Neuborne attempted to open a discussion, but in a matter of minutes egos flared. Swift and Weiss stood opposite each other in what looked like a Western shoot-out. As Swift threatened to take his twelve thousand clients and pursue their cases individually, Weiss began circling the doorway. Dressed in his long wool overcoat, Weiss, his red face tightened, dared Swift to try.[11]

Hausfeld watched his colleague pacing and shouting and felt reassured. Weiss was as committed as he was to this case.

Others watching couldn't help respecting Swift. It took a lot of guts to stand up to the "father of all class actions." After all, it wasn't just Weiss with whom Swift was facing off. It was his "eight-hundred-pound" firm.

On the plane back, Hausfeld, Gallagher, and Mendelsohn analyzed the afternoon. Korman's constant questioning of Swift was a good sign. The judge appeared to be leaning in their favor. It made no sense to break the case down into NGOs versus individuals. It had to be obvious to the judge that the Friedman complaint was broader and more comprehensive than the Weisshaus complaint. But what about Neuborne? The judge was relying on his leadership, and nobody knew where he stood.

Over the weekend, Hausfeld became tense and preoccupied. The more time he had, the more he worried. His optimism had turned to doubt. He had heard that Witten was going to Switzerland, and he began thinking that secret negotiations were going on between Witten and the WJC. Maybe Witten was making a separate deal with the WJC and Fagan. He thought of dragging the WJC into court and making it sign on to his suit as a "necessary member," but he quickly dismissed that idea. He really didn't want to be contesting that group.

He was angry at Witten for the May 2 delay. The more he thought about the case, the more depressed he became. There were too many people involved. All of them had different agendas. His depression was not helped by the fact that his daughter Wendi had begun making plans to spend her junior year of high school in Israel. He felt especially close to her, and the thought of her being so far away for so long depressed him more.

He arrived at his office early Monday morning and waited to hear from Neuborne. By late afternoon, he called him.

He had yet to receive the proposal from Swift and Fagan, Neuborne explained. He then added, almost as an aside, that Witten had called him.

Hausfeld hung up and began to pace. He was convinced that Witten had called Neuborne so that he wouldn't have to deal with Hausfeld. Even though Neuborne had assured him that he would let him know if Witten contacted him again, could he trust Neuborne?

Tuesday arrived. No word from anyone. Weiss was in Bermuda, Mendelsohn was unavailable, Lewis was in Tucson working on an environmental toxic case. Only Gallagher was left to sort through the uncertainty of the Weisshaus team's silence.

On Wednesday big news hit. The Swiss government announced a $5 billion fund to aid victims of catastrophes, human rights abuses, and Nazi terror. Swiss president Arnold Koller proposed the Swiss Foundation for Solidarity to the Swiss Parliament.

Rumors took hold. The end was in sight. The Swiss government was finally owning up to its share of history and the public relations disaster. Hausfeld told Kleiman to get him a copy of the exact text. Once again he suspected a secret deal. Did Witten have a hand in this? Was the WJC somehow involved?

He soon discovered that the offer was more complicated than the press releases had revealed. The SNB proposed to sell off up to $4.7 billion of its gold reserves at the market price instead of below the market book price held by the SNB. The difference, Koller had announced, would be put in a foundation to aid "victims of poverty and catastrophes, of genocide and other severe breaches of human rights, such as, of course, victims of the Holocaust."[12]

But $4.7 billion was the amount of the reserves, not the amount that would be given away. Georg Krayer of the SBA had announced that the gold would be sold over a ten-year period and that it would be the interest from the sale that would be put in the foundation. Only half of that interest would go to international charities; the other half would go to charities inside Switzerland. Perhaps the biggest complication was that the foundation would need to be approved by Swiss citizens in a public referendum. The legislation could be defeated. If passed, several years might pass before its implementation.

Hausfeld's phone began ringing. Leaders from the Wiesenthal Center and the World Council wanted to understand the implications of the foundation. Was the WJC connected to it? Who would control the money? How much money would actually be available?

He quickly organized a conference call with the few attorneys who were available. After discussing the complexities of the fund, he turned to the issue of the Plaintiffs' Executive Committee.

"What should we do about the fact that we have yet to receive any communication from Neuborne or Swift?"

A few suggested writing a letter to the court, advising the judge of their silence. Hausfeld hesitated. It was still twenty-four hours before the deadline.

"Let's send a letter to Neuborne, giving him one last chance to respond," Hausfeld suggested instead.

Wednesday evening. The Swift/Fagan blackout continued.

Early Thursday morning, Hausfeld entered his office and saw a fax on his desk. At last, he thought as he picked it up. The fax was a copy of a letter Swift had written to Korman in which he outlined the Weisshaus proposal for the Executive Committee: equal counsel from both sides, and one additional seat for Neuborne as chair and mediator. If this had been all, Hausfeld would have stayed calm. But there was more.

Swift repeated many of the same arguments he had argued in court: NGOs were detrimental (he experienced this in the Marcos case), the Wiesenthal Center was behind the Friedman case (he attached a copy of the Wiesenthal Center web page describing its support of the class action), the Weisshaus counsel represented twelve thousand individuals (half the class), pro bono shouldn't matter (pro bono lawyers might even be inclined to settle cheaply), and the Weisshaus lawyers were qualified (he had led the Marcos case).

Hausfeld, Swift continued, "has been secretive and divisive, and we would have no confidence in his judgment going forward."[13]

According to Swift, Hausfeld had reneged on their agreement in December. The two of them had decided to consolidate their complaints, have an equal number of counsel and co-lead the case, and Hausfeld had simply acted as if that deal had never happened.

Hausfeld was appalled that Swift had accused him of being "secretive and divisive" in an open letter to the court. He remembered the agreement he had reached with Swift, but to him it had never been definite. He had backed out after realizing that his vision of the case was different from Swift's. Now, he felt that there was no better proof of that difference than in Swift's claim that his twelve thousand clients represented half the class. That was a far cry from the six million victims Hausfeld believed the class included.

He faxed Swift's letter to the Friedman attorneys. Weiss and Wolfe shot off a response to the judge. They defended the Friedman proposal and repeated the arguments they had made in court. The judge called for a meeting. The deadline had passed, and the attorneys had failed to establish an Executive Committee. The meeting was short and Korman was direct. Hausfeld did not attend.

The committee would be divided equally, and Neuborne would act as leader and tie breaker. Neuborne declined, fearing that he would have to spend all of his time arbitrating small matters on which both sides would constantly deadlock. Neuborne proposed, instead, a more subtle version of the judge's plan: a ten-person committee on which the Friedman lawyers would have five votes (including the World Council), Weisshaus would have four, and Neuborne would have the tenth vote. This would give him the capacity to deadlock instead of break the tie. Sensing that the Friedman contingent was better equipped to deal with the case, Neuborne wanted to give Friedman the extra vote. Hausfeld and Swift would co-lead.

The judge accepted his proposal.

Upon hearing the news, Hausfeld laid his head on his desk. Extra vote or not, he had to co-lead with Swift and continue to deal with Fagan. And who knew which way Neuborne would lean? Added to this was his disappointment with the judge. Was Korman that unpredictable, or had Hausfeld missed an important sign?

He rose and began gathering his papers. He wanted to go home early. As he picked up his briefcase, his secretary appeared at his door. Burt Neuborne was on the phone.

"I had to do it," Neuborne told Hausfeld. Fagan had organized a substantial client base, and the judge would not have thrown him out. And, even if the judge had, Fagan would have filed a case somewhere else. "I needed to figure out a way to include him in a process where cooperation was necessary. The 5–4–1 setup accomplishes that."

He tried to allay Hausfeld's fears. "Unless you go off the deep end, the vote will always be six to four in your favor."

Hausfeld listened. How could he be sure this promise wasn't a face-saving gesture? Or a setup of some kind? Nevertheless, Neuborne's assurance felt like a fresh breeze. Maybe all wasn't lost.

"I'm not going to let Fagan or anyone else thwart what I know can be done in this case," he proclaimed in a renewed burst of confidence.

Neuborne commended him on his acceptance.

"Had it been me, and Swift had told the court that I had been secretive and divisive, they would've had to scrape me off the wall before I would have come down to deal with them."[14]

Hausfeld hung up the phone and sat quietly. There was a lot to be done. A meeting of the new Plaintiffs' Executive Committee needed to be called, tasks needed to be assigned, a strategy needed to be outlined. He looked at his watch. It was early. Opening his desk drawer, he pulled out a yellow pad and began writing.

6

A Rough Calculation

The Civil Action Declaration
I am son and heir of the first turn of my father, Piskokha Ivan Grigorijevich, which
was born in 1925 in Ukraine. . . . When my father was a child, he was drived away
from Vodjanoe village to Germany, where he was working from May 1942 till March
of 1945. In associate of this I beg you prescript for me, the son, . . . as the heir of the
first turn, the money compensacion for my father, . . . which was born in 1925 and
dead in of December 1992, in the rate of 32 657 989$ (thertu two millions six hun-
dred fifty seven thousand nine hundred eighty nine dollars) in the next rate:
   1. Work from May 1942 till March 1945 = 35 months = 140 weeks = 980
days.
   Because of working day was as long as 18 hours, my father worked in Germany
17640 hours. The minimum paid for an hour in USA = 6$ for hour.
   17640 X 6$ = 105 840$.
   So total = 105 840$

   2. My father had not taken any money during from 1945 to 1999 wich make up
54 years. I take the fixed years percent from the sum, my father must be given. The
fixed years percent in USA is 8 percent. As a result from the sum, my father myst be
given 105 840$.
   So 8 percent for a year myst be 8467,2$. From 1945 till 1999 total sum for 54
years fixed percent = 8467,2 X 54 = 457 228,8$. . . .

   3. Take into consideration, that my father . . . born in 1925 go through all terrors
the Second World War. When he was a child, an his young, not firm organism very
suffered as phisical, so psychologycal shocks. . . . Consideration make good the moral
damage, as a money compensation. . . .
   Total moral damage: 32 094 921$

All the sum, which will have been given the victim and his heir during years of Holochost from persecution with paid 105 840$ + fixed years percent 457 228,8$ + moral damage 32 094 921$ account = 32 657 989$

Total = 32 657 989$

August 5, 1999, Civil Action Declaration of
Piskokha Evgenij Ivanovich sent to the Court

The black limousine carrying Lewis and Hausfeld was not moving. It was nine thirty on a Wednesday morning, and the traffic from New York's LaGuardia Airport had ground to a halt. The two attorneys were talking in the back seat, oblivious to their driver's growing frustration. Hausfeld wanted to know about Lewis's case against an aircraft company in Tucson. Lewis had accused the company of polluting drinking water with the chemical TCE. To be successful, he needed to prove that TCE was responsible for the discovered clusters of cancer and leukemia. He was having trouble getting expert witnesses.

Lewis listened to Hausfeld's suggestions. Their meetings consisted of conversations on the fly. They discussed cases while boarding a plane or waiting for a taxi or sitting in the back of a limousine. The Swiss banks case was consuming both of them. Lewis needed more time to concentrate on the Tucson case. He had to get out, he told Hausfeld.

The two attorneys were engrossed in their conversation and hadn't noticed that their driver had exited the highway and was now weaving down the narrow side streets. Suddenly, they were jolted in their seats. They looked out and saw their limousine on the sidewalk with its hood resting against the rear of another car. The driver was cursing out the window.

"This is what I miss about New York," Hausfeld murmured as he looked at his watch.

They were a half hour late for the first meeting of the newly created Plaintiffs' Executive Committee that Neuborne was hosting at NYU's law school. They were only eight blocks from the university. The men grabbed their briefcases, got out of the car, and walked down the street. Neither one said a word to the driver, who was now standing on the curb, cursing wildly into his cell phone.

As they approached the university, they began to focus on the meeting. Fagan had informed everyone that, instead of participating in the meeting, he was going to be attending a press conference at the New Jersey State House. Two assemblymen were introducing legislation to impose economic sanctions against the Swiss banks, and he wanted to appear with several of his claimants.

The two entered the faculty conference room. Neuborne, Swift, and Weiss were among the dozen lawyers standing around, waiting for the meeting to start. The room's dark wood-paneled walls and warm colored carpet exuded a homey atmosphere.

The plaintiffs had meetings scheduled with Witten and the magistrate, and they needed to get organized. Although they couldn't begin discovery before May 15, Hausfeld wanted to make sure that they were ready.

"In your packets you'll find charts outlining the tasks that have been undertaken. We've had eleven researchers at the National Archives since the summer. We have amended our complaint, and just yesterday we had two historians review our fact section. We got all As."[1]

"We need to let the court know how aggressive we are. Our April 1 meeting with the magistrate is our opportunity," Neuborne chimed in.

They ran down a list of issues ranging from whether the judge would apply Swiss law or New York law to what to do with the WJC. Hausfeld noticed that, whenever they discussed legal theories, Neuborne got excited.

Once Neuborne had read Hausfeld's complaint, his original skepticism about the case had vanished. He believed that Hausfeld's suit was trying to accomplish much more than Fagan's and thought that the allegations not only were broader but were grounded in legal theories. He loved the idea of claiming that the banks had violated international law. The banks had had a special international obligation to protect the assets of Holocaust victims, and they had failed. The plaintiffs could use the Nuremberg Judgment and academic interpretations of customary international law to prove it. This was just the sort of thing he loved to contemplate.

Hausfeld reminded everyone of the $20,000 contribution they were to make to the case. So far, only half of the twenty firms had contributed. They needed the money to cover the cost of experts, researchers, and consultants. It would be reimbursed by the banks in the event of a settlement. Travel expenses would not be included, nor would legal fees.

"If any lawyer wants to collect a fee, he can file a petition and make an application to the court," Swift reminded everyone.

"It's a problem if some want a fee and some don't," declared Weiss.

"There are not many chances to give something back," Hausfeld began to preach. "We represent six million victims."

"If there are enough lawyers who can do it pro bono, then they should do it. Those who can't should step aside," Weiss added.

"So you're saying only comfortable lawyers can do it?" one of the Weisshaus lawyers countered.

"If we use the free enterprise basis, then yes. There are enough lawyers to do it for nothing," Hausfeld answered.

"I've been on both sides." Weiss tried to strike a conciliatory tone. "I argued against pro bono in another case, claiming that pro bono cheapens the work. You get what you paid for. But this case is different. We need a moral council."

Swift was polite and calm. Nothing was going to be resolved right now, so why let the discussion get out of hand? He listened as Hausfeld turned to the subject of Fagan and his pursuit of the press.

"He needs to have a title," Swift claimed. "He needs to have a role in this case."

"But he has to understand that he's lost his individual independence," Hausfeld argued. "There needs to be a P.R. committee, and it needs to be unified."

Again, nothing was resolved. After a break for lunch, Weiss brought up the meeting scheduled next week with Witten. Even though the meeting was not a negotiation, he wanted to have a ballpark figure he could toss into the ring.

"I think their proposal for a $5 billion Solidarity Foundation is a signal to us. It was their way of selling that figure to their country."

Hausfeld announced that he had put together a committee of experts to work on an estimate of the banks' liabilities. The experts were from separate disciplines and included a Dutch historian, a Swiss banker, an actuary, an economist, a professor, an expert on looted art, and a former CIA agent who specialized in the laundering of drug money. They were going to try to do what no one had yet attempted. They were going to estimate the pre- and postwar wealth of Switzerland and the Jewish communities in Europe. Volcker had expanded his search to include securities, safety deposit boxes, and vaults, but he was still not looking at looted and cloaked assets. Hausfeld's experts would be looking at looted and cloaked assets.

At this point they had one question that they wanted to ask Witten at their meeting. Would the three banks assume the liabilities of the other banks and institutions such as brokers, fiduciaries, and the SNB so that they could arrive at a global number? If the answer was yes, they could resolve this case.

By afternoon, Hausfeld was feeling better about the Executive Committee. Neuborne was so enthusiastic. He had creative ideas. The two of them could work together on a legal strategy.

"The WJC and D'Amato are out of documents," Hausfeld proclaimed. "There is only one story line, and we have it. If the press wants the story, they have to come to us. Litigation is the only story."

And now there was only one team of lawyers.

Hausfeld, Gallagher, Swift, and Weiss returned from meeting with Witten and Cohen in one of Wilmer, Cutler's conference rooms. The plaintiffs had outlined their conditions for a settlement. Plaintiffs' lawyers needed to be part of Volcker's audit, as well as conduct their own audit of looted and cloaked assets, and they needed to be included in the Bergier Commission's historical reconstruction. When the lawyers came to the question of money, they had been adamant.[2]

"We told them that we needed them to commit that the banks will assume the liabilities of the other banks and institutions," Hausfeld explained to a colleague back at the firm. "Mel made it clear to them that we have hundreds of lawyers. We have experts all over the world meeting and inviting organizations to join, and we're sending this message out. If the WJC wants to stand alone, then fine. Their standing is just distribution. Unless the banks tell the WJC to join together in one way, they're not going to get anywhere.

"Witten laid out his position methodically. He said that a fair amount of progress had already been made outside of litigation. He mentioned Undersecretary of Commerce Stuart Eizenstat's call for a summit and that they welcomed such a forum. In fact, they had invited it. I told him that we have an approach to reach a global resolution and that we can give the banks far more comfort because we will have resources to support the money sum. We can give releases to the entities involved. But Witten just didn't seem moved. That's when Mel decided to meet the issue head on. He told them that numbers much more than $5 billion were being indicated and that the public is titillated with $5 billion and there were indications that assets are larger than that. Dormant is just a sliver. We can't settle this for hundreds of millions of dollars."

"What did Witten do when Mel mentioned $5 billion?" Hausfeld's colleague asked.

"Nothing. He didn't say anything. I told him, we're compiling as much information from records as we can to come up with a dollar figure and that they should let us know what number they're contemplating because they must be thinking of one. That's when Cohen explained that the banks will pay whatever Volcker finds for deposited assets and as for looted assets, they will wait for the Bergier Commission report.

"But there are so many deposited assets that have been converted and misappropriated, and the court would have to take into account the magnitude of extermination. Volcker may be the best that can be done, but he may not be able to depict accurately what happened. They are taking micro. We're taking macro.

"So Witten asked, 'You want Volcker plus?' I said, no, global minus Volcker. I mean they are trying to compartmentalize. We need a global number." Hausfeld was growing irritated as he related the conversation. "Then Witten kind of smiles and asks, 'You want a 'B' number. If we find in the millions, will you refund us?' I told him, if they want to wait for the facts before arriving at a number then we have to be on the inside of the commissions. We're dealing with gross numbers. If they say just three banks, then we have to pare down the number."

"How did it end?"

"We told them, 'We need to know, is it a global resolution or not?'"

"And?"

"Witten said that he'd have to get back to us. As far as we were concerned the meeting was over. There was nothing more to say."

Twelve days later, Witten and Hausfeld met again, this time in New York in a hearing before Magistrate Marilyn Go. The role of magistrate was created in the 1970s to help relieve the work load of federal court judges. Magistrates spend most of their time resolving disputes over discovery issues.

Magistrate Go seemed eager to become involved with this case. As quiet and contemplative as Korman was, she was talkative and animated. She asked questions and kept trying to push for a timeline. She was not as enigmatic as Korman, and, as a result, the attorneys appeared more relaxed. They yelled and interrupted each other. Her meetings, at times, sounded like a free-for-all.

"What we learned about Witten yesterday in open court is that he does not discriminate in his judgments," Hausfeld told Lewis the day after the meeting with Go. He had taken Gallagher with him to the hearing, and the two of them were now regaling Lewis with anecdotes.[3]

"At one point Magistrate Go asked us what we wanted, and we said that we'd like a list of bank officers and directors from 1933 to 1952 who are still alive. She turned to Witten and said, 'Do it.' Witten became furious. 'How could we just run over the legal problems and make believe that this case won't get dismissed?'"

"She didn't blink. She wasn't intimidated at all," added Gallagher.

"The judge then asked me if I would be satisfied with the names, and I said yes and she said by April 24 and I said yes. She told Witten to give me the names. It was so uncalled for. I mean what am I going to get, a half of dozen names at best, of people in their eighties and nineties? It was a bunch of malarkey."

Hausfeld seemed oblivious to the fact that he and Witten were playing the same game with equal fervor.

"So did he come back? Did he take exception, or did he just sit down at that point?" asked Lewis.

"He sat down. He lost that one. But he didn't have to. All he had to do was say sure. Then there was the settlement discussion after Go's hearing. Witten tells me he's ready to answer my question. After a long introduction, he says that he is offering only the three banks. If Eizenstat can bring in others, that's great, but all he's talking about is the three banks. Burt explains to him that we're looking to determine the total of what the banks took in, estimate what they profited from, and calculate the gross amount that they've got to disgorge. Witten said that's not his position. At trial or settlement. At which point we said goodbye."

"Estimating damages would be acceptable in an antitrust case?" asked Lewis.

"This court, if we get past jurisdiction, is not going to restrict the nature of the evidence. Having said that, it doesn't mean that it won't happen or couldn't happen, I just think it's not likely to happen. Roger believes it will never happen. I think that's myopic.

"It was clear from listening to Swift yesterday that he feels that the money may now be in the insurance cases." (Swift and Fagan had filed against seven European insurance companies, alleging that they had failed to pay out the life insurance policies of Holocaust victims). "There are more companies, and they don't have to deal with us in not taking a fee. Burt and Mel both feel that he's going to push with Fagan for a swift settlement deal and then shift over to the insurance. That was the way he was acting yesterday. We should continue negotiations, we shouldn't get unreasonable, we may not have anything more than the three banks, let's see what the liability is for the three banks. Forget the cause, and just take the deposited assets.

"We have to think about how we can make the three banks responsible for all the banks." Hausfeld continued. His mind was racing. "We have to break that down into two separate categories. One is the deposited assets. I don't think that's a problem, because clearly the SBA was directing the banks' actions with these assets after 1945. I'm pretty comfortable that the exposure of these three banks is the exposure of all the banks. With respect to the looted assets, it's more difficult except for the fact that, by reason of the declaration of neutrality, all the banks had to get together and decide, this is how we're going to respond if we're going to be neutral. No one bank could have refused to deal with the Germans without breaching the neutrality. The Germans would have complained."

"But how do you know that they got together and discussed this?" asked Lewis.

"We know that they didn't act independently. We know that they never have, that they always act as a front. That it was critical for the Germans to use the Swiss banking industry to clear their money. If any of the big banks refused, they would have presented an obstacle."

Lewis wasn't satisfied. "Why wouldn't it be just an extension of what they were doing in the thirties? There was no real change. The war started."

"It's like the Passover question. Why is this war different from all other wars? In a traditional war of aggression, you have one side opposing another side for territorial gain or conquest. In this war, you really had two wars. You had your war of aggression, and you had your plans against humanity on a massive scale. It's the crimes against humanity that, in my judgment, deprive the banks from [*sic*] using the common assertion of just being neutral. There's no neutrality when you're dealing with crimes against humanity. You can't be the rock of Gibraltar for democracy when in fact you're feeding the very antithesis that is swallowing every other country around you. What was going to happen if Hitler won? The only democracy in Europe would be Switzerland? I don't buy it. It's senseless."

"But how do you apply all that to the facts?" This time it was Gallagher who expressed doubt.

"We know that the banks had interlocking directorates with the German banks. We know that the Germans were in Switzerland throughout the period of the war. We know that in 1940 the United States said we're going to block nonneutral assets in this country because we don't want to be the fence to launder looted assets by the Germans. If we knew that in 1940, you tell me the Swiss bankers didn't know that? You tell me the Swiss bankers had no idea as to where all this money that the Germans were running through their banks was coming from? I don't buy that. Now, Witten says you'll never be able to prove that the teller knew which asset was looted and which asset was not. If we get down to the teller, yeah, he's right. But the bankers knew. The directors and the officers knew where that money was coming from, and they all knew that they needed to maintain a common front to the Germans. They said, 'You got loot you want to exchange? Exchange it here. No problem.'"

Hausfeld was sitting on the edge of his chair. His face was flushed.

"If they all knew there was loot and it flowed from war crimes, why do we have to show that they had a common front?" Lewis protested.

"Because we want to make the three banks liable for all the others."

Hausfeld wanted to wrap things up. He was supposed to consult with his experts who were getting close to arriving at an estimate of damages.

Things would soon change. He was done trying to negotiate a settlement in which no monetary sum would be named until after Volcker's audit and the Bergier Commission's report. If the banks were refusing to let the plaintiffs be part of those processes, then he would do his own investigation. He would determine a number, lay it on the table, and say, this is it, this is what your clients owe. Without access to the banks' archives, he knew he was playing without a full deck of cards. Still, the time had come to force the banks' hand. Although he did not gamble, he approached negotiations with the confidence of a casino regular. Nothing excited him more than to place his bet and play the odds. With the Swiss banks, he not only wanted to play; he wanted to deal.

> The Committee of Experts was asked if it is possible to estimate the amount earned by Switzerland and its banks as a result of the actions alleged in the complaint entitled Holocaust Victim Assets Litigation. . . . It undertook this task realizing that no such estimate exists and the Swiss banks are not going to assist by opening their books during the course of this evaluation. Based on several days of discussions, the Committee reached the conclusion that an interim estimate could be devised, and it developed an analytic framework to achieve that objective.[4]

So began the report of Hausfeld's Committee of Experts. In its thirty-four-page study, which included ten pages of bibliographical sources, Hausfeld's experts (as they liked to call themselves) laid out the earnings made by the Swiss on wrongful Nazi activities.

They began by examining the wealth of European Jews before the Second World War. They used national income and wealth statistics for eighteen European countries, independent country assessments of Jewish wealth, the relative size of the Jewish population, and the proportion of Jews living in urban areas compared to the non-Jewish population. They arrived at $10 billion (in 1940–45 prices). The researchers determined that 40 percent of that consisted of real estate and household articles that the Nazis were unable to sell. European Jewry thus had $6 billion worth of movable assets.

Switzerland had the only foreign currency that could be freely converted into other currencies from 1941 on. The experts estimated that 60 percent of the looted assets moved through Switzerland. Sixty percent of $6 billion comes to $3.6 billion in looted goods. Of that $3.6 billion, they estimated that only 5 to 10 percent stayed in Switzerland. The rest passed through the country's middlemen. They attributed another $110 million to fees and commissions the Swiss financial community earned on the buying and selling of those looted assets.

They ran into problems when trying to determine the amount of deposited assets. In an effort to hide their funds, Holocaust victims often used third parties to deposit their money. The third parties ranged from professionals who charged for their services to acquaintances, friends, and relatives who were trying to help. Many of the third parties commingled their funds with those of others or placed the money in their personal or operational accounts. In addition, Swiss banks shrouded the true owners by commingling money entrusted to them for investment purposes. These custodial accounts were placed in the name of the bank. Volcker's committee was supposed to be looking into all of these deposits. Hausfeld's experts made their own estimate. They estimated that Jews had deposited some $100 million in Swiss banks, most of it in the name of third parties. Twenty-five percent of those Jewish deposits were returned after the war, thus leaving $75 million in unclaimed Jewish deposits.

The researchers calculated the cloaked and slave labor amounts by looking at Switzerland's imports from Germany. They determined that about one-third of the $800 million worth of imports were manufactured by slave labor, resulting in a value of $260 million, of which the Swiss, through trade financing, made a minimum of $10 million. Swiss companies also had subsidiaries in the Third Reich and occupied territories that employed nearly fifty thousand slave laborers. The researchers figured that each slave laborer would have saved the company five hundred dollars per year. Thus, over a period of three years, the companies would have earned an extra $75 million.

Hausfeld's experts added $110 million in earned commissions to the $180 million in looted assets, the $75 million in unclaimed deposits, and the $85 million from slave labor and arrived at a total of $450 million. They then added the 4 percent-a-year Swiss interest rate and figured out the appreciation of the Swiss franc from the war years to 1997 and came up with a grand total of $9.5 billion.

Hausfeld rounded $9.5 to $10 billion and took this as his magic number. He would later allude to the banks' accumulative liability during talks with Witten but wouldn't divulge the exact amounts. Better to drop a figure here, a reference there, than to hold up his experts' report and have it become a target. He knew that the report's gross estimates could present an easy aim for Witten, but he felt he had no choice. The plaintiffs were not allowed on Volcker's ICEP Committee or on the Bergier Commission. Ten billion dollars might be inexact, but he had to start somewhere. He had attempted to construct a number based upon documentary evidence and research. This was better than pulling dollar figures out of thin air, as he believed the WJC leaders were doing.

Nothing could convince the banks' lawyers that Hausfeld's and the WJC's numbers were based on anything other than illusions. Guesswork would never hold up in a court of law. Still, Witten didn't want to take any chances. On April 28, 1997, he wrote a letter to the judge asking him to dismiss the entire case.

"Some major historical problems can better be addressed through cooperative efforts outside a courtroom than through the adversarial process of a trial." The lawsuits would "wastefully duplicate" the cooperative initiatives under way.[5]

His sixteen-page letter was the first flurry in what would soon become a storm of pleadings and motions. The court battle had begun.

Armand Lakner lived in the wealthy suburb of Potomac, Maryland. He and his wife of more than forty years had decorated the rooms in their house with modern paintings and sculptures. A distinguished-looking seventy-five-year-old, he had several grandchildren. When relaxing in his brown leather chair in his living room, he looked like a typical successful retiree. His ordinary appearance did not reveal the fact that he had participated in two of the twentieth century's most extraordinary events. As a nuclear physicist, he had worked on the first Apollo lunar landing. As a Romanian Jew, he had survived the Holocaust. From Mauthausen to the moon, he had traveled the poles of grief and joy.

Most of the time, Lakner lived in the present, but, once in a while, during a conversation, a word would drift in and carry him back to his NASA days. Or back further. To the camp. At either memory, his voice would break, his eyes suddenly well up with tears until all he could do was bow his head and wait until the memory passed.

In 1992 Lakner gave his oral history to the United States Holocaust Memorial Museum. He seated himself in front of a video camera and recounted the events that had led him to Mauthausen and his eventual liberation.[6]

Lakner was born in Romania in 1922. When the Nazis came to power, his Hungarian-born parents thought that they would be treated better if they returned to their native country. They sent him ahead and were preparing to leave when the borders closed. His parents couldn't get out. Lakner, who had just graduated high school, was on his own.

He was transported in a boxcar to a labor camp, where he was forced to refuel German fighter planes. He had seen his first American while working at that airport—a pilot who had been shot down. His dead body had been badly charred.

Lakner had to march shoeless across the snow-covered Alps to Mauthausen. When he arrived at the concentration camp, he saw a pile of skeletons in front of the gates. Some of the bones had skin and were still moving. He watched as several inmates ate the corpses of other inmates.

"These people were hungry—what more can I tell you?"

On a rainy Friday, the Americans arrived. He had survived. He returned home and found that his parents had also survived. He finished his schooling, married, earned a Ph.D. in physics, and moved first to Canada and later to the United States, where he became the manager of the service and command modules for NASA's Apollo program.

When he talked about helping the Americans get to the moon, his voice quavered. How much the world had changed since that day he had come upon the downed pilot! The moon. The corpse. Both memories emanated in the same tear.

At the end of the interview, he held up a signed photo of the moon landing.

"Anti-Semitism is still here, all over the world." His eyes blurred.

"When nations and peoples learn how to co-exist, I think we are going to have a better world."

He had not recounted everything. There wasn't time. He omitted the day he had snuck out of the labor camp and met his father outside the Jewish ghetto in Budapest. His father, believing that his son had a better chance of surviving than he had, had slipped him a piece of paper with the number of his Swiss bank account. His father had deposited $54,375 in UBS.

Lakner returned to the labor camp and sewed the paper into the lining of his coat. In the chaos of the forced march to Mauthausen, he lost his coat. Neither he nor his father had any other record of the account. His father went to Zurich after the war to reclaim his money but was turned away. He died without receiving a dollar from his account.[7]

On October 29, 1996, Lakner wrote to Robert Studer of UBS. He had heard about the search for dormant accounts and thought the time had come to press the matter himself. He wanted the "gold and artwork, stolen from my family and millions of other Jewish innocent victims," and he wanted his father's account, which he estimated at a current value of $3.28 million.

On January 21, 1997, he received a letter back from the UBS's inheritance department. The Bergier Commission would address his gold and artwork claim. As for his father's dormant account, he would have to wait for Volcker's audit. Or he could write the banking ombudsman.

Lakner had no patience. Why should he have to use an intermediary when the assets had been deposited directly with UBS? He contacted the New York Banking Department, which was conducting its own investigation into Swiss accounts that had been transferred to the United States. He also called Hausfeld and Fagan. He signed on to both lawsuits.

He didn't care about the money. It was the principle. Why should the banks get to keep what wasn't theirs? The banks had had their chance in the past to make things right, and they had failed. Now it was time for American lawyers to demand justice. When they did, he planned to be in the courtroom watching.

Witten had written his sixteen-page letter in anticipation of the May 1, 1997, status conference with the judge (the date had been changed from May 2). Korman was to set the schedule for the case and discuss the plaintiffs' requests for discovery. Witten wanted to get a jump start. He would use the meeting as an opportunity to persuade the judge to dismiss the case entirely or, at least, stay (freeze) all proceedings, including discovery, until the defense motions were decided. In the letter, he reiterated the progress of the Volcker Committee and the Bergier Commission in redressing Holocaust victims' claims. He referred to the Humanitarian Fund, the Solidarity Fund, and the soon-to-be released report by the recently appointed undersecretary of state Stuart Eizenstat. Although the report was expected to be critical of the Swiss actions during the war, Eizenstat himself had consistently praised the recent efforts of the banks and government. The U.S. government, claimed Witten, viewed the lawsuits as "unnecessary and counterproductive."[8]

According to him, the plaintiffs could not use international treaties or international law as a means for claiming federal jurisdiction because none of the treaties allowed for an individual to pursue a private right of action (self-executing), none had been in force during World War II, and none were applicable to the alleged offenses.

He found numerous technical problems. The Friedman complaint had non-U.S. citizens (aliens) bringing claims against other aliens (the Swiss banks) in a U.S. court. It justified this by using the Alien Tort Claims Act, a two-hundred-year-old U.S. law originally meant to combat piracy. But Witten claimed that the Alien Tort Act provides for U.S. jurisdiction in claims by aliens against other aliens only for "'shockingly egregious' violations of 'well-established,' 'universally recognized,' and clearly defined norms of international law, e.g., torture, and not for the type of commercial conduct alleged here."

All three complaints—Friedman, Weisshaus, and World Council— invoked diversity of citizenship (aliens and nonaliens opposing each other), but in their complaints they had aliens as both plaintiffs and defendants and so did not fulfill the diversity requirement. In addition, the Weisshaus complaint named the Swiss Bankers Association as a defendant. The SBA had no office or presence in New York and thus, according to Witten, the claim should be dismissed for lack of personal jurisdiction.

He argued for dismissal based on *forum non conveniens*. According to this argument, a U.S. court would not be the most convenient forum to hold this trial. Most of the relevant documents and witnesses were in Switzerland and Europe, and translation would be "a burden." Many of the named plaintiffs lived outside New York. Besides, Witten argued, Swiss courts provided a viable alternative. He also asked to strike the punitive damages claim, since Swiss law does not recognize punitive damages.

He attacked the Friedman and World Council complaints for reading "more like manifestos than like pleadings designed to frame issues for a trial. They are rife with allegations that do not relate to the defendants and that are otherwise extraneous." He argued, finally, that if the court did not want to dismiss this case, it should, at least, stay all proceedings until the Volcker Committee and the Bergier Commission had had a chance to do their work, or until the court had made a judgment on jurisdiction. The defense was bent on preventing a court-ordered discovery.

The plaintiffs' attorneys had two days to respond. Hausfeld and Neuborne talked constantly. Every few hours one of them had a new idea or theory. They agreed that Neuborne would write a letter but would not address every argument. He would, instead, attack the banks' attitude.

Neuborne had a knack for simplifying arguments. In his letter, he declared that the defendants were "hardly the appropriate party to urge this court to refrain from proceeding against them because, in defendants' opinion, victims of Nazi war crimes will receive a better quality of justice elsewhere. Foxes are rarely a dependable source of advice on the best way to protect chickens."[9]

On May 1, the plaintiffs' and defense lawyers gathered in Korman's courtroom. Weiss, Hausfeld, Swift, and Neuborne sat at the table with the judge. Fagan and the other plaintiffs' attorneys sat behind them. Witten had come with Cohen and Peter Calamari, a New York attorney who was helping with the case. Magistrate Go sat off to the side.[10]

Korman looked irritated.

"This is not an efficient way for me to operate, to get letters at the last minute in advance of a hearing and then propose to act on the basis of it."

Witten started off politely. He repeated what he had written in his letter. Litigation would duplicate the initiatives already in place. He also announced several new developments.

The SBA had agreed to publish the names of dormant account holders that had been identified or would be identified by Volcker's Committee. And the Humanitarian Fund had appointed the Nobel Prize winner and Holocaust survivor Elie Wiesel as its international chairman. These initiatives "have a better chance to work than a shoot-out here in this courtroom."

He concluded with an alternative to dismissal. The court could freeze the proceedings.

"It would permit the cooperative, nonconfrontational efforts to go forward, unimpeded by this case. It would conserve the court's resources and the party's resources. It would damp down the adversarial fires that will inevitably ignite as a result of litigation, although I'm happy to say to the court all the lawyers are getting along just fine."

Although Neuborne, too, was polite and praised the cooperation among the lawyers, he was more emotional than Witten and opened with a quick jab.

"I hope that we do not have a recurrence of putting important issues on by letter, under circumstances that allow nobody an adequate opportunity to prepare. Having said that, much of the disagreement, I think, about the future of this case rests on the defendants' understandable insistence on characterizing the claims here as though they are some sort of Martian collection of norms that have been dropped on them from the other world."

He tried to convince Korman of the inadequacy of Volcker's investigation. Volcker was looking for existing bank accounts that had not been returned, but there were many more accounts that were opened by third persons or in custodial form or that had been transferred out of Switzerland. Those accounts would never be found. These vanished accounts were the black holes that had frustrated survivors and heirs for so many years. The linkage between putting money in and not getting money out should be sufficient evidence for a judgment by a court.

"I just want to be sure I see the difference clearly." Korman rubbed his face with his hand. "The remedy that you say is contemplated through the Volcker Commission is that somebody is going to have to show a relationship to an actual bank account."

"Or an unexplained account in a Swiss bank," interjected Neuborne.

"And under your theory here," the judge continued, "you have to just simply show that a deposit was made under the circumstances that you've suggested but not particularly linked to any—"

"And that no satisfactory accounting of what happened to that deposit can be made by the banks," Neuborne again interrupted. He explained that the looted and slave labor claims faced the same paradox. Their assets would not be found, either. Only a court-ordered discovery would be able to reconstruct the links between the banks and those lost assets.

"What you see," explained Neuborne, "are the defendants in this courtroom, urging the court not to go forward. I would do the same thing. I wouldn't want to be here. I would rather be in a forum where I had more control over the information and where I was able to use diplomatic cover. But in this kind of forum—this is a naked forum, where you can't run and hide—it is exactly the forum where this factual material should develop."

In reference to Eizenstat, he added, "The United States has not asked you to abstain. There is no likelihood that anyone seeking remedies from the plaintiffs' side, from the victims' side, is going to ask this court to stay its hand. It's the defendants that want the court to stay its hand, and, frankly, they don't have standing to tell us that we can get a better quality of justice somewhere else. It's this court where we think we can get justice, and it's this court where we wish to press our claims."

When he finished his explanation, Witten spoke again. He said that Neuborne misunderstood Volcker's Committee.

"They are not focusing simply on accounts that are today dormant. They are focusing on accounts that are today dormant and accounts that should have been, would have been dormant but for the conduct, including the misconduct of someone else, like a fiduciary or someone in the bank or anybody like that." (Volcker would soon name those accounts that "should have been, would have been dormant but for" the "but for" accounts.) He explained that Swiss banking secrecy was being waived for Volcker's investigation and that the auditors would be able to "look at any piece of paper they want in any of the banks. They can interview anybody they want."

So why can't the plaintiffs' attorneys look at Volcker's findings, Neuborne asked. "The discovery is complex, sure, but they've already admitted that the discovery that we're seeking is discovery that they are undergoing at the present time to the parliamentary committees, to the Volcker Commission. The only people they don't want to have see that material is us."

Korman thought about this. "Conceivably, one interim way to deal with this is for them to agree to make available to you what they're providing to others, at least to the extent that it's pertinent to this lawsuit. It's not necessarily all or nothing."

"That would be a major step forward, Your Honor," Neuborne jumped in. "We've offered to cooperate and participate with the Volcker Commission in the discovery, so that there would be a joint effort at finding this material. As I understand it, that is not acceptable."

"I point out that a month ago, these plaintiffs, who are in such a rush and pressing you at this point, a month ago Judge Go urged them to get their discovery on file," explained Witten later in the discussion. "Back on February 28, Mr. Swift was here talking about de bene esse depositions [Swift and Fagan had requested emergency depositions of elderly and ill survivors]. He raised it again on April 1. The plaintiffs have never served any discovery, Your Honor."

"We're prepared right now, Your Honor," responded Hausfeld.

"I'm sure you are, and I knew the minute I said it, you'd say that," Witten answered. "But the fact of the matter is here that we're talking about the next couple of months, when there hasn't been much evidence of a real rush over the last couple of months."

Hausfeld wanted to steer the discussion back to Volcker. The plaintiffs would like access to the materials from Volcker and the Bergier Commission.

Korman turned to Witten. "Was your response a flat no or is it, you'll see?"

"I think, for present purposes, it's a no, Your Honor," he answered.

"I understand why counsel would say that, but that highlights the impossibility of our position," stated Neuborne. "To stonewall on all facts, while asking the court to defer—"

"Don't do the stonewall thing," blurted out Witten.

"To resist discovery in a vigorous manner," Neuborne continued, "while insisting that the case then either be dismissed or transferred, it places us in an impossible position. That's what discovery is for, for us to at least look at this."

Korman didn't agree with Witten that Volcker's Committee was enough to stop the lawsuit or even discovery. Yet, the defense presented "more classic motions that I don't have a handle on right now, relating to jurisdiction and to the merits. It's awfully hard for me to deal with this in this way, in any rational way." He paused. "Let's set the schedule."

They agreed to dates for motions, opposition motions, replies to opposition motions. They scheduled the jurisdiction hearing for July 31, 1997.

Hausfeld wanted to slip in one last request.

"On a number of occasions, we have sought assurances from the banks that the Humanitarian Fund would be distributed by them with the purpose for which it was proclaimed to be intended, that is for humanitarian reasons. We have not only no objection to that, but we've urged that that distribution be made as quickly as possible on that basis.

"However, we had a concern. The concern was whether, in the distribution of that Humanitarian Fund to survivors, there would be an attempt to obtain a release of legal claims. We've asked the banks to affirmatively commit that, in the distribution of those monies, there would be no efforts to attach a release of legal claims in these proceedings. The banks have refused to make that commitment. . . . If the banks will commit that no such release will be attached to those funds, then we withdraw the motion because there is no reason for it. But if there's an attempt to distribute those funds before then, with an effort to relate the distribution to these claims, we think the court should consider enjoining the banks from making that attachment."

"Listen," Korman raised his voice, "this is not the way to litigate motions. You want to bring on a serious motion, you bring it on in a serious way. I don't have the faintest idea whether I even have the power to do anything."

"Your Honor, I apologize for miscommunicating. We're not asking for the motion to be decided now. That's the essence of the motion, and I think the motion should be set between now, possibly, and the date that the court has established for the hearing on the motion to dismiss, if in fact there is to be a distribution in that interim. I only raise it for that possibility."

"If you want a return date on the motion, I'll give you a return date on the motion, and we can have it briefed in an appropriate way. I don't know how else to deal with this. You'll let me know." Korman rose to leave.

The judge's reprimand was a reminder. There were protocols, deadlines, formalities. Despite Korman's rebuke, Hausfeld was relieved. The courtroom was still where he wanted to be. Worn out and frustrated from politics, he felt like a traveler who had returned home.

7

Arguments and Motions

Your Honor, Distinguished Guests,
I'm here as a survivor. I lived through the war and in 1939 when the war broke out I
was 14 years old. . . . I had two sisters, four brothers, my parents. When the war was
over just my father and I had survived. I lost the rest of the family. It was a living hell,
I was in camps, I was in Krakow . . . where I was running a factory. In that factory,
we were getting in clothing from people that were murdered. Clothing full of blood. We
were made to tear apart the clothing to . . . look for treasures and we found lots of di-
amonds, gold, money, hidden in the seams, behind the linings. Germans were coming
in every single day to collect the treasures. I'm sure, that I don't know but I'm sure that
some of the money was deposited within the Swiss banks or someplace else. . . .

I was told that the Swiss banks are making available a certain amount of clai-
mants only sixteen thousand or whatever. And there are so many more. I would ap-
preciate to see that the Swiss bank would make gesture, this moral gesture to the sur-
vivors and reveal all the claims, all the accounts that are available because I don't
think that anyone could understand or realize what it means for a survivor to see, to
find a name that is familiar or a relationship that had an account or whatever way. I
was left from my whole family, everything was looted. I have nothing left, not even a
picture of anyone. And how welcome it will be to me to see that anyone in my family
or any one of my relatives or ancestors had an account within Switzerland or some-
place else. I don't think that anyone could understand this, the meaning of it. Only a
survivor could do so.

November 20, 2000, Swiss Banks Fairness Hearing

On May 7, 1997, Stuart Eizenstat published his study on gold and assets
stolen by Germany during World War II. The two-hundred-and-seven-
page report covered everything from Operation Safehaven to the 1946
Allied-Swiss Washington Accord to the Tripartite Gold Commission.

Eizenstat and William Slany, the State Department historian, coordinated researchers from eleven federal agencies. Together, they examined hundreds of thousands of pages of documentation in the National Archives. Although the report examines the role of all the neutrals during the war, its light shines the brightest on Switzerland.

People had been reading about the Swiss/Nazi relationship in the newspapers for almost two years now. D'Amato's hearings had generated articles on the 1946 Washington Accord and on gold looted by the Nazis. It was now common knowledge that Switzerland had returned only a fraction of its looted gold and practically none of the hundreds of millions of dollars it had acquired in German assets. The Nazis had depended upon the neutrals for the importation of key war materials, and Switzerland had provided Germany the currency with which to buy those materials as the German Reichsmarks had become useless outside Germany. Eizenstat's report did not provide news. It attempted to put the pieces together.

The study did contain one revelation. The Nazis not only had confiscated gold from the central banks of occupied countries but had seized gold from victims of Nazi atrocities. The victims' gold, which included dental fillings and jewelry, had been incorporated into the gold stocks of the Reichsbank, Germany's central bank. Researchers found that much of the victims' gold had been deposited in an account in the name of S.S. Officer Bruno Melmer. Some of the victims' gold had been resmelted into gold ingots. Those gold ingots had been mixed with looted gold from central banks and sold to Switzerland and other neutrals. Eizenstat's report posits that the Swiss had no way of knowing that they were accepting victims' gold. The victims' gold ingots were indistinguishable from those of monetary gold. The report does allege, however, that the Swiss had to have known that they were accepting looted monetary gold from the occupied central banks. By 1943 all the countries knew that Germany had depleted its own gold reserves.

The report details the Allies' failed attempts to get Switzerland to freeze German assets and to halt trading with the Axis powers, and the painstaking discussions that resulted in the 1946 Washington Accord. Despite these details, Eizenstat's report, with the exception of the revelation about victims' gold, was no more damning than other historical accounts that had been published on the subject. The Swiss might have even resigned themselves to its contents had it not been for Eizenstat's ten-page foreword in which he interpreted the study's findings. It was there that he declared that "the Swiss were the principal bankers and financial brokers for the Nazis." Neutrality had "collided with morality," and trade with Germany "had the clear effect of supporting and prolonging Nazi Germany's capacity to wage war."[1]

Facts were one thing, but conclusions—in the eyes of the Swiss, Eizenstat had crossed the line. Thomas Borer and Swiss Federal Councillor Flavio Cotti publicly repudiated Eizenstat's conclusions. Neutrality had saved Switzerland from invasion and had allowed it to become a land of refuge for displaced persons. Why hadn't Eizenstat even mentioned the fact that, between 1944 and 1948, the Swiss people had donated more than 150 million Swiss francs to relief projects for victims of the war? Swiss neutrality had provided services to the Allies, such as protecting prisoners of war and gathering intelligence. When it came to Eizenstat's statement that trade with Germany helped prolong the war, Cotti was defiant. In a public address, he claimed that "the body of the report contains not a single element which bears out this statement."[2]

Swiss government officials rallied in opposition. Swiss citizens who had not been initially sympathetic to the banks were now lining up behind the officials. It was one thing to be insulted by a politically motivated individual or by biased attorneys or by a special interest group— but by a member of the Clinton administration? A representative from the U.S. State Department? This was not acceptable.

Eizenstat hadn't expected the Swiss to respond so harshly to his foreword. He thought his report was evenhanded. The Swiss had taken his words out of context. He hadn't said that Switzerland *alone* had prolonged the war or that Swiss neutrality *alone* had collided with morality. In his foreword, he had written "that Argentina, Portugal, Spain, Sweden, Switzerland, Turkey and other neutral countries were slow to recognize and acknowledge that this was just not another war." It was the cumulative role of the neutral countries that helped support and prolong the war. If the Swiss had read his foreword carefully, they would have seen that he was critical of the U.S. government, as well. He blamed the United States for restrictive and inadequate immigration and postwar policies.[3]

Eizenstat's assertions fell on deaf ears. The Swiss were entrenched in their own defense. They were as angry at the messenger as at the message. When Slany went to Switzerland to discuss the report with the Swiss Parliament, he was met with a barrage of criticism, most of it directed at the foreword.

Slany was later invited to attend a conference for historians in Ascona, Switzerland, along with Greg Bradsher, the archivist from the U.S. National Archives. State Department officials gave them strict orders before they left. They were not to speak to any reporters. Even a "no comment" was off limits. Sponsors of the conference had assured Slany and Bradsher that the press would not be there. When they arrived, they found dozens of reporters eager for comments. They snuck off to the mountains and hid until they were confident that the last reporter had left.[4]

Two weeks after his report was made public, Eizenstat appeared at a D'Amato hearing and tried unsuccessfully to shift the focus from Switzerland to the Allies. He pleaded on behalf of the double victims who had lived under Communist regimes. He asked that the Tripartite Gold Commission freeze its remaining $70 million worth of gold, since it was tainted with victims' gold. He asked that the claimant countries voluntarily donate their portion of that gold to surviving Holocaust victims. He also added that the Swiss banks and companies should bolster their Humanitarian Fund, now worth $180 million.

D'Amato held the first of two hearings on the Swiss banks the same week that Eizenstat's report was published. On May 6, Christoph Meili appeared before the Banking Committee. He recounted his experiences during and after his discovery in the shredding room of UBS. He had received death threats and a warning that his children would be kidnapped. He had been blacklisted from jobs in Switzerland. In response to his plight, Bronfman had offered him a position in the United States.

Meili pleaded for help.

"Please protect me in the U.S.A. and in Switzerland. I think I become a great problem in Switzerland. I have a woman, two little children, and no future. I must see what goes on in the next days for me. Please protect me. That is all."[5]

His plea resonated in the United States. President Clinton signed a bill several weeks later, granting Meili and his family permanent residence. The fact that he was the only Swiss citizen who had ever been granted political asylum in the United States was a testament to how strained relations had become between the two countries.

D'Amato held another hearing on May 15, 1997. This time his list of speakers included Israel Singer of the World Jewish Congress, Rabbi Hier of the Wiesenthal Center, and Ambassador Borer of Switzerland, among others. A group of twenty-five Holocaust survivors belonging to the World Council of Orthodox Jewish Communities had come from New York and was seated in the back of the gallery. The Orthodox men, with their long white beards, weathered faces, and melancholy eyes, provided reporters with good photo opportunities.

Rabbi Hier demanded an investigation of perpetrator accounts in Swiss banks.

"Yesterday, the second largest bank in Switzerland announced that they have found a secret account in their bank maintained by Henrik Himmler. And the Credit Swiss Bank announced it twenty-four hours ago. So when we talk about dormant accounts of victims, that's not where we're going to find the money. You're going to find the money when you look into the accounts of the perpetrators and their agents, not in the dormant accounts of victims."[6]

Borer reiterated what he and other Swiss officials had been saying all month. His tone was angrier than usual. The Swiss were doing a lot to compensate for past lapses and should be given credit. He refuted the conclusions in Eizenstat's report.

Singer spoke in his usual dramatic tone. "Senator, if all the trees in the world were quills and if all the oceans in the world were ink, we wouldn't be able to produce enough words here today to thank you."[7]

In addition to these hearings, Eizenstat's report, and the class actions, the Swiss were confronted with another challenge. In May the comptroller of New York City, Alan Hevesi, had traveled to Switzerland on a fact-finding mission. Hevesi had been using his position as chief trustee for New York City's $70 billion pension funds to question the Swiss banks. He had written Swiss companies asking them to disclose how much, if any, money they had contributed to the Humanitarian

Fund. The pension funds had investments totaling approximately $460 million. Although he hadn't yet threatened the banks with sanctions, everyone knew that he had the potential to initiate a boycott.

Hevesi was Jewish and had a close relationship with Singer. He also had a relative who had been a Holocaust victim. He was up for reelection in November. He might even run for mayor one day.

A year earlier, Hevesi had written to the CEOs of the three major banks asking them to investigate their records. Dissatisfied with their responses, he had decided to meet with the bankers and Swiss government officials on their own turf. During his visit, he had asked about the Humanitarian Fund and the proposed Solidarity Foundation. Did the SNB's contribution to the Humanitarian Fund need to be approved in a referendum? Would the Solidarity Foundation really benefit Holocaust survivors? Although the Swiss officials were careful to allay his doubts, they were not careful enough. One of Hevesi's aides who spoke fluent German found himself in an elevator with two Swiss officials. The two men had just come from a meeting with Hevesi and were discussing the Solidarity Foundation. Unaware that their German was being understood, they talked freely. The fund was unrealistic, one remarked. It would have to go through several referendums and even then it would never be approved. The entire proposal was a farce.[8]

Hevesi returned to New York with a new level of distrust. It didn't help matters when, shortly after, he read a statement by Robert Holzach, the honorary president of the board of directors of UBS, in a recent issue of *The New Yorker*. In the article, Holzach voiced his belief that there was a Jewish conspiracy to take over the world's "prestige financial markets."[9] Hevesi wrote to Studer, demanding that the bank dismiss Holzach. He received no adequate response. Hevesi became more agitated as the weeks wore on.

Hausfeld felt vindicated by Eizenstat's report. The study validated the complaint that he had written almost a year earlier. Switzerland's banks were the chief financiers of the Nazi regime. He was still waiting for the contributing agencies to respond to his subpoenas for individual documents, but the report as a whole supported his claims. He went to D'Amato's May 15 hearing but became bored. Everybody kept saying the same things. The Swiss kept trotting out Volcker and the

Humanitarian Fund. D'Amato and the Jewish leaders kept talking about justice.

But justice without a court? He perked up when Senator Christopher Dodd, of Connecticut, spoke about his father's role at the Nuremberg trials. Dodd's father had helped convict the German banker Walter Funk, former head of the Reichsbank.

Funk, along with the German bank officials Emil Puhl and Karl Rasche, had become fixtures in Hausfeld's mind. During the past month, he had been thinking constantly about them. If he could convince the judge that the same principles of customary international law responsible for the convictions of those German bankers at Nuremberg applied to the Swiss banks, then maybe his claims pertaining to slave labor and looted assets would survive. At night he would lie awake, reviewing every possible argument. He'd then rise early in the morning, seat himself at the dining room table, and plod through another volume of the Nuremberg transcripts.

He needed to prove not only that the banks had violated international law but also that violations of international law fall under the jurisdiction of a U.S. court. Three grounds exist for such jurisdiction: violation of a U.S. treaty, violation of customary international law, and/or violation of a specific U.S. statute. Although there were many treaties and statutes, he could not point to one specific treaty or federal statute that covered conduct during World War II. At that time, the world had not imagined that a belligerent would enact such a systematic genocide of a portion of the civilian population. He would have to rely instead on a loose and evolving body of law known as customary international law.

Composed of scholarly writings and academic treatises, customary international law is a consensus among civilized nations on what constitutes appropriate and ethical behavior among nations, one to the other. It provided the basis upon which the International Military Tribunal at Nuremberg drew its judgments, including those related to the war crimes of enslaving and plundering a civilian population.

Even if one recognized the relevance of customary international law to the Swiss banks, could one apply it in the United States? Hausfeld and Neuborne were determined to prove that they could. They found past cases in which U.S. courts claimed that customary international law was part of federal common law—in other words, that the United

States recognizes international law as governing the rights of its citizens. They then pointed to the Alien Tort Claims Act, which allows an alien in the United States to sue another alien in the United States for violations of international law.

On May 15, 1997, Witten submitted close to a thousand pages of motions to the court. He picked apart each of the plaintiffs' claims until he found inconsistencies. Some contradictions were more glaring than others. He attacked all details with equal emphasis.

The plaintiffs' complaints did not satisfy legal requirements. If they were going to invoke the Alien Tort Act, then no U.S. citizens should be in the class. If they were going to invoke diversity of citizenship, then no aliens should be in the class. They couldn't have it both ways. The Alien Tort Act (for looted property and slave labor) did not apply to the behavior of the Swiss Banks, since the banks did not commit egregious violations of customary international law. And, even if they had, customary international law is not self-executing. The Nuremberg Charter did not apply to the Swiss banks. It was used to prosecute war criminals, not to impose civil liabilities. How could the plaintiffs compare what the Germans had done to what they alleged the Swiss banks had done? The Rasche and Puhl decisions did not support plaintiffs' claims against the Swiss banks. Besides, Rasche was acquitted. The plaintiffs' arguments for customary international law did not hold water. Looted-property and slave labor claims should be dismissed.

Witten knew that the plaintiffs had more traditional arguments when it came to dormant accounts. He turned to a Swiss academic named Pierre Tercier to help him argue against the deposited-assets claim. Professor Tercier stated in a written declaration that, under Swiss law, claimants must be able to trace their assets to a specific bank before they can sue for breach of contract or destruction of property or fraud or make similar claims. They must be able to identify the bank that is holding their assets. Swiss law does not require a bank to identify and return deposited assets to their rightful owners if there has been no request for the assets' return.

This requirement of having to trace one's assets to a specific bank posed the ultimate Catch-22 for Holocaust survivors and heirs. Most of them had no contracts identifying a particular bank. They needed to conduct a search to find out which bank was holding their families' assets. Swiss banking secrecy made such searches impossible. Witten and Tercier acknowledged this paradox and held out Volcker's ICEP Committee as the solution. The ICEP audit was the appropriate forum, not the court. The deposited-assets claims should be dismissed.

On May 19 the plaintiffs' attorneys assembled in Hausfeld's conference room. Fifteen folders stuffed with Witten's motions were piled in the middle of the table. Nobody engaged in small talk. The attorneys had one month to file opposition papers.

Hausfeld had invited his Committee of Experts to present its findings. The attorneys were skeptical of the experts' report. It was based on so many assumptions.[10]

"It won't be met with credibility," one attorney challenged.

"There's no alternative," retorted Hausfeld. "We can't have exact numbers because nobody really gave a damn. It's the only process we have."

"We may fail in respect to damages," another one joined in.

"I don't think any of us have any illusions—but it's all we have," Hausfeld repeated.

Neuborne turned to the motions.

"We're going to have to replead. We need simplicity and clarity. There's a lot less than meets the eye to Witten's 12(b)(6) claims." Neuborne's comment led some to suggest that they file a Rule 11 misconduct motion. Witten's thousand pages were excessive.

"We must stay focused," Hausfeld reminded everyone. He was standing by a blackboard behind the table. He went down the list of motions. When he got to the international law claims, he stopped.

"What are we claiming under international law? We are not seeking criminal liability; we are seeking to apply the principles of Nuremberg. We want a new remedy to international law, that of civil disgorgement."

"Seems risky for a judge to make a new entity," Gallagher interjected.

"I don't know of any case asking for a commercial entity to do what we're doing," Neuborne concurred.

Hausfeld continued down the list. He drew up a timeline and assigned tasks to the law firms. Swift would be responsible for dormant assets. Hausfeld and Neuborne would take on the international law claims. Weiss would be the most important player at the negotiating table.

"All we need to do is state a claim and stay alive," Hausfeld concluded. "We've got to convince the judge that he's got nothing to be embarrassed about."

The lawyers worked at a frantic pace. Hausfeld called Neuborne in the morning. He called him in the afternoon. He called him on the weekend.

"I'm sorry to bother you at home," he would tell Neuborne's wife apologetically. The next weekend, he would make the same apology.

He sent Kleiman to the National Archives, then to the Holocaust Museum, then back to the National Archives. She brought him the Nuremberg transcripts. He plowed through twenty-four volumes. He found that the German banker Rasche was acquitted of one count, as Witten had claimed in his briefs, but that Rasche was convicted of another count later in the trial. On the basis of his role at Dresdner Bank, Rasche was found guilty of espoiliation of civilian property. He had, among other activities, Aryanized property in Czechoslovakia.

He wanted documents, books, newspaper articles. Kleiman had to search through cartons of loose papers, looking for a single quotation. Her desk became a mound of memos and folders. No sooner had she found what she needed than he'd call her in with another request. Timing couldn't have been worse. Her wedding was in several weeks, and she still had a lot to do to prepare.

She wasn't the only one working double time. Gallagher had to put his other cases on hold. He no longer had Lewis working by his side, since Lewis was working full time on his Tucson environmental case.

Gallagher began arriving early in the morning and staying into the night. Sequestered in his office, he wrote and rewrote the briefs. As the deadline approached, he began coming in on weekends.

Neuborne decided to write his own abbreviated memorandum to the court. He wanted to respond to Professor Tercier. He relished an academic battle over legal theories, but his time was at a premium. The semester was coming to a close. He found himself working on his brief between grading students' final exams.

Swift made several trips to Washington, D.C., to work on his briefs. He sent two summer interns to Cohen, Milstein to help sort through documents. For the moment, he and Hausfeld were getting along. With deadlines looming, they had no choice.

On July 2, 1997, Hausfeld and Mendelsohn traveled with their wives to Geneva, Switzerland. The Wiesenthal Center had invited them to speak at a conference on property and restitution. They planned to spend a few days vacationing after the conference.

Hausfeld was still preoccupied with his claims regarding slave labor and looted assets. He began his speech quoting from the Bible but quickly segued into a disquisition on the Nuremberg Tribunal.

"To remove any doubt about the complicity of both the banker and the perpetrator, the tribunal simply and unequivocally stated that the receipt, acceptance and disposal of plunder was not the business of banking. It was the business of crime."

He reminded everyone that the tribunal invoked moral principles. "As explained by the tribunal at Nuremberg, it is no defense for the soldier to say he was only following orders. The very essence of inviolable international human rights is that individuals have duties which transcend obligations of obedience."

Hausfeld, like Singer, leaned toward the theatrical. He quoted the governor-general of Nazi-occupied Poland, Hans Frank, at the Nuremberg trial. "'A thousand years will pass and this guilt of Germany will not be erased.'" He then concluded with his own remark.

"For the banks of Switzerland, there has, as yet, been no accounting for their offenses. For the banks of Switzerland, the mark of a thousand years' shame has not even begun to fade."

He talked to a number of Swiss who had come to the conference but were not involved with either the government or the banks. Many of them feared that if there was a large settlement against the banks, the government would impose a tax to raise the money for the judgment. Such a tax would be unfair. They were not the wrongdoers. Hausfeld realized that in order for the banks and government to arrive at a settlement, both the banks and the government were going to have to convince the Swiss public of the necessity of such a settlement.

At the end of the day, a Swiss government official approached him. He had read his complaint.

"I disagree with the nuances," he told Hausfeld.

Hausfeld looked at him but said nothing. He took his comment as an admission. And that admission, he believed, was a breakthrough. The question was now no longer whether they were going to settle, but when.

When Hausfeld and Mendelsohn returned to their hotel, they found a message from their secretaries. Eizenstat wanted to meet with them upon their return. It wasn't until they got home that they learned that Eizenstat had already met with representatives of the Swiss government and the banks, in particular Lloyd Cutler.

Cutler carried political weight. He was not only the founding partner of Wilmer, Cutler but had served as legal counsel to the Clinton administration. Hausfeld figured that Witten had only one reason for sending Cutler to meet with Eizenstat—Cutler could persuade Eizenstat to write a letter to the court declaring that it was not in the U.S. interest to hear the case. Everyone knew that an objection from the State Department could kill the case.

When a tense Hausfeld arrived at the State Department, he, Mendelsohn, and Neuborne found the room filled with officials from the State Department, the Justice Department, and the Commerce Department. It didn't take him long to understand the purpose of the meeting.

The State Department, on behalf of the U.S. government, might like to express an opinion to the court, and, before it did, it wanted to give the plaintiffs the chance to express their views. The different officials posed a series of questions. Why isn't the Volcker Committee sufficient? What interests would not be covered if this case were resolved outside court? How did the plaintiffs expect to prove their case in terms of damages?

Hausfeld and Neuborne recited their usual answers. They were approaching the case from a top-down as opposed to a bottom-up position. They were looking at how much wealth was confiscated by Germany and passed to Switzerland, as opposed to trying to find a particular Jew's or gypsy's assets and tracing those assets to a particular Swiss bank. They addressed all the major issues until finally Eizenstat asked the big question.

Should the United States request that the court delay the hearing until a meeting was set between all parties, under the auspices of the United States, to see if a resolution could be reached?

The plaintiffs' attorneys were quiet. If they refused, Witten could accuse them of walking away from an opportunity to negotiate. If they agreed, the hearing would be delayed. Hausfeld thought back to the Nuremberg Tribunal: "He who participates or plays a consenting part therein is guilty of a crime against humanity." Only a court could make the Swiss banks accountable. He and Neuborne looked at one another.

"No," they answered. "No more meetings."

He returned to his office and waited for Eizenstat's decision. At three o'clock, he got a call. Could the plaintiffs send over their filed pleadings, as well as their initial settlement proposal?

"This can't be good," he thought.

The day dragged on. Still no response.

The next afternoon, an official from the Commerce Department called Hausfeld.

"You can relax," she told Hausfeld. "Eizenstat will not be taking any position on the issue." She explained that he had initially drafted a letter asking the court to stay a decision but decided, after meeting with them, to hold off and let the court decide.

Hausfeld breathed a sigh of relief. They were free from the vise of the U.S. government, but they were still far from claiming victory. Witten had done an excellent job of slicing the issues apart. The judge could throw out the case or weaken it by dismissing the claims regarding looted property and slave labor. Without the threat of discovery, the bankers would not be motivated to come to the table. The plaintiffs needed to keep the political fires stoked.

Hevesi told the lawyers that he had spoken to certain managers of the large pension funds across the country and that they were willing to act if the banks continued to take positions that were inconsistent with obtaining justice. He had also written a letter to Swiss ambassador Defago, who had assumed the post after Jagmetti resigned. Defago had written to Judge Korman in June, asking him to dismiss the case. Hevesi refuted Defago's claims that the issues were being resolved outside litigation. Weiss planned to send a copy of Hevesi's letter to the judge.

The plaintiffs' attorneys watched contentedly as others fanned the flames.

The Swiss bankers came up with one more plan to show their good faith. This plan, they were sure, would work. The SBA would publish a list of dormant accounts that had been found during the past months' investigations. The Volcker Committee had completed its preparatory work and was now embarking on its pilot audits. These pilot audits would lay the groundwork for the auditors to complete more comprehensive audits of all the relevant Swiss banks. Since Volcker's audit would take a year to complete, the bankers believed that publication of these most recently discovered accounts would make a significant statement. They would be telling the world, in effect, that they were willing to lift banking secrecy and publish actual names. This would quell any doubts about their commitment to Volcker's audit. It would also provide the court with one more reason for dismissing the case.

The SBA officials didn't realize the enormity of this task. Their underlings were not equipped to deal with the coordination and paperwork. Representatives from individual banks had to come and assist. Witten and Cohen flew to Switzerland to help.

The publication of the list was costly both in terms of time and money. One full-page ad in the *New York Times* cost $74,000. The SBA used three pages and ran them in twenty-eight countries, as well as on a newly established Internet site. On Wednesday, July 23, eight days before the court hearing, the bankers published 1,756 names. These accounts had shown no activity since May 9, 1945, the day after the Nazi collapse. They belonged to non-Swiss citizens. The bankers listed a toll-free telephone number. Potential claimants could call and request an information kit about filing a claim. The international auditing firm of Ernst & Young had been hired to process the claims.

The list contained an assortment of names. Some belonged to European Jews. Some belonged to people who held powers of attorney over foreign accounts. And some, as Rabbi Hier, of the Wiesenthal Center, revealed, belonged to prominent Nazis. This last discovery proved to be the most embarrassing for the bankers.

Hier discovered exactly what he had said, at D'Amato's hearing, that he had feared. He found the name of Hitler's photographer, as well as the name of the Nazi leader of Slovakia and the alias used by an aide to Adolf Eichmann. They all apparently had stashed money in Swiss banks.

The bankers tried to put a positive spin on Hier's discovery. The publication of these Nazi accounts proved how genuine they were in their effort to reveal all dormant accounts. After all, they could have scanned the list first to avoid such embarrassments, but then the list wouldn't have been as complete and truthful.

They had no explanations for other embarrassments. Journalists found that some of the account holders could have been located if the bankers had just looked in a telephone book. One depositor had lived at the same address in France from 1936 until his death in 1982. His widow was still living there. Another man's grandmother was on the list. She had lived near the Swiss-German border for years. And then there was Madeleine Kunin, the U.S. ambassador to Switzerland, who found her mother's name on the list. In addition to these embarrassments, there was the fact that the bankers had found 1,756 dormant accounts, more than twice the number they had announced to Bronfman back in 1996. Krayer of the SBA offered a feeble apology. "No fig leaf is big enough to cover the negligence of my colleagues in the postwar era."[11]

The majority of the survivors and heirs who were relying on the class action did not find their names—Greta Beer, Jacob Friedman, Armand Lakner, Lewis Salton, Estelle Sapir, Gisella Weisshaus. Many did not expect to see their families' names, yet some felt a surge of hope when they opened their newspapers and scanned the list. When they reached the end and did not find their families' names, they couldn't help being disappointed.

"I'm extremely disappointed and completely—what shall I say— more than frustrated," Beer told the *New York Times*.[12]

The banks' lawyers had a response to these class-action claimants. The plaintiffs' lawyers should submit a list of their plaintiffs' names. Volcker's auditors would search for their accounts. After all, Fagan and Swift alone claimed to have twelve thousand names.

The plaintiffs' lawyers refused. They did not trust ICEP to protect their interests. Its mandate was too narrow. A day after the SBA publication, they had even more reason for their distrust.

On July 24, 1997, Volcker sent a letter to Judge Korman. The letter was written on ICEP's official letterhead and contained a list of ICEP members. Volcker told the judge that a court-ordered discovery would have an adverse impact "on the ability of the Committee to carry out its mandate and investigation." He outlined the broad mandate of the committee and emphasized that it would be able to reconstruct disappeared accounts. The class action could have a "potentially crippling effect on the Committee's ability to do its job."[13]

The three hired auditing companies, Arthur Andersen, KPMG, and Price Waterhouse, were worried about potential leaks. These leaks could result "in a reluctance of Swiss banks—especially, the over-whelming majority of Swiss banks who do not see themselves as subject to the jurisdiction of U.S. courts—to cooperate with the work of the Committee."[14]

Avraham Burg, who was an ICEP member, wrote to Volcker. The committee had not given Volcker permission to send the letter, and it did not express the views of all the members. Volcker must inform the judge immediately.

Volcker refused. He had written "my personal observations" and "my concerns" and did not need to send another letter to the court stating that the letter expressed only his opinion.

Witten and his team were feeling confident. The banks had shown their good faith with the publication of accounts. Volcker had told the court that discovery would interfere with his audit. The dormant accounts claims were covered. As for the claims about looted property and slave labor, surely the judge would see how vulnerable they were, based on such a far-fetched theory as customary international law. They would not be surprised if the judge threw them out during the hearing. The legal case would fizzle before the plaintiffs' eyes. Nothing would please Witten and his associates more.

On July 25 the plaintiffs' attorneys gathered for a final meeting before the court hearing. They had wanted to hold a mock argument, but they had too many issues to discuss. Weiss had invited a high-profile attorney named Arthur Miller to come to the meeting. Miller was a Harvard professor who had established himself as a prominent consultant. He had appeared in court many times, for many sides. Weiss's firm had hired Miller in the past. As a favor to Weiss, Miller had agreed to lend his advice to the case pro bono. He planned on attending the court hearing. Neuborne was excited about having him by his side. They had also solicited the help of another academic, Neuborne's fellow NYU professor Andreas Lowenfeld.

Neuborne stood at the head of the table in the faculty room at NYU. He and Hausfeld were eager to tell the others about their conference call earlier with Korman. The judge had encouraged them to file amended complaints. The new complaints would eliminate the technical problems Witten had seized upon. Neuborne was hastily working to reorganize their complaints into four new complaints. He explained that it was just a matter of "rearranging the deck chairs." Each complaint would have plaintiffs who were either aliens or citizens and thus avoid the problem of mixing the two. He also planned to delineate their complaints according to deposited-assets claims and slave labor and looted-property claims. They didn't have much time, and they all feared that Witten might use the last-minute amended complaints as an excuse to ask for a delay in the hearing.

Swift was growing unhappy. He didn't like the idea of having Miller and Lowenfeld joining the hearing. The Executive Committee was unwieldy enough without throwing in attorneys who had no relationship to the case. Bringing in academic heavyweights created an air of sensationalism. Neuborne and Hausfeld were taking over too much. They were putting together amended complaints without input from the rest of the Executive Committee.

"The judge is working with Burt's memorandum," Hausfeld announced as he wrote down the different claims and classes on the blackboard.[15]

Neuborne was pacing around the table. "That's a classic Rule 12(b)(6) motion to dismiss. That claim falls under 1332. That one applies to Rule 23(b)(3)."

He paused and closed his eyes. When he talked about folding aliens into a diverse class, his hands folded the air, over and under, as if kneading dough. He cited the Ben Hur rule, which allows aliens in a class that is headed by a named plaintiff who is a U.S. citizen. An alien can be in the class and not destroy class diversity. He put his glasses on. He took them off. All the while, Hausfeld scribbled on the board.

The two attorneys looked like a pair of scientists. Absorbed in their legal theories, they were oblivious to their surroundings. They were discovering not only new directions to go with the case but their own shared passion for the law.

"Do we want to push the allegation that the Swiss banks financed the war so the Nazis would win?" Hausfeld turned to the table of seated attorneys. "Eizenstat implied in his report that they extended the war a year. We could claim that they were an accessory before the fact."

The others shook their heads. That would be too risky.

A half hour into the meeting, Miller strode in, dressed in a navy three-piece suit. Beneath his buttoned vest, he wore a blue and yellow striped shirt and a red tie. He immediately entered the discussion, advising the lawyers to keep their arguments loose. They shouldn't get bound too tightly to one theory. Not at this stage of the game, anyway. He had a hint of an English accent, an affectation that suited his Harvard credential.

Korman had informed both sides that the hearing would be held around a table. He would not be on a bench. They took this arrangement as a hint. He wanted no grandstanding or rhetoric. Only a few of them would speak at the hearing. Hausfeld, Swift, and Neuborne would make the principal presentations. The chorus would enter only on important issues.

When the meeting ended, everyone agreed—Swift, Fagan, the lawyers for the World Council—that if they could survive the motion for jurisdiction, the banks would come to the table. But they had to survive.

On July 28 and July 29 Witten responded just as Swift had predicted. He sent letters to the court asking to delay the hearing. The defense needed more time to study the plaintiffs' newly amended complaints. There were too many changes. The defense's efforts to prepare for the hearing were being "completely disrupted."

Neuborne wrote to Korman.

"Defendants cannot have it both ways. They cannot seek to prevent discovery while seeking additional time to move to dismiss." Nothing of substance was added to the complaints. "If, however, the price of filing the simplified complaints is to delay the oral argument scheduled for July 31, and thereby extend the discovery stay, plaintiffs will stand on the existing complaints. . . ."[16]

Witten made one more attempt to persuade Korman, but Korman could not be swayed. The issues remained the same. The hearing would go on as planned on July 31.

Hausfeld arrived at his office on July 30 as the sun was coming up. He spent the morning organizing his papers. He sat alone at his conference table and leafed through two stacks of thickly bound notebooks. Each notebook was filled with charts, facts, and documents. As eight thirty approached, the office came to life. Gallagher and Kleiman began rushing in and out of the conference room.

The amended complaints were still not finished. Neuborne had decided that they should simplify the complaints even more. He wanted to take out the facts and include only a brief summary of them. He believed Korman did better with less paper. Hausfeld trusted Neuborne's intuition and agreed to the changes.

Swift objected. The revised complaints presented too drastic a change. Such change would add fuel to Witten's argument and perhaps delay the hearing. Besides, Neuborne and Hausfeld had not received approval from the entire Executive Committee.

Neuborne continued to revise the complaints.

Hausfeld flew to New York later that morning. He went straight to his room at the Waldorf-Astoria Hotel and stationed himself by the phone. He kept calling Gallagher, who was still in D.C. revising the complaints. As he leafed through his papers, his leg, once again, bounced nervously under the desk.

Where were his handouts? He had prepared a series of definitions about customary international law and had planned to distribute them at the hearing. Each handout had a heading in black boldface with quotes written underneath. The definitions were set in bright blue ink. Key words were highlighted in red.

"Who's got the charts?" he barked over the phone.

"Maybe Paul has them," his secretary told him calmly.

Gallagher had already left to catch his flight to New York.

As the afternoon wore on, more people arrived. Mendelsohn sat back on Hausfeld's hotel bed and mused about the importance of this case.

"Justice delayed is justice denied," he quoted Robert Kennedy.

Kleiman joined them. Hausfeld had flown her to New York for the hearing.

"What would you say if you could say anything to the court?" he asked her.

Kleiman thought about all the phone calls she had been receiving from survivors. The survivors were elderly and spoke with thick accents. Some were hard of hearing. Others were ill. Many sounded depressed. They had been recently widowed or had just come out of the hospital. They kept asking the same questions. How much money could they expect? And when? Would the banks apologize?

"The need to get money to survivors before they die," she answered reflexively.

By early evening, Gallagher had arrived. He was carrying copies of the amended complaints, as well as the handouts.

Hausfeld grew restless. He wanted to get out of the room. They had made plans to meet the other lawyers for dinner. It was a nice evening, so they might as well walk.

They gathered at Trattoria Dell'Arte, an elegant Italian restaurant. Weiss had selected the restaurant, even though he himself would not be coming. He was celebrating his birthday. They laughed when they entered the restaurant. A large, white mold of a breast hung on the wall alongside a giant ear and nose.

Inside the reserved Candle Room, tall candelabras flickered against mauve walls. Soft jazz played in the background. Swift, Fagan, and Neuborne were chatting in front of a large painting of a nude woman with a parakeet on her foot.

Against such a romantic backdrop, the lawyers talked shop. Most of the conversations centered on the case. When they did relax, they traded tales of past battles like war veterans. Swift talked about how he had recently been denounced by the Philippine Congress. Neuborne amused everyone around the dinner table with anecdotes from his first case before Judge Weinstein.

Only Hausfeld remained solemn. He kept pushing the conversation back to the Swiss case. Were there any problems? Any questions? Did everyone understand, he glared at Fagan. We need to keep things calm. No talking to the press.

8

The Hearing

Dear Mr. Edward Korman,
We are still alive. We are the Living witnesses of the most horrible event in the history
of the Jewish people, the Holocaust.

Many years after World War II life brought us to different countries and even dif-
ferent continents. Hundreds of those who survived were welcomed by America. Among
the residents of Philadelphia, there are 115 from the former Soviet Union who during
the war lived in ghettos, concentration camps, labor camps or in hiding. They've lost
their loved parents, relatives, neighbors, friends. They've lost their homes, household,
clothes, jewelry, money etc.

Thanks to America we've SSI payments, food stamps, medical service.
God bless America.

Among our 115 survivors there are many aged, sick, single ones, they suffered so
much in their childhood and youth. They need good rest and treatment at rest homes or
sanatoriums, they need to buy shoes, clothes, but can't efford all this because rent, util-
ity and energy are very high. That's why all the members of the Philadelphia Organ-
ization of Holocaust Survivors from the former Soviet Union ask you very much to
take into account our hard situation.

Dear Mr. Edward Kormanm, we believ you, we trust you, we rely on you. We're
sure that all our claims against Swiss Banks will be fully satisfied.
God bless you in your life and your work.

November 20, 1999, Letter to the Court from Klara Vinokur

Hausfeld stepped out of the taxi in front of the Brooklyn courthouse. It
was eight in the morning. The sun was beating down, and the summer
humidity had already begun to settle in. He glanced across the street. A
group of Orthodox Jews dressed in knickers, black knee-high socks, and
long black coats were holding hand-drawn signs protesting the lawsuits
against the Swiss banks. They called themselves Neturei Karta of

America, and they had come as "true Jews according to the Torah." Believing that the Torah teaches Jews to live peacefully during their exile, they wanted to put a stop to the Swiss bashing. They were a small group, but their unexpected message caught Hausfeld off guard. He grabbed his briefcase from the backseat and walked inside the courthouse.

"It's going to be a long day," he murmured under his breath as he made his way to the fourth floor.

Attorneys from both sides were gathering inside the courtroom. They looked small beneath the giant marble seal looming over the judge's bench. Some were standing off to the side, leaning their backs against a wall-length mural depicting scenes from the American West.

Witten had brought Marc Cohen and Carol Clayton to help argue the motions. A large contingency from Wilmer, Cutler firm had come to watch. They were young attorneys and paralegals who looked fresh and energetic as they mingled and joked among themselves.

Hausfeld and Mendelsohn talked with Weiss and Miller. Weiss was flying to Salzburg, Austria, and would be staying for only part of the hearing. Swift was speaking to a colleague in a hushed voice. Gallagher stood in the background. Neuborne was smiling and talking excitedly to colleagues from both sides.

Fagan was standing among his group of survivors in the corridor. He was ushering them to their seats in the spectator gallery. Like a tour guide, he waved the last few stragglers over. Gizella Weisshaus was at the front of the pack. Other survivors and their families had already taken their seats. Lewis Salton and Armand Lakner were among them.

When Judge Korman walked in, the room grew quiet. Once again he abstained from wearing his judge's robe and opted for a coat and tie. He signaled everyone to sit. He took a chair at the head of the table.[1]

"How do you want to proceed?" he asked in his usual muffled voice.

After lamenting the fact that he had just received the plaintiffs' newly amended complaints, Witten gave an overview of their plan for the hearing. He ended his summary with an appeal to the plaintiffs.

"They chose this forum because they wished to invoke the truly awesome powers of the federal court to take broad discovery across oceans, in search of claims to certify enormous, worldwide classes, to threaten, frankly, the defendants with unimaginable financial risks, all of which is possible only in a federal court proceeding. That's why they're here.

"But since they're here and since they want to do that, they have to play by the rules, and they should not be heard to claim foul or to call odious arguments presented by the defendants which are responsibly invoked on the basis of the Constitution, statutes, and precedents. I think that kind of response to our arguments ought to be out of the case, and I hope we won't hear any of it today."

He began by arguing that the court should abstain in deference to the national interests of another country. The Swiss government was behind the Volcker Committee and the Humanitarian Fund and so was addressing the matter. Holding up Volcker's letter, he asserted that court discovery "would be an incredibly clumsy and ineffective way to go about trying to do what Mr. Volcker is doing. And why try, when he's doing it comprehensively, independently, fairly and costlessly to the claimants, by all accounts?"

"It may be that they don't have to duplicate it," Korman challenged him. "Maybe they could rely on it. But when this came up, when we were here the last time, that was unacceptable to you. In other words, as I recall, one of the issues that was raised was their simply monitoring in some way or having access to documents that were being—materials that were being made available to Mr. Volcker, you said that that was prohibited by Swiss bank secrecy laws, if I recollect your answer correctly. What if that's all that happened here, and there was a confidentiality order to boot?"

"Your Honor, first of all, that would run right in the face of what Mr. Volcker has said to the court, which is that the greatest potential damage to the committee's investigation would be the possibility of public disclosure of the documents, and I believe that's not solved by a confidentiality order with respect to the plaintiffs," Witten responded. "But now to answer the question you really started back a minute ago, if we're happy to work with Volcker, why aren't we happy to work with the plaintiffs?

"It is one thing, Your Honor, for the banks voluntarily, but also under the directive of the Swiss Federal Banking Commission, to work with a group that is objective, independent, professional, and holds out every promise that the job will be done comprehensively and cooperatively.

"It is quite another thing, legally, factually, and psychologically, to say, oh, yeah, those folks who are suing us for several billion dollars, and every time we turn around it's another billion dollars, those folks who are threatening boycotts and those folks who are threatening to put the banks out of business, sure, we'd love to cooperate with them, too. We'd really particularly love to cooperate with them, even though it's a complete duplication of the significant commitment we've already made to the Volcker process."

"But limiting ourselves here, there doesn't necessarily have to be duplication," Korman contested.

"I don't know how there would not be duplication," answered Witten.

"It's like making an extra copy," explained Korman. "If that's duplication, I suppose—"

"Literally, it is duplication, Your Honor, but I don't rest on the copying machine for my position. First, there are Swiss legal problems."

Korman kept hounding him. Why couldn't the court order a limited discovery for dormant accounts? The discovery could work with, not against, Volcker.

Witten cited Volcker's letter again and again. And if Volcker wasn't enough, he brought in Eizenstat. The undersecretary of state "expressed concern about these class actions because they were interfering with the administration, which after all has a responsibility for foreign policy—with the administration's efforts—objective of bringing closure to this issue."

"Why haven't I heard from anybody in the government of the United States directly about what the position is of the government of the United States?" Korman questioned.

"Because you haven't asked . . ." Witten answered.

"But the government only asserts its interest when it's requested?" wondered Korman.

Neuborne listened as Witten reiterated Eizenstat's concerns about the lawsuit. He had predicted that Witten would try to convince the court that Eizenstat was opposed to litigating the case. Remembering his meeting at the State Department, he could not hold his tongue.

"That's a factual misstatement, and I must interrupt. Both of us have spoken to the State Department, and the State Department has chosen not to discuss this case with the court until the court reaches a decision on the motions to dismiss."

"That is not right." Witten raised his voice.

"We don't have to argue about it. If I ask them, they'll tell me," Korman intervened.

"Neither of us should be talking about our private conversations with the State Department," scolded Witten.

"But you can't state something that contradicts them," Neuborne shot back.

"It's not important, this particular little dispute. Go on." Korman rubbed his forehead.

Witten continued with another long explanation regarding Volcker and the payment of dormant accounts. He suggested that the court could stay the proceedings and receive detailed reports from Volcker. He also berated the plaintiffs for not submitting their plaintiffs' names to Volcker.

"What these guys are doing is claiming sour grapes. . . . They say, we're not going to participate, we're not going to interfere. But they haven't told you what they are going to do, and when you look at what they have tried to do by way of discovery, it is a direct and would be a direct interference."

When he finished, the plaintiffs got their chance. Neuborne wasted no time in challenging Volcker's letter. He waved a copy of Burg's letter in the air.

"This is a letter from Avraham Burg, which has been made public, who is also a member of the committee and who strongly disagrees with Mr. Volcker's presentation to the court."

Hausfeld then explained that they had tried to work out a cooperative agreement with Volcker, but it went nowhere. Volcker did not want to expand his investigation or involve the plaintiffs.

"Think of what would occur if any company accused of wrongdoing could literally escape accountability in a court which had jurisdiction over it and in which a claim could be validly asserted, if the defendant could merely say, 'I'm taking care of this myself, and don't look at me.' That's what they're saying."

The argument over Volcker and discovery went on and on. Korman kept trying to explore ways that discovery could become part of Volcker's audit.

"One way might be to use the Volcker Commission as a kind of a special master to oversee discovery, with whatever additional obligations to the court and to the parties that that might impose. But at least it would be an entity that the Swiss government would have some confidence in."

Witten would consider that, but "there is no particular enthusiasm for a U.S. court role in this process, for the reasons I've said."

He did not want to give an inch. If he opened the door for even a limited court discovery, he would be opening the doors of the banks. His clients wanted no such thing.

After more arguments from both sides, Neuborne asked whether Arthur Miller could speak.

"But . . . I must whine just a little bit," Witten broke in. "We had no notice that half the faculties of the Northeastern Law Schools were going to be brought here. He hasn't signed any briefs, we don't know whether what he's going to say is in any brief. Of course the court should hear him, but I think this is a little bit of a stunt."

Miller used his lofty academic voice. He invoked the power of the Constitution and referred to past cases and decisions. He used the Paula Jones case in an attempt to convince Korman that a judge did not need to abdicate from making a decision in order to be sensitive.

Weiss addressed the judge next. His gravelly voice resonated through the courtroom.

"We need the oversight of this court . . . and as lawyers we ask this court to ignore the statements that we're just a bunch of class-action lawyers and that we're increasing transaction costs. That is not a dissuasive answer when we're dealing with these kinds of claims, and Your Honor knows full well, as does Mr. Witten, that these lawyers are working pro bono."

After more discussion, Fagan walked over to the table.

"Judge, since the action was filed in October, our office has received phone calls at the rate of one hundred to three hundred a day. We represent tens of thousands of clients. On July 28, I received the following letter, which I'm going to give to the court, but I'd like to just paraphrase, I'd like to read one section of it."

The letter was written by Paul Frenkel of Connecticut. It read, in part: "As one of the few survivors who survived the German concentration camps, I am dismayed and angry that here we are in 1997 and we cannot have our representation made in court before an impartial judiciary because someone thinks that he can take care of our interests better. I respect and admire Mr. Volcker for the job that he has undertaken, but he should stay out of our civil rights to have our interests represented and aired by the judiciary. . . . Please request Judge Korman not to dismiss or delay this case. . . ."

Korman scratched his eyebrows and called for a short break.

Fagan hustled to the hallway. His group of survivors gathered around him.

"Why does the judge mumble so much?" one woman asked.

"You call this a public hearing? Who can hear?" another one complained.

Speaking loudly and slowly like a school teacher, he tried to explain what was going on. Reporters were accustomed to seeing this scene. They had watched Fagan and his small group of survivors at court, at congressional hearings, and at press conferences. To many, his parading of survivors appeared to be nothing more than a publicity stunt. He seemed to need his survivors as much as they needed him.

Despite such criticisms, several of his claimants raved about their attorney. He provided a liaison to a judicial or political process they did not always understand. After all, no other attorney was escorting them around.

Attorneys were beginning to concede that his grassroots efforts were proving helpful in pressuring the bankers—attorneys other than Hausfeld, that is. He never would admit that.

When the attorneys and judge reconvened, Witten addressed the subject of aliens and diversity of citizenship. Legal technicalities were a strength of his. He could take a complaint and keep picking at it until a thread finally pulled loose. In this case, he had found that Estelle Sapir was not a citizen of the United States. She was a permanent resident, and yet she was included in a complaint that named U.S. citizens. Thus, the new complaints still lacked complete diversity. He also complained that the plaintiffs had not proven that each class member had sustained a loss equaling at least $50,000, which was the minimum required for jurisdiction (the amount had been raised to $75,000 after the filing of the complaints). The plaintiffs had to prove that they met this minimum before taking discovery. They could not use discovery to prove that they could meet it.

Korman and Witten carried on a legal debate over this issue for a good twenty minutes. This case was unusual, Korman explained. The plaintiffs did not have access to the information that they needed in order to prove that they could meet the amount.

All the technical terms began to confuse reporters and observers. The judge's inaudible voice did not help matters. Many spectators grew restless.

Neuborne spoke. Sapir would not destroy diversity because, under a congressional statute, permanent resident aliens are to be treated as citizens of the states in which they reside as long as there is an American citizen co-party. Miller joined in by citing a list of past cases. When they were finished, Korman called for a lunch break.

Hausfeld collected his papers and left. Fagan was already outside the building, standing in a park across the street. He was surrounded by a group of reporters, leaning into their microphones, happily answering questions.

Hausfeld shook his head and walked on. He was encouraged by the morning's proceedings. Korman had to believe that the dormant accounts claims had merit; otherwise, why would he have kept challenging Witten? Now, they just had to stay alive with the claims related to slave labor and looted property.

"The good news, Your Honor, is that over lunch we received no new complaints," Witten jabbed. "The bad news is that there turned out to be three new complaints and not two and the only one we received on Monday has been changed quite a bit and . . ."

When he finished complaining, he introduced Carol Clayton. She would be arguing the *forum non conveniens* motion.

"It's important for me to state up front that the purpose of this motion is not, as the plaintiffs would claim, to deprive Holocaust victims of a forum or of remedy," Clayton contended. "As Mr. Witten has described, these defendant banks have made and they continue to make very substantial efforts to address the claims of Holocaust victims. We have moved to dismiss on *forum non conveniens* grounds, because the plaintiffs have an adequate alternative forum in Switzerland and because a trial in New York would be truly oppressive to these defendants and would intrude on very important Swiss national interests."

According to the defense, having a trial in the United States would present a "massive burden." It would be "a tremendous expense to translate all this information so that U.S. lawyers can understand what it is we're dealing with."

From the outset, Korman made it evident where his bias was in respect to this motion.

"This complaint would be dismissed in Switzerland."

"We believe this complaint should be dismissed here," Clayton repeated.

"Yes, but if it's not dismissed here, it clearly would be dismissible in Switzerland." According to their own Swiss expert, Korman explained, the claims would be dismissed under Swiss law since the plaintiffs couldn't trace their assets. He was trapping the defense with their own arguments.

"It's really no forum, that's what you want, no forum, because they could not, this complaint, the pleading in the alternative, in looking to discovery to assist in a more precise pleading would not survive in a Swiss court if your experts are accurate."

Clayton kept to her rehearsed argument and offered little rebuttal. When she talked about the documents being in Switzerland and Europe, Korman pounced on her.

"I don't understand, I've never been able to understand why it's important where the evidence is. I mean, some of these concepts go back to a different time, and they get repeated over and over again. You know, documents that are in Switzerland today can be in the United States in six hours, notwithstanding time zones. These are all, there can be a document on the president of one of your clients' banks and it can be in my office in thirty seconds. These are all to a large degree antiquated concepts."

Korman could not have been clearer. *Forum non conveniens* was doomed to fail as a motion to dismiss.

Swift was supposed to argue *forum non conveniens*. When he got his turn, he conceded that Korman had beat him to the punch.

"Your Honor, you anticipated most of the arguments that we were going to make on *forum non conveniens,* specifically with regard to the adequacy of the forum." He argued the motion anyway. Within minutes, he had slipped in the Marcos case.

Marc Cohen had sparred earlier with the judge over the plaintiffs' inability to trace their assets to a specific bank.

"Well, we are aware of no case where someone comes into court and says I think I may have a contract with a Swiss bank when there are four hundred possible defendants. I think I may have a claim against them. I find three up the street, so I'm going to bring them in and take discovery of them to see if I have a claim against them. We have no such case. Breach of contract requires identification of the parties to the contract before you get in the door."

"This is kind of an extraordinary case, though, in terms of requiring people to plead in advance of discovery," the judge had countered. "They allege, and I don't accept for the moment that it's true, that they've got here, representatives of 75 percent of the banks that were in business in Switzerland in the relevant time period and probably a greater percentage of the ones that would have been likely depositories of money. And . . . this is not the usual case in terms of the ability of people to identify or have access to the ability to identify particular bank accounts, given the circumstances under which these accounts were open."

Korman was articulating what the plaintiffs had been trying to argue for months. One couldn't apply the requirements of an ordinary lawsuit to the extraordinary conditions surrounding this particular lawsuit.

The defense's response had always been, Then don't bring the suit to court. Let the plaintiffs use Volcker and the Bergier Commission to resolve this, not a U.S. court.

Hausfeld had spent a lot of time thinking about this conflict. Over the years, he had found more and more cases that fell into this gray area. He had come to believe that the courts were adhering too strictly to written laws. Equity, or what he liked to refer to as the conscience of the law, was all but disappearing. This disappearance was leaving a hole in the law. He feared that the Swiss banks would disappear into that hole. If the judge was going to rule, he was going to have to decide which was more important—the written rules or the principles behind those rules.

He was determined to remind Korman of this discrepancy.

"Your Honor has said something repeatedly throughout the day about this being a most unusual case, and yet the banks' response to that is in the most usual of ways. Where is the contract? Where is the bank? Where is the passbook? Where is the death certificate? These are not usual circumstances, and there is a tragedy in attempting to pigeonhole the staking of a claim at the very beginning of a litigation with the fact that you can't bring forth the proofs that you otherwise would have had possibly in the usual circumstances."

When discussion turned to the claims, based on the principles of customary international law, of slave labor and looting of assets, Hausfeld again came back to this theme.

"The violation, as Mr. Witten has said, cannot be a garden-variety tort, and I don't mean to demean these particular torts, but garden-variety torts would be murder, theft, and false imprisonment. That would be garden variety. What we have claimed here is a knowing participation of the banks in a common plan of genocide, plundering, and enslavement. Those aren't garden variety. Those aren't garden variety for the first part because they apply to entire populations, not to just single events. They are the foundations upon which all civilized nations have agreed each has to live by, if there's going to be some peaceful order."

And again.

"The banks tried to distinguish the convictions at Nuremberg of Puhl, Funk, and Rasche, but they can't get away from the language, which is applicable to anyone of any nationality, regardless of his status as a belligerent or neutral or whether it is a state act or a civilian, that the plunder engaged in by the Nazis was an integral part of genocide and that knowing participation and consent and complicity in the disposal of the plunder itself was a crime. That's the principle, that is the fundamental norm, that is universal, that is not garden variety. . . . The military court acted on the principle that any civilian who was an accessory to a violation of the laws and customs of war is himself also liable as a war criminal."

"But what makes one an accessory?" asked Korman.

"That's a question of fact, Your Honor, and this is a motion to dismiss," answered Hausfeld. "What the banks are arguing is that we can't prove those facts. That's not the issue here. Do we state a claim? Clearly, we have stated the same claim for which those individuals not only were indicted but convicted, under the same principles. . . ."

"At the time as well, if we're going to look at the facts, the Allies warned the Swiss banks about their trafficking in polluted assets and in slave labor. At the end of the war, the Allies requested, demanded, and was ignored, that the Swiss banks disgorge and restitute all looted assets and all profits of slave labor. The banks understood that. In fact, what the position of the banks was at the time was that under their interpretation of international law, the Germans were allowed to loot and enslave, because they were the occupying powers and to the victors belong the spoils. That was their position. There's no debate that they didn't understand that the Allies had a different position and that was the law that the Allies said was the law of nations. If in fact, under customary international law, under Section 1350, the crimes of genocide, plundering, and enslavement as pled—"

"Are you saying these banks are guilty of complicity in the crime of genocide?" Korman asked incredulously.

"Under the express decisions of the International Military Tribunal as applied to German bankers, yes," Hausfeld answered. "Unless you can distinguish and separate the tribunal's decision of the conviction of Rasche and Puhl that he who participates in the disposal of the fruits of genocide is himself or herself an accessory to that crime. We're not saying they have the same degree of guilt."

"Suppose, in our domestic law, somebody murders someone and steals something from the person who is murdered and another person knowingly purchases it, is that person an accessory—is he guilty of murder?" Korman asked Hausfeld.

"Would he be guilty as an accessory after the fact if he refused to reveal—" Hausfeld replied.

"Accessory after the fact is entirely different," Korman retorted. "Is he guilty of murder? Is it quite the same?"

"The Swiss banks, Your Honor, are not being charged with the actual execution of individuals."

"I understand that," replied Korman.

"The German bankers weren't, either," Hausfeld tried to explain. "But as part of the plan of genocide—"

"But their complicity was much more significant." Korman was leaning forward, more intent than ever.

"That is a question of fact, Your Honor. That is a very serious question of fact. As the Eizenstat report raises, no one has really uncovered at this time the full extent of the complicity of those private banks with Nazi Germany. How can we say at this time that we have failed to state a claim based on facts which have not yet been developed, but which, under the test for a motion to dismiss, that there may be facts that would establish that precise connection, we have not stated a claim."

"What facts would you say would state the claim, would support the claim?" Korman kept prodding.

"Very simple, Your Honor. If there were facts to support the allegation, which we believe there will be, that there was a common plan between the Swiss banks—"

"What does that mean, a common plan?"

"That there was an agreement—" Hausfeld continued.

"The agreement between the Swiss banks and the Germans was, okay, you go kill people and we will process the plunder," Korman interrupted. "Was that the agreement?"

"Your Honor, that's what the evidence at this time seems to point to."

Neuborne came to Hausfeld's aid.

"Your Honor, can I state what I understand our claim to be, which is a little less ambitious than that? What we have alleged and are prepared to prove is that the banks knowingly acted as a receiver of looted property, knowing that the property had been obtained under circumstances that sink to the level of war crimes."

He became animated as he talked about the crimes. "In every community in which the Nazis took power, there was an organized stripping of the Jewish community of all its property. The property was accumulated in depots, it was carefully indexed, it was melted down, and it was turned over to the Swiss banks that earned profits by laundering it.

"The question is, do they keep those profits or do the survivors of the camps have standing in an American court to ask at least that those profits be disgorged? Whether it's under customary international law, whether it's under New York or whether it's under Swiss law, we think we're going to be able to prove that, under all three of those laws, the defendant banks' activity creates a right at least to get the profits back, because it may be too late to get anything else, but at least to get the profits back."

Korman turned to Witten to see whether he had anything to add.

"Apart from observing that I think my friend really goes a little too far, though not as far as Mr. Hausfeld, I think I can rest on what we said earlier with respect to the international law issues."

"I apologize for getting emotional about this," Neuborne replied.

"This is an emotional case, and I do want to keep it at the level of reasoned discussion and legal discourse."

It was five thirty. Everyone was worn down. Korman was slouched in his chair. Neuborne's few wisps of hair were out of place. Shirts were wrinkled. Ties were crooked. A few hearty spectators remained in the gallery.

"Standing, I guess would be the next point," Witten smiled. "Is anyone left standing? That's the question we want to ask, Your Honor."

After a five-minute break, they dug in for one more round. Witten attacked the claims related to slave labor and looting of assets on the ground that they had no causal connection to the banks.

"None of the, at least in the complaints I'm familiar with, none of the looted-asset plaintiffs even allege any more than that they believe their assets were stolen. Some of them aren't even sure that their assets were stolen. None of them even allege that the assets are in Switzerland, let alone that they're in a Swiss bank, let alone one of the banks they sued. As wide as the gap is with respect to looted assets, it's even wider with respect to the slave labor allegations, which apparently have been drastically changed."

Neuborne took his turn to challenge Witten's reasoning.

"Let me suggest that if what we had here was a huge burglary ring that engaged in a lot of thefts, and they used three fences to move the items, and a victim came in one day and said, you can't get the burglars, they're gone. They're all in jail, they don't have any money. The property probably isn't left with the fences anymore. The fences probably moved it. I don't know which of the three fences moved my couch, but somebody moved my furniture. But I can show you that these fences have made very substantial profits in dealing with the fruits of the burglary. I would like those profits.

"That's what this case is. It's nothing more than that. This is a situation where the Nazis are the big burglary ring, the banks are the fences, and the plaintiffs are the victims. All they want is the profits from the fences. What the banks are saying here now is there's no connection. Of course there's a connection."

Cohen returned to this analogy later. "But, given Mr. Neuborne's hypothetical, a plaintiff would have to show that his or her property ended up in one of the defendants, as a requirement under Swiss law."

"I'll just say that Swiss law is not as archaic—the absurd suggestion that the defense keeps the money and the hypothetical that I suggested will not be the law in any civilized nation and it is not the law in Switzerland," Neuborne argued. He was agitated. "If you look at Professor Tercier's affidavit and read it closely, he as much as admits that when he says you can't find out from large numbers of people, it's large numbers of people, it's not three. When they've acted together as part of a common plan, he doesn't suggest that you can act as part of a common plan and then insist that you're treated as individuals."

"Are you alleging they're all—I'm trying to understand this conspiracy. Each of the three banks were conspirators with each other in addition to conspiring with the Germans?" asked Korman.

"No," Neuborne answered. "I think it's really more a hub and spoke. The Germans are the hub and the banks are the spokes. It may well be—we'll see if they conspired with each other. They may have divvied up the market, for all we know. I don't know that at this point. But they certainly were each in communication with the Germans and in a very parallel way."

Cohen told Neuborne to study Professor Tercier's affidavit.

"Why don't you give Professor Tercier Mr. Neuborne's hypothetical?" Korman asked.

"I'm curious," said Neuborne. "I'd like an answer from Professor Tercier on what will happen in my hypothetical. We'll provide you answers from Swiss experts, as well."

"Are you going to pay his bill?" Cohen remarked.

"So far you guys have been very helpful, and we think that that should continue. But we'll provide Swiss experts to answer the hypothetical," Neuborne sighed.

"I thought that's what this briefing was about," Cohen added sarcastically.

Everyone was tired. Discussion turned to the schedule and reply briefs.

"Having spent most of May reading the thousand pages that hit me originally and the seven hundred pages that hit me later, do you think we could talk about page limits?" Neuborne jabbed.

"Sure. I offered nine hundred and ninety," Witten answered in an affectless tone.

"I like everything in one," Korman said. "As I told you before, I don't find the way this was briefed very helpful in terms of the compartmentalization of all of these issues, except of course for Mr. Neuborne, who put it all in one brief."

"That had nothing to do with the complaint," Witten added.

"It does now," replied Neuborne.

Korman continued. "There are two issues that we sort of left, and that is—I don't know whether it could await the outcome of your submission or not, but the extent to which the Volcker Committee can be used here in terms of discovery with respect to the deposited assets. And then you had a suggestion about possible settlement discussions, if I heard you correctly, a long time ago, many hours ago."

Both sides agreed that the next step would be to meet with Volcker and see whether they could agree on a plan where the plaintiffs' and the committee could cooperate. The judge would wait to hear from them. He issued no other orders. The stay of discovery remained.

The attorneys began gathering their papers and coat jackets. Witten approached the table.

"We're sorry to bring you back. Magistrate Go has scheduled a discovery conference tomorrow, as against the chance that it will be time to talk about discovery. We thought it was perfectly clear from the way things were just left that it wasn't, but we were just told by Mr. Fagan that tomorrow morning he's going to ask Magistrate Go for massive discovery."

"Mr. Witten, with respect, that is not true. All I told you was that Magistrate Go has a discovery conference scheduled for ten o'clock. Please, don't misrepresent me," Fagan argued.

"I asked the question, what are you going to ask, and the answer was discovery," Witten countered. "All this petulant stuff is horrible to be brought up at the end of the day and with the court, but I don't think that's where we are, and I don't think that's where Mr. Neuborne thinks we are."

Neuborne didn't quite agree. For instance, why couldn't they take the deposition of Meili, the bank guard? That discovery wouldn't be too threatening.

"If you have an affidavit from him that Mr. Fagan procured, probably in violation of Swiss law, but be that as it may, I don't know what the pressing need for a deposition is now," Witten contested.

"The difference between an affidavit and a deposition is that it allows his testimony to be preserved," explained Korman.

"Exactly," said Neuborne.

"He's not going anywhere," Witten said.

"What do you mean, he's not going anywhere? If he's hit by a truck tomorrow, what are we going to do?" Neuborne asked in disgust.

"That's true of everybody," answered Witten.

"This happens to be an important witness."

Witten would not relent. "My suggestion is, again, if they want to serve some discovery, rather than at seven twenty-five at night, but at a time when I can consult with my clients, we'll review it. If we agree there's no dispute to be resolved by anybody —"

"When will you get back to him on it?" Korman asked wearily.

"I suppose I can get back on Monday or Tuesday," Witten mumbled.

"Fair enough," nodded Neuborne.

"I don't think there's any need to go to the Magistrate's tomorrow," Korman said.

"Thank you, Your Honor," Witten sighed.

After everyone left, Neuborne and Hausfeld sat in the back of the courtroom, reviewing the day. To them, this case had everything to do with Nuremberg. They had tried to make the judge understand that, but Witten had done a good job of removing the controversy from its context. Maybe they should have tried harder. Maybe they had been too afraid of becoming emotional. After ten hours of discussion, Korman had given no indication as to when a decision might come or when the stay of discovery might be lifted. Hausfeld was troubled. This case needed to be dealt with expeditiously. The judge had not offered any hints that he would do that.

Hausfeld and Neuborne hugged outside the courthouse. They both felt consumed and exhausted by the past year.

Hausfeld returned to the Waldorf and collapsed on his bed. As tired as he was, he could not fall asleep. He kept trying to devise ways that some form of discovery could go ahead. If the plaintiffs could show that what they wanted would not conflict with Volcker's work, they would have a chance. Volcker was focusing on the identification of names and amounts of dormant account holders. He was not looking into why these accounts remained dormant and why he was finding many more depositors than accounts. That "why," Hausfeld thought to himself, goes to issues outside the accounts. What did the Swiss bankers discuss at each bank and among the banks, in the 1940s and after, to ensure that, in light of the fact that so many persons would not be returning to claim their assets, they could keep those assets for themselves? The Volcker Committee would not be looking into the why behind those lost accounts.

By morning, he was feeling better. He had not only come up with an approach to Volcker, but he had several items he wanted the Executive Committee to discuss at the meeting that morning.

He arrived late. As he entered the room, one of the lawyers pulled him aside.[2]

"Bob and Ed just laid into Burt. They accused him of ramming through amended complaints and trying to take over the case. They said that he monopolized the hearing and intruded on their arguments. Bob was upset at having Miller and Lowenfeld at the hearing. He said it looked as if they were there so the judge could recognize that they had celebrities on their side. He found their presence demeaning."

When Hausfeld entered the room, Neuborne was standing by the door. His face was bright red, and his hands were flying.

"I don't have to put up with this," he yelled.

"Those kind of accusations were petulant and unproductive," he later remarked when recalling the incident. "I told them, I'm carrying you guys on my shoulders. If I left you alone, how long do you think you would stay afloat? You'd be at the bottom of the Hudson River by now, and you're telling me you're annoyed because you didn't get a chance to make noise in court?"

Hausfeld took his arm and led him back to the table.

"What's all this Mickey Mouse? The only reason in large part that we were there was because of Burt's instincts and because the court does listen to Burt no matter what the rest of us say or how we say it. Even though the court probably does listen to us, Korman has a long-term relation with Burt, and he listens to him a little more. And that's fine. Burt is one of us, not separate, following his own agenda."

Fagan was angry. They were supposed to have had a hearing with Magistrate Go, but both Neuborne and Hausfeld had opposed it at yesterday's hearing. Because of their opposition, the rest of them did not feel that they had the support to request the hearing, and thus the hearing had been canceled.

"A hearing on what?" Hausfeld bellowed. "We need this meeting today to decide what we want to do and what we want to ask for. Are we going to go before the magistrate and act like what, a bunch of clowns, not knowing ourselves how we want our house ordered?"

Swift and Fagan did not back off. They were angered by Weiss's comment to the court that the class-action lawyers were working pro bono. Neuborne and Hausfeld had not included a separate claim for attorneys' fees in the new amended complaints. It appeared that the pro bono attorneys were trying to undercut the fee-based attorneys. Swift and Fagan were going to write a letter to the judge listing those firms that were not working pro bono.

The tight alliance between Neuborne and Hausfeld was an irony not lost among the squabbling lawyers. Swift had brought Neuborne to the case, and to some it looked as if Neuborne was turning his back on Swift and Fagan at every chance he got. Instead of acting as a bridge between the two camps, it appeared that Neuborne was pitching his tent directly adjacent to Hausfeld's.

Tempers settled enough to discuss a few topics. They all agreed that they needed to find an area outside Volcker's jurisdiction in which they could ask for discovery. They wanted to file a motion requesting a lifting of the stay, at least with regard to deposited assets. They also talked about renewing settlement talks. Hausfeld would write a letter to Witten telling him that before they would meet with him, they would need a written framework of the banks' conditions. No use getting together if the banks had nothing new to offer.

On Monday, August 3, 1997, Neuborne sent a memo to the Executive Committee. After addressing several of the committee's decisions regarding Volcker and discovery, he revealed his real reason for writing.

> I also want to answer Bob Swift's accusation that I rammed the amended complaints through without adequate consultation. I raised the probable need to amend months ago. The Executive Committee decided to stand on the initial complaints until after the motion to dismiss was argued. Although I disagreed with such a strategy, I attempted to execute it. One week before the

argument, Judge Korman raised the need to amend on a conference call. Bob and I may have heard different things, but I
heard Korman deride the original complaints. He laughed
when I said we would stand on them. We then attempted to
amend while keeping the structure of the original complaints. It
became clear during the drafting process that we could not do
so without filing cumbersome and vulnerable pleadings. I took
the opportunity to draft simplified pleadings that do not give
away a single theory. The amended complaints are an example
of notice pleading. I circulated the amended pleadings to Mike
and Bob. Given the enormous time pressures, there simply
wasn't time to do more. I am certain that the oral argument on
Thursday would have been much worse if we had not taken
Roger's best issues off the table, without losing anything in the
process. Je ne regrette rien. . . .

I'm off for vacation. Maybe I'll cool off. But my current intention is to rethink my participation in the litigation. I have
three options. The least attractive option is to continue in my
current posture as a member of the Executive Committee. I
find myself immersed in distasteful personality conflicts, and
am unable to respond to a crisis without precipitating the abuse
that I took on Friday morning.

The most attractive option for me is to inform the Court
that I have done all that I can do in the case, and ask to be allowed to return to my academic work.

Third, I can resign from the Executive Committee, continue
as Court-appointed co-counsel for the plaintiffs, and file my
own papers, if necessary.

Let's see how we all feel in a couple of weeks.[3]

Most did not take his threat of quitting seriously. They knew how
emotional he could get. Swift had no doubt that Neuborne would remain. The memo was just his way of getting attention and sympathy.

Hausfeld read the memo and sat quietly for a few moments. He
understood how Neuborne could contemplate leaving. He too felt frustrated and worn out by the constant personality clashes. Every decision
took so much energy. He did not like to think of continuing without
Neuborne. The delicate balance of the Executive Committee would be
destroyed if he were to leave. The judge knew that, Hausfeld knew that,

and Neuborne knew that. Neuborne would have to come to his own decision. There was nothing left to say.

Late in the afternoon, Neuborne was preparing to leave his office
when he heard a rustling at his door. He looked up and saw a gorilla
standing at his door holding fifty balloons.

"I have a telegram for a Burt Neuborne," the gorilla announced. He
handed the bouquet of balloons to Neuborne and gave him a small
note. Neuborne opened it and smiled.

"If you leave me alone with these people may you suffer eternal Jewish guilt."

Signed, "Michael."

9

Stucki's Ghost

Your Honor,

Ladies and Gentlemen

It is after 5:00 already and I understand that you are a little bit tired. But please, I would like you to listen to me very attentively. . . . Me and my husband twice were victims. The first time, we were victims of fascist occupation. We flee and we ran away in order to save our lives. We flee in summer clothes. We didn't take any belongings with us. In addition, they were bombing. Bombs were falling on our heads. This time, on the road you could see a lot of corpses just laying around, people who, like us, were running for their lives but they died. Among the people was my sister. She died, she perished.

The second time, we were victims when we flee Communist Regime. Once it came that the Jews got the possibility to go abroad from that Regime, to escape that Regime. I'm a doctor and I worked thirty-eight years as a doctor. This time, me and my husband was allowed to take from the Soviet Union, while we were coming here to this country, only two suitcases, twenty kilograms or forty pounds each. Was I allowed to take some valuables with us? No, I wasn't.

We came here at an older age and we couldn't bring much valuable stuff with us. Also, I couldn't . . . my diploma in order I couldn't get a job here, as far as my specialty. So me and my husband had to apply for SSI and collect public assistance from the government, and it was essential to us, to pay our bills, to pay the rent and just basic things, providing our life. You know what? We had no money to put to the bank or to accumulate some savings in the bank. . . . . I am eighty years old and it can happen that I will never see the justice. . . . I have relatives in Minsk and they have a very terrible hardship. Sometimes they have a choice what to buy, either some food or some medication. They were also evacuated, they also lost their property. . . . Please distribute the money in a fair way. Thank you.

November 29, 1999, Swiss Banks Fairness Hearing

168

Hausfeld and Gallagher landed in Zurich early in the morning on Friday, December 12, 1997. They had been flying since the previous evening and were hoping that they would be able to take a nap and refresh themselves before beginning the day. When they arrived at their hotel, their rooms were not ready. They put down their bags and walked up the street to the elegant Savoy Hotel, where the negotiations were to be held. So this was it—the place where they would have their first encounter with the banks' CEOs. Hausfeld picked up a brochure. The Savoy had been built in 1838. It was owned by Credit Suisse. He should have known. The CEOs would never have agreed to meet on someone else's turf.

Hausfeld walked over to the winding stairwell, with its gilded railing and heavy gold chandelier. The lobby had a stately, conservative air. Its conference rooms were decorated with wood-paneled walls and soft turquoise carpets. Everyone was talking in low voices. He felt as if he were interrupting a secret. He had experienced this same sensation during his June trip with Marilyn. Whether he was visiting a mountain hamlet or walking the streets of Geneva, he had always felt as if he were on the outside of some whispered reality. Maybe the country appeared muted compared to New York or Washington, D.C., or maybe it was just that his perception of Switzerland had changed. As a child, he had thought of Switzerland's quiet not as some sinister secret but as an alternative to the hype of the Cold War. If things got really bad, he used to tell himself during those school drills when he and his classmates were told to crouch under their desks and wait for a siren to signal that no nuclear bomb had exploded, he could go to Switzerland. It was one of the few countries in the world that was neutral. He had seen pictures. The country always looked so peaceful, so blissful, so unaffected by the world's turmoil. And now he had discovered that the country he had secretly held in his mind as a refuge held a much different secret. No wonder the hotel felt to him more like a private country club. He couldn't help picturing Swiss bankers whispering behind closed doors.

Zurich is known as one of the quieter, more picturesque cities in Europe. It has a lake and nearby mountains. Its most distinguishing feature is Bahnhofstrasse, Switzerland's version of Fifth Avenue, only cleaner and without the constant noise of traffic and taxi horns. Looming over both sides of Bahnhofstrasse are the stone buildings of Switzerland's three largest banks: Credit Suisse, Union Bank of Switzerland, and Swiss Bank Corporation.

Gallagher had heard about the Franz Carl Weber toy store located on Bahnhofstrasse and was eager to look around for something for his son. He and his wife had recently found out that she was pregnant. Now that the plaintiffs were going to meet the bankers face to face, he was sure the case would be over soon and he would have more time at home.

It was cold and drizzling. Hausfeld and Gallagher did not pause to look at the window displays of Cartier watches and Yves St. Laurent clothes. They ducked into the toy store and became absorbed in playing with the toys. When they left, they realized that they had only a few minutes to get to their lunch date. Hausfeld had agreed to meet a woman he had never met. He knew only that she was Swiss and that she wanted to help him with the case. She had been sending him cards and letters over the months with tidbits she had gleaned from Swiss journals. Each note contained a few glowing words about him. Curious as well as flattered, he had agreed to meet her when he came to Zurich. Gallagher had reluctantly agreed to accompany him, but he couldn't believe that, with all they had on their minds, they were going to spend time meeting some Swiss woman who had for some inexplicable reason become interested in the case.

Ursula Erber (her name has been changed upon request) was waiting for them. She was an older woman with short, white hair and glasses, hardly the picture of an infatuated groupie. Serious and intense, she wanted Hausfeld to know just how strongly she believed in his pursuit. She offered to translate documents and to keep him abreast of news in Switzerland.

Her attention made Gallagher uncomfortable. Why was she so eager to help? Hausfeld didn't ask any questions. He was absorbed in talking about the case and was delighting in having a captive audience.

What Ursula did not tell them was that she was not Swiss but German. Even though she had been living in Switzerland for more than thirty years, she was a German citizen who had spent her childhood in Germany. She did not tell them that she had been a member of Hitler's Nazi youth movement and had awakened to find her half-Jewish best friend suddenly gone. She did not tell them that her older brother had fought for Germany, that she had wanted to believe that he had not participated in the horrors but had found a photo he had taken at the entrance to a Polish ghetto. She did not tell them that, over the years, her guilt at being part of such a system had grown, that guilt never goes away. And she did not tell them that when she had heard Hausfeld's voice on the television, she had become enamored. She felt destined to do whatever she could to help him.

The two lawyers returned to their hotel. Talking about the case had reinvigorated Hausfeld. Instead of napping, he looked over the settlement books he had prepared for the meeting. He was surprised at how numb he felt. He was neither hopeful nor discouraged. When an aide from the State Department had originally called him to suggest a meeting between the banks and the plaintiffs, with Eizenstat, now an undersecretary of state, as the coordinator, he had been skeptical. Nothing had changed since the July court hearing. Volcker was still reluctant to let the plaintiffs play a role in his audit. Witten still wouldn't discuss a money figure. The WJC was still acting independent of the lawyers. Korman still hadn't ruled on jurisdiction or discovery, and Eizenstat was still fluctuating between praising the banks and supporting the plaintiffs. Hausfeld felt as if he were on a treadmill. Every time he stepped forward, he moved back. There were so many meetings and phone calls, yet he kept returning to the same spot. He was afraid to hope that this time things would be different. But . . . the bankers had agreed to meet. This had to be a sign of something. He couldn't help feeling that maybe, just maybe, the scenery was about to change.

In October he had gotten excited when Hevesi had made a bold move and had denied UBS the chance to provide a routine letter of credit to back up New York City's borrowing of $1 billion. The action was mainly symbolic, since UBS would have gained only $450,000 for arranging the financing. Still, financial officers from other cities had begun talking about following Hevesi's lead. Within days, Matt Fong, the Republican state treasurer of California, had imposed a moratorium on his own state's dealings with Swiss banks and two Swiss-owned brokerage firms. On December 8, Hevesi had hosted a conference on the Swiss bank accounts at the Plaza Hotel in New York. Singer had risen to speak and, to Hausfeld's surprise, had proposed a ninety-day

moratorium on all sanctions. Singer wanted to give the banks a chance
to resolve the issues on their own without actually having to impose
sanctions. For some Jewish leaders, sanctions were disagreeable. They
reminded them of the Arab boycotts of Israel. Hevesi had agreed to the
moratorium. People understood that the threat of sanctions could be as
powerful as sanctions themselves. This threat would hang over the
bankers like the sword of Damocles.[1]

Hausfeld disagreed. He looked upon the moratorium as another
delay and believed that the bankers would do nothing unless they felt
some pain. As always, he took it personally. He remembered that Singer
had assured Weiss and him that he was with them, and then he had
gone and declared a moratorium. Hausfeld had listened to Steinberg
and Singer at the conference. One had praised the banks while the
other had scolded them.

Bronfman added to Hausfeld's confusion. "Let's forget all this non-
sense about great funds and commissions and the committee that's looking into bank accounts," Bronfman had told a reporter. "Let's just say
there's a figure at which point we could just settle the whole damn thing,
which includes of course the class-action suits in New York."[2]

Hausfeld had grown weary of everyone. He had listened to bank
representatives at the conference declaring that the circumstances of
the Holocaust were so exceptional that normal banking processes didn't
apply. But how could they use this defense when in court their lawyers
had argued just the opposite—that, under the rules of normal commercial banking, the plaintiffs must be able to trace their assets? He couldn't
believe that the Swiss envoy, Borer, had the nerve to insist that sanctions
by state controllers would not be consistent with international law.
Among all the places for the Swiss to hide, international law shouldn't
have been one of them—not after their arguments in court that international laws were not part of U.S. federal laws.

Hausfeld had enjoyed Weiss at the conference. Reporters had
hounded the lawyers to name their figure. What would it take to make
this issue go away? Marc Cohen had even approached Hausfeld, dig-
ging for a number. Weiss aimed his daggers straight at the banks'
pocketbooks.

This was not an issue that applied to survivors only, he remembered
Weiss claiming. This was an issue that applied to all victims, and just

because the survivor population was dropping off rapidly was not a reason to sell the issue short. He threw out numbers nobody else would have dared to say aloud. Surely the banks, which were worth $560 billion in assets, could address the issue of Holocaust victims' assets. If the tobacco companies could pay $360 billion, surely the banks could pay. If Exxon Corporation could pay $5 billion for its wrongs, surely the banks could pay. When he finished, Hausfeld turned to the defense lawyers.

"Did that clarify it for you? The number is somewhere between $5 and $360 billion."

Another disappointment to Hausfeld had come with the announcement that UBS and Swiss Bank Corporation were planning to merge. The proposed merger would form a single bank with assets of more than $590 billion. The bank would be the second largest in the world. To Hausfeld, the merger was a slap in the face. The banks wanted to carry on business as usual, regardless of the allegations swirling outside their walls.

The plaintiffs could write the Federal Reserve and the New York Banking Department to protest the planned merger. They could tell the regulators that they must confront the Holocaust issue before approving the merger, that the issue was not separate. Hausfeld had written down some ideas in a spurt of anger and excitement. He had wanted to discuss them with Mendelsohn when he returned from the conference.

He had reread accounts of the 1946 Washington Accord during the days preceding the Zurich meeting. He had been especially interested in a Swiss official by the name of Walter Stucki. Stucki had been aptly named, as he was a stubborn and intransigent negotiator. During negotiations with the Allies, he had refused to admit that Switzerland had received any looted gold. He had argued that even if his country had accepted gold, Nazi Germany had had a legal right to that gold, since it had been looted from central government-owned banks. Stucki had approached every issue, from gold to the liquidation and distribution of German assets, with a legalistic and narrow perspective. He had believed that his country was being unfairly sanctioned by the Allies, especially by the Americans. In the end, he agreed to return $58 million in gold—a paltry sum compared to the $289 million in looted gold the Americans claimed Switzerland had absorbed. Still, $58 million had been too much in Stucki's mind. He made no apologies. He accepted no responsibility. His only justification for signing the accord was to enable Switzerland to resume normal relations with the world trading community.

Hausfeld couldn't get over the similarity between Stucki's position and the position of the Swiss bankers fifty years later. Kleiman had found the original letters between Stucki and the U.S. negotiators. Hausfeld had studied them before coming to Zurich. He had used Stucki's responses and words to prepare himself. He wanted Stucki's ghost with him, sitting at that table on Sunday, warning him of what was to come.

Weiss arrived in Zurich impassioned. He and Hausfeld went for a drink and talked about the different possible scenarios. Cutler was going to be at the meeting. They could view his presence two ways. The optimistic view was that Cutler was there to bridge the gap—to help his clients understand the law in America, their exposure, and what they had to do to get peace. The pessimistic view was that Cutler was going to play the role of the bad cop. He would represent the banks' hard line. Whatever the case, Weiss was adamant that this was their chance to move the discussion from dormant accounts to the totality of wrongs committed and, ultimately, to money.

Over the past several months, Weiss had become more and more determined to make the case encompass more than just dormant accounts and survivor payments. This case needed to be settled on a grand scale, with a financial number large enough to make a grand statement. The Swiss banks were unrepentant. Admission of their behavior during and after World War II would come only through the gesture of money. Many of the other plaintiffs' lawyers appreciated Weiss's larger vision of the case. He seemed to understand the symbolic significance of money more clearly than others and was constantly reminding both the Plaintiffs' Executive Committee and the defense. Unlike Hausfeld, he had no expectation that this Zurich meeting would be any more fruitful than their past discussions with the other side—with one exception. This time he would be able to look the Swiss CEOs directly in the eyes. For someone as adept at negotiations as Weiss was, this was an opportunity to seize.

Weiss and Hausfeld talked about an article by the attorney Alan Dershowitz in *California Lawyer*. The essay discussed the profound impact of Jewish lawyers on the general practice of law in America, and on the social conscience of the law in particular. Even though the article made no reference to the class action against the Swiss banks, it was natural for the two of them to draw comparisons and realize how interrelated their Judaism and their work as lawyers had become.

Gallagher watched with amusement as Weiss made his way through the streets of Zurich. To Gallagher, Weiss appeared completely at home in the expensive stores. While Gallagher was stunned by the high price tags, Weiss did not seem to give them a second glance. Gallagher remembered watching Weiss buy a new overcoat after deciding that he didn't like the condition of his old one. He bought several hundred dollars worth of cigars and purchased a new knife while turning to Hausfeld and Gallagher and telling them to pick one out for themselves. He seemed comfortable with Zurich's high style and empowered by his mission.

Swift arrived on Saturday, along with several other attorneys. Swift, Hausfeld, and Weiss were the designated negotiating team. Hausfeld had told Gallagher that he wanted him at the negotiating session as well, even though Gallagher was uncomfortable with that decision. He knew that his inclusion could anger those who would be left outside the room, primarily Fagan and the World Council lawyers.

As the meeting drew near, the attorneys began to feel anxious. To calm themselves, they reminded each other that they would take no more excuses from the banks. Witten and his team had been talking about process for over a year. The plaintiffs no longer wanted to hear about how the WJC was not cooperating or how the banks were not getting enough credit for the Humanitarian Fund. The bankers had to accept the fact that they were going to need to pay a specified amount of money. All the talk in the world would not make that fact go away. The time had come. Hausfeld, Weiss, and Swift were ready to reveal that amount. No more excuses.

As tense as the plaintiffs were, the defense lawyers were calm. Almost a year had passed since the Meili affair. Swiss officials had not offended anyone in a while. The Humanitarian Fund was preparing to issue its first check. The SBA had published its second list of dormant accounts, and the Bergier Commission had issued a preliminary report in which it had found that the majority of the looted gold had gone to the SNB, not to the private banks, although the private banks had received more gold than previously estimated.

Neither Witten nor Cohen was worried about the class action. They were sure Korman would throw out the claims about looted assets and slave labor. Volcker would take care of the dormant accounts. Why Korman was taking so long to make his decision they didn't know, but they weren't concerned. Only the threat of sanctions worried them, but now, with the ninety-day moratorium, that too had eased.

The defense lawyers had agreed to meet with Eizenstat and the plaintiffs as a good-faith gesture. They had no intention of getting down to the nitty-gritty of money. In their minds, this was not a settlement meeting. They weren't even sure that they were going to bring their clients to the table. When they heard that the U.S. ambassador to Switzerland, Madeleine Kunin, was planning on attending, they decided that the CEOs would show up, out of respect for her.

Of course, they knew better than to relax completely. They were never sure what would come out of Weiss's mouth. The Swiss lawyers were especially wary of Weiss. To them, he exhibited none of the reserve and self-restraint that they were accustomed to among their Swiss colleagues. They had heard stories of his ranting and raving. Some viewed him as a crazy American lawyer, while others acknowledged his brilliance as a negotiator. Either way, they did not relish coming up against him.[3]

Eizenstat was late to Zurich. He had been attending the London Gold Conference, and his flight had been delayed. Participants at the conference had come to discuss how to distribute the remaining bars of Nazi gold that were still in the Tripartite Gold Commission's accounts at the Federal Reserve Bank of New York and the Bank of England. At the conference's opening, the British foreign secretary, Robin Cook, had announced that the British government would head a new international fund to help Holocaust survivors. The United Kingdom would contribute £1 million, and the United States agreed to contribute $25 million over four years. By the conference's end, disagreements had emerged. Several countries had announced that they had no intention of contributing to the fund. Eizenstat concluded the conference by announcing that another conference would be organized within six months in Washington to address the issue of stolen artworks.

As the plaintiffs' lawyers waited for the Zurich meeting to begin, they listened to the newly arrived Fagan. Rumors were flying. News of the meeting had leaked, and there was talk that an agreement had already been reached for $1.7 billion.

Hausfeld panicked. Maybe the banks had already settled. Maybe the plaintiffs' attorneys were being played for fools and Eizenstat was actually going to announce a done deal. Maybe . . .

The four plaintiffs' attorneys entered the Savoy's conference room and surveyed the scene. Close to sixty people were assembled around a giant rectangular conference table. The banks had stacked the room with their lawyers and accountants. Such a show of force surprised Hausfeld. It was as if the bankers wanted to make sure that the plaintiffs understood just how enormous their resources were.

Hausfeld's eyes turned to a man sporting a sky-blue tie with big red dinosaurs on it. When he learned that the man wearing the tie, who was seated at the end of the huge table, was Mathis Cabiallavetta, the president of UBS, he couldn't help thinking that his whimsical tie was a sign. No serious agreement would be reached today.

Lukas Muehlemann, the CEO of Credit Suisse, welcomed everyone.[4]

"The bankers are open to dialogue, but we have been overwhelmed by the publicity, and this is making it difficult to do anything more than just listen."

Hausfeld had just received his second sign.

"We are here to engage in noneconomic structural terms of preliminary negotiations," Witten announced.

His third sign.

Witten's words were shrouded in legalese, but the message was clear: no money would be discussed around this table. Witten also made it clear that only the three banks would be involved in these talks and nobody else—not the Swiss government, the SNB, or the SBA. The banks had "absolutely zero tolerance" for threats of boycotts or sanctions. He looked at the plaintiffs' lawyers, and then he pointed at the banks' three officers.

"That type of conduct doesn't and won't work with these guys."

"This is all a show," Hausfeld thought. "Witten brought us here so he can show his clients how he can lecture us like two-year-olds."

How little progress they had made in a year. Once again, the banks were drawing a line in the sand. The plaintiffs could have the three banks but no more. How did the banks expect to achieve a true peace without all the entities involved? The banks still didn't understand—this was not just about dormant accounts.

Cutler made sure everyone understood that charges related to anything other than dormant accounts could not be proved. Witten then talked about structure and how they needed a mechanism to distribute all the unmatched deposited assets. That mechanism, he asserted, should be the Humanitarian Fund. He did make one major concession. While the claims related to looted assets and slave labor had no legal merit, some agreement might be reached on a rough justice number and that that money, too, could be turned over to the Humanitarian Fund.

Weiss, Hausfeld, and Swift asked for a break.

Hausfeld could hardly wait to get outside.

"What a bunch of malarkey. This is not a negotiation. This is nothing more than Roger and Lloyd performing in front of their clients. Their position hasn't changed. There's nothing new in this whatsoever."

Weiss agreed, as did Swift. In fact, Swift was visibly angry. His discontent with NGOs had continued to grow with the Marcos case. He was adamant that no NGO, especially the WJC, should become the primary distributor of the money. Yet this would occur if they let the Humanitarian Fund become the mechanism for distribution.

Hausfeld repeated the same principle he had been repeating from the beginning.

"The Humanitarian Fund is for humanitarian purposes. Putting settlement money into the Humanitarian Fund would allow the banks to save face; it would make a settlement appear as if it was a charitable gesture instead of a moral obligation."

Weiss then suggested something brash. Why not throw a number out? Make them confront an actual number at the beginning of negotiations.

Even if the bankers didn't respond, having a number out there would be a major accomplishment.

The four returned. Witten and Cutler's proposal was unrealistic. Period. Swift rejected the Humanitarian Fund.

Weiss then leaned forward and spoke calmly.

"It appears clear from these discussions that the banks and the plaintiffs are far apart in terms of process and that the banks are not discussing the amount. You can't build a bridge between the process and the amount without a discussion of what both need to be, and without that discussion there will never be an understanding." Then he turned to Hausfeld for an explanation of what their process was for finding an amount that the plaintiffs believed represented a level at which a global resolution could be achieved.

Hausfeld looked up and noted that Witten's face had turn ashen. It was as if the angel of death had entered the room. He watched Witten shake his head in unusual animation and turn to Eizenstat.

"We thought we had an understanding that there would be no discussion of economics. We won't talk numbers, we cannot have an economic discussion."

People from the State Department held their breaths. It was true. Money was not supposed to have entered this discussion. At least not yet, not at this meeting with the CEOs.

Eizenstat began to speak. His soft voice, with its slight southern drawl, had a calming effect. "We need to listen to the plaintiffs' exploration of the issues, even if," and he looked at Witten, "you don't want to respond. You've at least got to hear what they have to say."

Hausfeld explained what had gone into his experts' report. He talked about all three types of assets and how they accounted for the total.

"The total sum"—he paused to give the number its full effect— "amounted to $10 billion."

The bankers shifted in their seats, their eyes fixed ahead. Eizenstat returned the conversation to the role of the Humanitarian Fund and how money should be distributed, but, for all intents and purposes, the discussion was over. It was early afternoon, and Eizenstat had to catch a plane. Witten used Eizenstat's departure as an opportunity to ask for a break. He said he would call the plaintiffs at two thirty and let them know whether or not the banks wanted to reconvene.

Hausfeld heard only the "or not." He and the others had come all this way for two hours of discussions? What had been the point?

The CEOs all said goodbye. When Muehlemann approached Hausfeld and Weiss, he extended his hand.

"This is not going to be easy," he said.

So what was he really trying to say? Was this his way of indicating that the banks were heading toward a resolution? Hausfeld wanted a sign, anything, to indicate that something had been accomplished. He analyzed those seven words as if they were an encrypted code that had just been pressed into his hands.

The negotiating team returned to their anxious colleagues waiting at the hotel. They filled them in on the meeting and waited for Witten's call. Everybody was disappointed. They had hoped that the discussions were going to open a window. At three o'clock, Witten called. The banks had heard enough. They would assess their position and get back to the plaintiffs in January. The negotiations had ended. The door was closed.

Even though he had told himself not to have any expectations, Hausfeld couldn't help himself. He had wanted something to happen. He had allowed his hopes to soar, and now he was hitting rock bottom.

Gallagher listened from a distance as Weiss tried to reassure Hausfeld. Weiss had said from the beginning to expect little. Before meeting with the banks, he had warned Hausfeld to stay calm and to keep his emotions reined in. Now that the discussions were over, he assumed a paternalistic air and tried to bolster him. He reminded him of how much they had accomplished and how they wouldn't give up, and, yes, they were making progress.

Before returning home, the plaintiffs' lawyers discussed their plan. They would move ahead of the banks and devise their own plan for settlement and distribution and send it to Witten. For once, the plaintiffs' side was in agreement. Nobody accused anyone of manipulating or dominating or deviating. Despite the disappointment of the talks, they were getting along surprisingly well. They had talked and laughed over meals. They had gone shopping together. They had taken walks by the lake, and they had articulated their doubts, fears, and goals for this case.

"The boys have bonded," Hausfeld had told Gallagher earlier. "I even heard Fagan refer to the Executive Committee as a team. We've all come to Zurich to represent the same claimants and the same demands."

Maybe, just maybe, the battle of the Weisshaus lawyers versus the Friedman lawyers was a thing of the past.

The Swiss defense lawyers had gotten to watch their American counterparts in action. They had known about Weiss, but Hausfeld. . . . To them, his passion bordered on fanaticism. He appeared possessed. How else to explain this guy who, in an American courtroom, had accused the banks of being accomplices to genocide? His rhetoric and emotional tantrums were an anomaly to the understated Swiss. They took to calling him Ayatollah.

Swift was the only one among the three American plaintiffs' attorneys with whom the Swiss attorneys felt comfortable. He was rational and calm and diplomatic and . . . well . . . more like them. He did not push the extremes. This was not to say they liked him. After all, he was still fighting the banks over the Marcos assets. But Swift, when compared to Weiss or Hausfeld or the flamboyant Fagan, was the most approachable.[5]

Witten and the bankers were not disturbed by the abrupt ending of the talks. The CEOs had made their appearance. They had shown Ambassador Kunin and Eizenstat that they were involved. They had also made it clear that they were not ready to talk about money and were nowhere near accepting the amount the plaintiffs were demanding.

In reality, the CEOs had other concerns. The merger between Swiss Bank Corporation and UBS had provoked a rash of negative publicity and was causing unease in Switzerland. The Swiss economy had been hurt by a recession, and the banks were first in the line of fire. Rumors that the merged bank planned to reduce its Swiss work force by as much as seven thousand people had added to the public's disdain. How could the bankers justify paying the Jews a billion-plus dollars when they were laying off their own people?[6]

UBS had its own problems. The bank had not been performing well and was facing increased competition from American institutions. Some in UBS were calling for Studer's resignation.[7] In addition to its own losses, the Swiss Bank Corporation, had reported a loss of $1.4 billion. And, just recently, the New York State Banking Department had issued a consent order against Swiss Bank Corporation for not acting with "appropriate speed and diligence" in responding to requests for information about the bank's wartime accounts held in New York.[8] The two

CEOs of the proposed combined bank, Marcel Ospel, of Swiss Bank Corporation, and Cabiallavetta, of UBS, knew they would need to create a new image for their banks. The Holocaust conflict was not helping, but they didn't think that the issue should affect their plans to merge.

Muehlemann and Gut of Credit Suisse were more concerned than UBS and Swiss Bank Corporation with trying to resolve the Holocaust conflict. They had been suffering losses over the past few years, and they didn't want this Holocaust scandal to keep gnawing at their image. They had hired Frederick Schwarz from Cravath, Swaine to cast about for solutions, but the negative reaction of his colleagues at the firm had weakened his position from the start. Schwarz had talked to Neuborne, whom he knew from a former case, but none of his proposals had gotten off the ground. If a settlement was going to be reached, it became evident that all three banks were going to have to initiate it.

There was one person, however, with whom Credit Suisse officials were trying to make a separate peace.

"Credit Suisse took our money and refuses to give it back," Estelle Sapir told reporters outside Credit Suisse's New York branch, where she, Weisshaus, and several other survivors whom Fagan had organized were demonstrating. "They owe me the money, they owe me interest, and they owe the profits they made from withholding my father's money for over fifty years. I'm old, sick, and what Credit Suisse has done and is doing is making me sicker. I need my money now!"[9]

Despite her weakened condition, Sapir kept appearing at hearings, demonstrations, and on the news. To Credit Suisse officials, she was like a tough weed.

Robert O'Brien was managing director of Credit Suisse in New York. He had met Sapir several times and had come to believe, as did other officials at his bank, that her story was true, or at least partly so. They believed that she had been turned rudely away from their bank's doors in 1946 and 1957. They just weren't sure whether her father had an account with Credit Suisse and, if so, whether a member of her family had already emptied it. A call from Sapir's sister-in-law in France added to the confusion. The sister-in-law claimed that she too had a right to the account. Credit Suisse employees were ordered to search for Sapir's father's account. The problem was that they had few leads. The documents D'Amato had referred to at his hearing with Sapir turned out to be less than productive. One card represented defunct Polish bonds, and, although the other had the name J. Sapir written on it, no account address or amount was cited.

Sapir had memories and circumstances that were credible. She just didn't have the necessary documents. Her situation was hardly different from those of Weisshaus or Lakner or Salton or Beer. But she had what the others didn't. She had D'Amato, and he was putting increasing pressure on the bank to find an equitable solution. Sapir was losing weight and getting sicker. Money from her father's account could help pay for extra health care, maybe even get her into an assisted living program.

Her tenaciousness captured the attention of everyone, including the bankers. This little woman had made repeated trips to Credit Suisse between 1946 and 1957. Each time, bank officials had refused to deal with her. Now, more than fifty years later, Credit Suisse was admitting that, yes, there was a card under the name of J. Sapir.

O'Brien liked to boast that he and Sapir were friends. After all, before walking through the front doors of his bank, hadn't he walked over to the demonstrators picketing on the sidewalk and given her a hug? But he also knew, as did the others, that if the class action ever went to a jury, it would be Sapir who would gain the hearts of the jurors.

Since no account had been found, Credit Suisse officials had only one other choice. They could settle with Sapir privately. This option began to look more and more enticing. If they could cut a deal with her attorneys, they could remove her from the scene and get D'Amato off their backs. O'Brien had met with Sapir and Fagan back in July, but Fagan had refused to make any private deal. Witten had approached Fagan and Swift several months later, and again the attorneys had refused. They had a problem. Sapir was a named class representative on their complaint. How could they broker a separate deal for one of their named plaintiffs? The two did not share their dilemma with Hausfeld. He would only complicate matters.

Sapir was not the only survivor who had urgent needs. Many survivors were living alone in rundown apartment buildings or without proper health care. Sapir put a face to the plight of U.S. Holocaust survivors who had not been able to rise above their pasts and achieve the riches of the American dream. They couldn't all be like Salton or Lakner. Some of them clamored for money from the Swiss banks because they needed it, not because they were chasing after some esoteric notion called justice.

Nowhere was this need more evident than in Eastern Europe. Survivors in Eastern Europe were the "double victims" that Eizenstat had been invoking. They had been released from Hitler's trap only to be ensnared by the Communists. They were Jews and gypsies who had had their properties Aryanized and their homes looted. Many of them had worked as forced and slave laborers during the Nazi regime. They had received no money from Soviet authorities or from Germany's reparation payments. Many of them were living in poverty and, as the years passed, dying in it.

The Humanitarian Fund was supposed to be the banks' and the WJC's quick fix. The fund was going to get money quickly to these needy survivors. The banks had hoped it would fix their public relations problem, and the WJC leaders had hoped it would be the first step in getting the banks to reach a final settlement. Whether the fund was really going to fix anything was debatable, but, if nothing else, it was supposed to be quick. Survivors were dying. The Humanitarian Fund Committee's goal was to identify needy Holocaust survivors and distribute the now nearly $200 million it was holding. Almost a year after its inception, the committee had distributed only $32,000. For the first time in the Holocaust payments conflict, the Swiss accused the WJC of dragging its feet.

The Humanitarian Fund was designed to have a seven-member executive committee. The committee was to comprise three non-Swiss and four Swiss. Rolf Bloch was the fund's president; the Swiss officials believed it would be a good move to name a Swiss Jew as the president. Similarly, the World Jewish Restitution Organization leaders thought it would be advantageous to place Elie Wiesel in one of their committee slots, with some sort of special role. Because the bylaws of the Humanitarian Fund required the fund president to be Swiss, there was a period of two weeks during which officials haggled over a title for Wiesel, and the Swiss government finally agreed to name him doyen international chairman. Days later, Wiesel declined the job, saying that he didn't want to have to "quantify the suffering of others." Bronfman was named as Wiesel's temporary replacement.[10]

More delay ensued when Burg demanded that the fund be turned over entirely to the WJRO, thus angering the Swiss. The structure had already been established. Back and forth the argument went. The Swiss government accused the WJRO of delaying and failing to submit proposals for allocating the money. A meeting to receive the WJRO's proposals was set, but Singer got sick and the other WJRO members stayed away. The Swiss government attributed the missed meetings to political fallout. Bloch insisted that the delays were logistical.[11]

The Swiss government did not escape without blame. For months, the SNB had debated whether to contribute to the fund. Its chairman, Hans Meyer, had pledged in March to give $70 million to the Humanitarian Fund but had said that it would need orders from Parliament to do so.

Government bureaucracies proved another obstacle. The WJRO would need a large database or system in place to identify survivors in Eastern Europe. In many countries, this task was tremendously complex. Each country had to create or provide an organization that could identify needy survivors. The Fund Committee had to make sure that, once that organization had accepted those survivors, the payments would not disqualify the recipients from receiving welfare.

The Fund Committee decided that it would make its first distributions in Latvia, since this was a small country with relatively little bureaucracy. On November 18, 1997, the Humanitarian Fund made its first payment. Bloch traveled to Riga, Latvia, and handed a survivor named Riva Sefere a $400 check. He promised that $600 would come later.

Sefere was one of among eighty survivors in Riga who received money. She was a seventy-five-year-old Jewish survivor of a Nazi labor camp in Latvia. She had survived by slipping away from a column of prisoners being marched to the forest of Rumbula, outside Riga. Twenty-five thousand Jews had been shot in that forest on November 30 and December 8, 1941.[12]

The Latvian distribution did not play out in the press as Swiss government officials, Bloch, or even the WJC had hoped. Instead of heralding the first distribution of Swiss money, the papers concentrated on the small amount. They broadcast Sefere's initial disappointment upon learning of the amount.

"What I really need is a washing machine because all my life I had to do the washing by hand. Unfortunately, this sum isn't even enough for a washing machine."[13]

Reporters got hold of Yosef Burnstein, an eighty-six-year-old survivor, who lamented over his $400.

"It's nothing. It's enough to go to the sanitarium for twenty-four days. The doctor said I need to go."[14]

"The fund is misunderstood," Bloch said. "It's not a matter of compensation."[15]

It was the humanitarian aspect, the symbolic gesture.

Jewish leaders concentrated on the fact that it was the first time Holocaust survivors in formerly communist Eastern Europe had received any assistance.

They were right. But the survivors felt that they were also right. Whether one lived in Latvia or the United States, $400 or even $1,000 just wasn't very much. It would not change anyone's life, and it would not compensate for anyone's past. And, without an apology or punishment, one could hardly proclaim justice. So what was the purpose? And had the talk about the large amount of money in Swiss banks raised survivors' expectations unfairly? Was the money worth the painful memories it had forced survivors to retell? Were survivors being used as pawns in this game of cat and mouse? The Latvia allocations were a prelude to such questions. The survivors' dilemma began to cast a shadow over the case.

10

A Victims' Fund

I and my family lived in Crimea, in steppe, on Jewish collective farms, organized by JOINT. I want to describe briefly the life of Jews during those hard years.

Now very few people know about those events. Very few witnesses of that horrible tragedy are alive today. The collective farm workers worked very hard from dawn to dawn without days off, without medical assistance. But with the time those Jewish collective farms became rich. They were growing rich crops of wheat, corn, grapes, sunflowers and other agricultural products. Livestock farms were established. In the beginning of the war the young people went to fight. On September 19, 1941, the Government had issued an Order to leave our houses and our village immediately because the Germans were approaching. We left behind our homes, our belongings, large amounts of bread, grains, agricultural machinery, poultry, feed for animals, wines, oils and other things.

We took our own and collective farm's livestock and began to walk through the steppe towards the Kerchenskaya Pereprava. We took the livestock with us and hoped that soon Crimea will be free and we will return to our homes.

It was very frightening and very dangerous because they already began to bomb us. In Kerch we loaded our livestock on the self-propelled barges and thus, by water, we reached the Caucasian shore near Taman'. . . . 3 days and 3 nights we were at sea. In Taman' we unloaded the barges. It was very difficult. The animals didn't have enough water to drink and again, we began to walk and we walked through the rest of Krasnodarskyi Kraiy. The fall had arrived, but we were still walking, hoping that soon we will return home. The herds were getting thinner. We were very scared. The old people and women with children had returned to the village. They were killed and tortured in Bagerevskyi Rov (second Babyi Yar).

All our wealth was taken away by the Germans and by the Romanians. We were experiencing hunger, but continued our journey through the Northern Caucasus. Near Nal'chik we were surrounded by people on horses and with machine-guns. They took our herd away and ordered us to leave immediately, otherwise they will kill us all. In the evening some people crossed on foot the mountain river Malka and then continued to walk towards Ordgenikidze. Then they reached Baku in Central Asia. We were very hungry and scared. We returned to Crimea after its liberation on April 12, 1944. We returned in July. Nobody was waiting for us. All our possessions, our wheat, agricultural machinery, seeds, wheat, corn, oats, barley, sunflowers were transported to Germany, were eaten up by the occupants. We had experienced terrible hunger. We had no clothes. We were very poor, sick, helpless and homeless.

Several families would buy one cow and, in turn, will feed it and collect milk from it. We were making clothes from the old military coats. We were making fire like prehistoric people—with a flint. We didn't have dishes, soap. Nobody helped us.

With regards to the Swiss compensation, I am sure, we must receive our bloody share.

Letter to the Court from Nizker Mariya

Hausfeld left Zurich and flew to Israel to see his daughter Wendi. She had been gone since August, and he couldn't wait to see her. They met in Tel Aviv, where she dragged him from store to store. He browsed while she stocked up on clothes and toiletries to get her through the rest of the year. He tried not to think about the case, but he couldn't help it. While standing around, waiting for his daughter, his mind kept returning to the case. Was this the beginning or the end? Sometimes the Swiss bankers' conversations, silences, denials all seemed so frustratingly familiar, as if 1998 were 1946 and the controversy were replaying itself.

He was sure of one thing. He was relieved to be out of Switzerland. He found Tel Aviv, with its noisy streets, a refreshing contrast. Compared to the Swiss, the Israelis were boisterous and unmannered. They waved their arms and laughed loudly. They argued and yelled on busses and sidewalks. He found himself enjoying the discord, even craving it. He had had enough of Zurich's muted tones. As soon as he had stepped off the plane, he had felt as if someone had turned up the volume. He was basking in the noise of people bantering and badgering one another. If only the bankers had shouted, banged their fists on the table, and said this is what we'll pay, not a penny more, he would have known where they stood and where they needed to go. Instead, the bankers had sat in silence while Witten talked about how they would not talk about money. But money was the dark secret everyone needed to talk about. Money was the only key that would break the deadlock of denials and demands.

Hausfeld returned to Washington and went to work hammering out a structure for a global resolution. If Witten wouldn't talk about money until he had a structure, then, okay, he would give him a structure. The Zurich mantra replayed in his head: No more excuses. In a letter to Witten and Cutler, he outlined the plaintiffs' key demands. He reiterated what Witten had implied at the doomed Zurich meeting. There must be a single lump sum that would include three components: matched deposited assets (actual deposits found by Volcker), unmatched deposited assets (assets estimated to have been deposited by Holocaust victims but that could not be found by Volcker), and rough-justice payments (for looted assets and slave labor claims). He listed the plaintiffs' other conditions. They wanted a Victims' Fund, which would distribute the money under the supervision of the U.S. District Court, and they wanted a presence on the Volcker Committee and the Bergier Commission. If the lump sum were large enough, however, these last two demands could lose their urgency. Of course, he did not tell that to Witten.

He also did not mention how things could change if Korman were to issue a decision. With every passing week, that possibility seemed more remote. Nevertheless, he couldn't stop fantasizing about it.

"If Korman would rule favorably on our discovery motion," he kept thinking, "the banks would come crawling to the table, begging to talk dollars."

But Korman had yet to rule. Since the summer hearing, he had remained silent on every motion. His silence made the lawyers desperate for news. They grabbed onto any scrap of gossip they could find. When Neuborne heard that Korman had hired a third law clerk, he called Hausfeld immediately. The lawyers pounced on the information.

"It could be, he's trying to write a detailed opinion that will withstand the scrutiny of time," Hausfeld suggested hopefully. At the same time, he worried that the hiring of a third clerk meant nothing more than that the judge was getting ready to dismiss the case altogether.

Whatever the judge was doing, the plaintiffs wanted to be sure that nothing would deter him from issuing a decision. They wanted a decision, even if it was negative. At least then they would be able to prepare an appeal. All meetings with the defense were to be kept quiet. The judge was not to be informed that anything even resembling settlement talks was occurring. Witten, Cutler, and Eizenstat had all agreed to that.

As far as Korman was to know, the Zurich meeting had never taken place.

The plaintiffs' lawyers discussed their proposals during conference calls. The camaraderie that they had felt in Zurich had disintegrated as soon as they had stepped on American soil.

Neuborne was once again in the picture. He had been drawn slowly, phone call by phone call, into the vortex of negotiations. The lure of constructing a global settlement was a challenge too enticing to resist. He knew, however, that because of the Executive Committee, which he himself had helped structure, he would be forever hitched to Fagan.

Among the Friedman lawyers, Weiss was viewed as one of the most diplomatic toward Fagan. He, like the others, agreed that the young lawyer could go overboard, especially with statements to the press, but his public demonstrations and his rallying of survivors were helpful. As long as the conflict stayed in the news, the banks would continue to feel the heat.

But Fagan could alienate even his own supporters. On January 13, 1998, members of the Executive Committee received a press release. "CHRISTOPH MEILI AND GIUSEPPINA MEILI SUE UNION BANK OF SWITZERLAND (UBS) FOR MILLIONS IN COMPENSATORY DAMAGES, BILLIONS IN PUNITIVE DAMAGES (FOR CHARITY) AND TO RECOVER INFORMATION RELATED TO THE DOCUMENTS WHICH UBS DESTROYED JANUARY 8, 1997."[1]

Fagan was suing UBS on behalf of the Meilis "for damages they suffered as a result of the activities of UBS and its representatives from January 7, 1997 to the present."

This was the first Hausfeld and Weiss had heard of the suit. Word spread quickly. Members of the Executive Committee began calling one another. Why hadn't Fagan given them a heads-up?

"It's from our own goddamn ranks," one lawyer grumbled. "We need to know what the other is doing. He didn't even let us know."

"Eizenstat is livid over this," Hausfeld added. "He's afraid the banks will use the suit to show how they will never get closure."

Swift hadn't signed on to the suit, but he was not opposed to it. After all, Meili and his family had suffered. The Swiss prosecutor had dropped the charges against him, but UBS had yet to apologize. UBS's actions and response had left the former security guard estranged from his own country.

Fagan's suit wasn't the only news that hit the wires that day. The Wiesenthal Center released a report entitled "The Unwanted Guests: Swiss Forced Labor Camps, 1940–1944." Like Fagan, the Center had not informed the plaintiffs of its latest move. Alan Morris Schom, an American historian, had written the report. He claimed that local Swiss camps set up during the war were really "forced-labor camps" designed specifically for Jewish refugees. Schom described brutal living conditions within the camps and Swiss anti-Semitism. He also claimed that Switzerland had made foreign Jews fill out a special form listing their bank holdings and secret codes for their accounts. He suggested that the banks might have used this information to loot Holocaust-era accounts that now contained only small sums.[2]

Almost immediately, Swiss leaders and former Jewish refugees attacked the study, calling it one-sided. The report was "nothing but an anti-Swiss polemic," Ambassador Borer wrote to Rabbi Hier of the Wiesenthal Center. "I believe it would be constructive to all concerned for you to disassociate your organization from the Schom report."[3] Several former refugees wrote editorials in newspapers thanking Switzerland for saving them from the Holocaust.

For the bankers, these two developments proved useful. Switzerland could, for once, charge a Jewish agency with foul play. The Wiesenthal Center report was unfair and unbalanced. The Meili suit, coming from Fagan, was an act of sensationalism.

Hausfeld had heard little from the banks since sending them his proposals. After speaking to an aide to Eizenstat, he understood why. He quickly wrote a memo to the Executive Committee.

"In college basketball there used to be a strategy called four corner stall. That was utilized when a team was at least one point ahead and could dribble and pass the ball on their side of the court for four to five minutes of the remaining game time. Everyone understood that although there was a lot of movement, no one was going to be driving to the basket. Although the banks may think we have made great progress, until they address the issue of what they are willing to pay, they are not driving to the basket."[4]

As much as he disagreed with the timing of Meili's suit, he knew that the bankers were using it as an excuse for a four corner stall. Of course, even if they were talking, he was not naive. Both sides remained far apart. In the one meeting that had taken place after Zurich, the defense had made it clear that it would not agree to the plaintiffs' demand that a Victims' Fund be the sole distributor of the money. They kept insisting on including the Humanitarian Fund.

"One thing is clear," Hausfeld told his colleagues. "Eizenstat is the catalyst for moving this forward. Witten's last letter to us was go screw yourself on rough justice, and now it's a part of every discussion because it's part of Eizenstat's view."

Hausfeld, Weiss, and Swift had had several meetings and phone calls with Eizenstat since Zurich. With each exchange, Eizenstat was acting more and more like an arbitrator. Not only did he relay messages between the plaintiffs and the banks, the banks and the WJC, and the WJC and the plaintiffs, but also he looked for areas of agreement around which they could rally. He tried to play all sides. Sometimes he lost them all.

On Friday, January 30, 1998, Eizenstat traveled to Davos, Switzerland, to address the World Economic Forum.

> This is my third visit to Switzerland in as many months, and I am very encouraged by the character of the dialogue we have established. This dialogue is based on mutual respect and fundamental shared interests. . . . But let me reiterate our view that among the wartime neutral nations, Switzerland has taken the lead in the international effort to face the past and, where appropriate, provide justice in the present. . . .
>
> I also brought the parties in the class-action lawsuit against Swiss banks together in Zurich in order to explore with them the possibility of achieving a prompt and fair settlement.[5]

In his speech, he urged an end to all threats of boycotts and proposed a permanent moratorium on sanctions. First Lady Hillary Clinton was also in Switzerland and had, like Eizenstat, praised the country for its strides in serving the cause of justice.

Less than a week after Eizenstat's address, Witten sent Eizenstat's Davos statement to Judge Korman. Whatever anyone uttered was fair game in the battle between the banks and the plaintiffs. Any words could be used by either side to gain advantage.

Hausfeld called Mendelsohn.

"Witten's sending the letter seems to me to be a total breach of every understanding that we had from Zurich. It was the banks that insisted that these talks be characterized as exploratory only, that there be no reference to the word negotiations, and that nobody inform the court directly or indirectly that the talks or negotiations were ongoing. What do you think about my writing a letter to Eizenstat, stating that these two events were a serious breach of our understanding?"

Mendelsohn concurred, and Hausfeld began constructing the letter. He wanted to get it out that day, knowing full well that he would not have time to get the assent of the Executive Committee. He would sign only his name. After all, Fagan hadn't thought anything of it when he filed Meili's lawsuit without his consent.

> Dear Secretary Eizenstat:
> . . . as every member of Plaintiffs' counsel could have predicted based on the banks' previous actions—the banks would use your statement to further their primary argument before the Court that the banks' liability is a *political* issue that should not be litigated in a United States court. The banks have wasted little time in doing just that.
>
> Speaking personally, I consider this a serious breach of the protocol under which the parties were attempting to resolve their disputes, both by the banks and the State Department.[6]

Swift was angry when he saw Hausfeld's letter. Not only did Hausfeld use inappropriate language to a high-ranking U.S. diplomat, but the Executive Committee should have been consulted first. Swift was conciliatory when it came to Eizenstat. He understood the pressures that Eizenstat was under and why he might have felt compelled to say those things.

A week later, the plaintiffs' negotiating team found itself sitting at a table at the State Department waiting for Eizenstat. When Eizenstat walked in, Hausfeld noticed that he looked tired. He was naturally slender, but he appeared to Hausfeld to be unusually thin. He also noted that on top of the pile of papers he was carrying was the letter Hausfeld had written him.

The plaintiffs learned that there were two reasons that Eizenstat had had to make that statement. One was that the First Lady was coming to Davos, and he had had to lay the groundwork. There was a lot of pressure on the White House to retain good relations with Switzerland, as well as to avoid any more controversy given the current situation at the White House (i.e., the Monica Lewinsky affair).

The second reason was the Meili suit and the Wiesenthal slave labor report. Relations between the United States and Switzerland had worsened, and he needed to say something positive to improve them.

Hausfeld listened as Eizenstat defended himself. Eizenstat had invested his time and effort to bring the parties together to get a global resolution. He had not foreseen that Witten would bring his words to the court's attention, nor had he calculated that those involved would react as strongly as they had. For that he was sorry.

Hausfeld was taken by surprise. People rarely apologize in this business, much less an undersecretary of state. He appreciated his candor. Nevertheless, the plaintiffs wanted Eizenstat to write a letter to the court explaining that Witten's letter was a breach of their understanding and that it was not as it appeared on the face of it. He should let Korman know that the State Department did not intend to convey any position on the merits of the motions before the court. More important, Eizenstat should get Witten to respond to the plaintiffs' proposals. It had been more than a month since they had given him their structure, and they had heard nothing.

"We want a letter from the banks by the close of business Monday, bringing us totally up to date as to where we are now. We are willing to consider a three-week time period in which we have to reach agreement on all structural aspects of a global resolution; the Volcker Committee, and the Bergier Commission, as well as distribution. During that three-week period, we have to agree on the process for the appointment of a settlement judge and go to the court to announce it." Hausfeld wanted to be perfectly clear. If the banks didn't come through with their letter, the plaintiffs were ready to walk.

On Tuesday, February 10, a day after the designated deadline, the plaintiffs had still not received a letter from the banks. Hausfeld sent a fax to the Executive Committee.

> Roger Witten called yesterday to advise me that we would not be receiving the banks' letter as of the close of business. He could not tell me with any probability of certainty when we would receive it. . . .

> He then asked me if Bob, Mel and myself will be at the meeting convened by the State Department on Monday, February 23rd. I told him we had made no commitment. His entire tone then changed. He said, "Well if you made no commitment then I have to rethink sending the letter. Are you going to be there or not? If you're not, I'm not giving you the letter." I replied that it wasn't us that walked away from the table, but him. We wanted to evaluate what, if anything, he had to say. He insisted that if I don't commit to being at the State Department he was withholding the letter. At which point I made the unfortunate decision that we would be there. He said "Fine. Now we can both put our guns back in our holsters. . . ."[7]

That night Hausfeld went to watch Marilyn perform *Dear Esther* at the Jewish Community Center. He walked to the back of the small auditorium and seated himself behind a group of whispering teenagers who had come as part of their social studies assignment. He spotted several people he knew across the room but did not get up to join them. He preferred to be alone. He had seen his wife perform Esther more than a dozen times and had memorized the play.

Watching it had become a ritual for him. Sitting in the dark, listening to Esther's story, he felt reflective. The Swiss banks case was the most important case of his career. He would not let it dwindle to a million-dollar political settlement. As determined as he was, he felt as if everything was blowing apart. He had heard that Weiss was talking to Singer, who was talking to Eizenstat, who could not get the banks to produce a letter on time. And where were Hevesi and the rest of the financial officers? Two Chicago aldermen had indicated that they were willing to propose a boycott, but they couldn't do it alone. And D'Amato? He had written a letter to Alan Greenspan, chairman of the Federal Reserve, opposing the UBS merger, but why wasn't he holding another hearing?

On February 11, two days after the deadline, the plaintiffs finally received a letter from Witten. Before the banks would discuss money, they would need the consent not only of the plaintiffs but of other interested private and governmental parties, namely the WJC. Witten outlined the structural terms.

All matched deposited assets would go directly to the identified claimants. The remaining unmatched deposited assets, as well as a rough-justice amount, would go to the Humanitarian Fund. The plaintiffs could then create a Victims' Fund, which could apply to the Humanitarian Fund for money for distribution. As for the plaintiffs' demand to have a nonvoting member on ICEP, that would be up to Volcker. The banks did not agree that the plaintiffs should be allowed on the Bergier Commission, and they definitely did not want to heed the plaintiffs' request for a settlement judge.

Hausfeld called Neuborne.

"Their proposal on the distribution plan is what we discussed and rejected as being unworkable. They just persisted in resubmitting it as if we had had no comments and had not spent an hour or so discussing it. And didn't we tell them a month ago that we needed to have discussions with Volcker and Bergier, but Eizenstat said we should wait for the banks' response. In essence, we just lost an entire month."

Neuborne was equally angry. "Roger's insistence on community support before there is agreement on a dollar amount is premature. His categorical rejection of a settlement judge is a bad sign. The banks have no intention of discussing money."

Hausfeld got a phone call from an aide in the State Department. The State Department was encouraged. Things were moving toward a settlement.

"Given the alternatives, litigation would be extremely protracted," the aide reminded Hausfeld. "These negotiations might be long, but they might be less than where we would be in litigation. Your clients will know it's close."

"My clients are dying," Hausfeld muttered.

"I know they're dying. They are dying either way."

"My clients will be happier dying if this is in litigation than if the settlement discussions are going nowhere," Hausfeld replied, vaguely aware of the absurdity of his response.

After numerous conference calls, the Executive Committee signed off on a letter to Eizenstat. Since "the banks may desire a face-saving gesture," the plaintiffs would be willing to allow the banks to pay a lump sum settlement amount to the Humanitarian Fund, on condition that the fund then transfer, within five working days, the entire amount to a Victims' Fund.[8] It was a convoluted compromise, but a compromise nonetheless. Now, maybe they could move forward. They committed to meet on February 23.

Hausfeld was constantly on the phone. Every day he heard something different. Hevesi was ready to impose sanctions. Hevesi was hesitating on sanctions. Singer was moving closer to joining the litigation. Singer was meeting with the bankers separately.

Swift called him on Wednesday. He and Fagan were getting closer to reaching a settlement for Sapir. All signs indicated that it would reach six figures.

Hausfeld hung up the phone and went straight to Gallagher's office.

"Fagan insisted that Sapir be included as a class rep, and now he's gone ahead and settled her individual case. Class reps aren't supposed to use the class device to settle their individual cases. Does this mean that he's going to go through the rest of his twenty thousand or whatever clients he says he has and negotiate separately for each one of them while he supposedly has an obligation as fiduciary to the class?"

Gallagher sat at his desk and shook his head in weary agreement. He had had enough of this case. It was too consuming, and he hated the politics, as well as all the egos. He'd have quit the case long ago if Hausfeld had let him.

On Monday afternoon, February 23, Hausfeld, Weiss, and Swift went to Eizenstat's office at the State Department. Witten was standing in the room with Cutler, Cohen, and two Swiss lawyers. Hausfeld could not take his eyes off Cutler. He was wearing a white and blue striped shirt. The collar and cuffs were starched white, and his tie was blue with loud white polka dots. Hasufeld tried to reap some meaning from the outfit, but he couldn't figure out what message he was supposed to be getting.

They went inside Eizenstat's conference room, where Eizenstat took a seat at the head of the table. He summarized the two sides' convergences and differences. Fifteen minutes into his speech, he made an announcement. He had been talking to Singer, and Singer preferred that no amounts go through the Humanitarian Fund. Singer was willing to let Korman decide whether there should be a relationship between the Humanitarian Fund and the Victims' Fund. Singer would accept Korman's decision as binding on all issues raised by the WJC. According to Eizenstat, Singer expressed a willingness to bind the WJC to the entire structure as approved by Korman.[9]

Suddenly everything changed. The banks no longer needed to insist on using the Humanitarian Fund. They had believed that Singer was committed to the Humanitarian Fund and therefore, to win his support, they had needed to place the fund in the center of the settlement. Now that he was throwing his support to Korman and the plaintiffs' lawyers, the banks could let go of this requirement.

Hausfeld, Weiss, and Swift were confused. For the past year and a half, they had been trying to unite with the WJC and had been rebuffed. Suddenly, Singer had changed his position and had used Eizenstat to communicate his change of mind.

The defense lawyers were disbelieving. They wanted a face-to-face meeting with Singer.

Eizenstat assured them all. He had known Singer for more than twenty years. A face-to-face meeting was not necessary. He would re-confirm Singer's acceptance of a Victims' Fund and court-directed distribution.

The plaintiffs were pleased. If Singer was truly allying himself with them, the banks had no more excuses. They couldn't pin their unwillingness to talk money on anything but dread. Even if the defense would not agree to get a settlement judge to help with the financial negotiations, Hausfeld and the others were prepared to accept Eizenstat as the facilitator. Korman was too risky. If settlement talks failed, and everyone knew that they could, Korman would have to go back and decide the motions. He might be influenced by the failed negotiations. Better to have Eizenstat, even though he too was not risk-free. At any time, he could write the court and ask to dismiss the case on behalf of the U.S. government. Nevertheless, if they had to choose between Korman and Eizenstat, they would choose Eizenstat. The known was more comforting than the unknown.

Hausfeld looked out of the airplane window and rubbed his temples. He could feel another massive headache coming on and hoped that this one would not debilitate him as so many others had. He had been having a lot of headaches lately. Sometimes the pain would get so bad that he had to pull the blinds and sit motionless in his darkened office. Other days, he went home and tried to sleep it off. Once the headache had settled in, it lingered, despite the aspirin, the sleep, and the dark. It was his body's way of telling him something was wrong.

"What's wrong is that you're going against your instincts," Mendelsohn told him.

They were on their way to Whittier Law School in Costa Mesa, California, to speak at a symposium on Nazi gold and justice.

Mendelsohn was right. Everything relating to the settlement talks felt wrong; from the fight to get a representative on the Volcker committee and the Bergier Commission, to the role of the Humanitarian Fund, to the impasse over discussions about money. All those things felt wrong, yet he continued to meet and discuss them. The most distressing part was the bankers' attitude. They delayed and delayed as if they had more important issues with which to deal. Their sheer arrogance was getting to Hausfeld. His most recent meeting with Witten was a prime example. All he had to do was to think about it and the throbbing inside his head increased.

"He asked me why I oppose money going to the Humanitarian Fund," Hausfeld recounted to Mendelsohn, "and I said for all the reasons we've been writing since December of '97. You set up the Humanitarian Fund as a charity. What these people are asking for is the return of money that rightfully belongs to them, not a charity.

"Witten then says, 'Okay, so let me get this straight. When people go to the Victims' Fund and they have no proof that they have an account, they just have a story that they think their great-grandmother may have had some money in a Swiss bank, you're going to give them money? So what you're saying is, you don't want your people to ask for charity from the Humanitarian Fund, but it's okay if your people ask for charity from the Victims' Fund.'

"He said that he could not commit to the Victims' Fund. He would need to meet with his clients and that wouldn't happen until March 9, when he would be in Zurich. So I asked, 'You can't find out before then?' and he says no, decisions like that are made only by the CEOs in person and he wasn't going there before March 9. 'After all,' he said, 'it's not easy to get the attention of the busiest bankers in the world.' That statement says it all."

Surprisingly, the more he talked, the more his head began to feel better.

"I should pay you a fee," he joked to Mendelsohn.

That night, the two of them met Neuborne and his wife for dinner.

Neuborne had flown in for the conference, and they had decided to get together Saturday evening. Hausfeld was committed to keeping the dinner social. He promised himself that he would not talk about the case. In fact, he was so determined to make sure that the evening started out warmly that he had spent two hours looking for a florist.

"This is for all the times I called Burt at home," he apologized to Neuborne's wife and handed her a small bouquet of flowers.

She told him how glad she was that her husband was working with others who felt as strongly as he. Nothing more needed to be said.

After dinner, Mendelsohn and Hausfeld waited outside the restaurant for the valet to bring their rental car. They were eager to get back to the hotel so that they could go to bed. Tomorrow was going to be a busy day. They had arranged to meet Matt Fong, the treasurer of the State of California, before the conference.

They heard car brakes. The driver who had parked their cherry-red Mustang rental car had come to a screeching stop in front of them. The young man got out and looked around. When Hausfeld and Mendelsohn stepped forward, the driver looked at them in disbelief. "This is not a car for two old farts like you," he laughed and handed them the keys.

The next morning, Hausfeld and Mendelsohn met Fong. Immediately, the two attorneys realized that they had found a soulmate. They knew that the treasurer had been a strong advocate of sanctions against the banks, but they hadn't realized how strong.

A tall, handsome man of Asian descent, Fong was charming, personable, and committed to this issue. But he was confused. He did not know what exactly the plaintiffs needed and wanted at this time. Hausfeld grabbed a piece of paper and began writing.

1) The banks must reach agreement by March 31,1998, that money paid into a settlement be paid to a Victims' Fund under the jurisdiction of the court.
2) The banks must withdraw all demands that there be no boycotts, sanctions, or opposition to mergers as a precondition to negotiations.
3) The banks must withdraw all demands of silence as a precondition to negotiations.

4) The ICEP and the Bergier Commission must be integrated as part of a global resolution.

5) By May 1,1998, there must be a resolution on the amount of the Victims' Fund.

The attorneys brainstormed on how Fong could take these five points and create the first ripples in what they hoped would become a wave of action. Perhaps Fong could hold a news conference or send out a press release on Yom HaShoah, Holocaust Remembrance Day. The treasurer seemed ready to do what he could. If California were to call for sanctions, then maybe Illinois and Florida would follow. State by state, they could begin a movement.

Hausfeld had one other idea he wanted to discuss with Fong. He had already run it past Mendelsohn, Gallagher, and Neuborne. With each positive reaction, he got more excited. What if Hausfeld were to file a separate suit against the banks in California under the California Unfair Competition Act? This act allows people to sue for restitution from any company doing business in California that has gained a competitive advantage as a result of engaging in illegal or unfair business practices. The California Supreme Court had just recently ruled favorably on a case in which a nonprofit organization had sued a grocery chain for illegally selling cigarettes to minors and thus gaining an unfair advantage over other stores. He believed that the same arguments could apply to the Swiss banks. The banks, by illegally acquiring assets looted by the Germans, as well as illicit profits from slave labor, had gained an unfair competitive advantage over other banking institutions in California.

What really excited him was the fact that the claim had to be brought in California state court and could not be removed to Korman's federal court. It was different from the international law violation claims and thus would not conflict with any rulings by Korman. Even if the banks tried to remove it to federal court, there'd be decisions and activity. That would be fine. Activity was precisely what he wanted.

Fong appeared to be excited about the idea.

Hausfeld and Mendelsohn had to get to the conference. They shook hands with the treasurer and assured him that they would send him a formal version of their five points.

When they arrived at the law school, they took their seats and waited for their turn to speak. Hausfeld reread his speech. Officials at the State Department had implored him not to say anything that would cause the bankers not to return to the table.

Hausfeld labored over one line in particular. He had used it before. Maybe it was a bit harsh for this conference. He drew a line through it, then sat back and listened as Victor Comras, an aide to Eizenstat, spoke.

"As a matter of general principle, the United States government sees little wisdom in increasing pressure just when progress is finally being made, and just when the desired results are finally nearing its reach."[10]

Progress. Results. Hausfeld shot a look at Mendelsohn, then listened to the other speakers. When his turn came, he walked to the front. Pausing at the podium, he scanned the audience of attorneys, government officials, professors, and survivors. Midway through his speech, he glanced at the line he had crossed out.

"If, as it is said, that money is the root of all evil, then Hitler was the world's evil and the private banks of Switzerland were his root," he read aloud.

There. He had said it. He then read the rest of his prepared speech.

"Generally, people say lawyers cannot and should not speak with emotion or from their hearts because they have none. I'd like to try. I'd like to share with you an event that occurred to a survivor that she shared with me."

Dear Esther was never far from his thoughts.

"After speaking at high schools, she received a very moving letter from a student. The student wrote that she was saddened at listening to her story, about the years she had spent at a death camp, and that she was truly sorry that people could act like that. But, this student wrote and concluded, 'I hope next time more of you survive.'"

A few people in the audience let out a laugh.

"It's not funny because there can be a next time. If the knowing financiers of atrocities are not held responsible for their guilt, who will remove the ability of those who want to perpetrate those atrocities from doing so? If the world, if the perpetrators, if the victims and others remain silent, that guilt will never be made a standard for all others. I and others with me have chosen not to remain silent."[11]

Hausfeld returned to his seat, folded his speech, and tucked it into his coat pocket. He felt as if a veil of self-doubt had suddenly been lifted. Everything had crystallized. He was not afraid to walk away from the talks. He would have no problem waiting for a decision from the court. No longer would the bankers and Witten dictate the rules. He was ready to litigate, ready to fight. He knew what he needed to do. Everything felt right. From now on, he would follow his instincts.

"I'm from Texas, and I'm a new kid on the block," Fagan proclaimed to the audience.

> I have no organizational affiliations. I have no Jewish communal organizational commitments. I used to be Orthodox. My life changed a lot, and I thought I was really happy until a sixty-seven-year-old lady named Gizella Weisshaus walked into my office on a Friday afternoon when she was going to pay me as she normally paid me in a kugel and a cake on a Friday afternoon.
>
> . . . And I was naive, I guess when it comes to Holocaust education I don't have the privilege of representing clients as significant and as important as the Wiesenthal Center like Marty, my colleague, does and did. I hadn't been working, I didn't even know Michael Hausfeld was working on a lawsuit at the same time that I was working on a lawsuit. I knew who he was, everybody knew who he was, but we didn't know that we'll be sitting together in the same case. . . .[12]

Hausfeld and Mendelsohn looked at each other. Why was Fagan making a point to distance himself from organizations right now when the WJC was close to joining them?

Fagan's voice grew shrill. "But from 1995 until the present, millions of documents are declassified within our own government and there are still millions more to be declassified."

Upon hearing this statement, Mendelsohn and Hausfeld picked up their pens and scribbled on their legal pads. They glanced over and laughed quietly. They had both, literally, written the exact same words. "And he hasn't read a single one."

"Let me give you the best quote I've ever heard in my life," Fagan concluded, "from an insurance company, from one of their former heads who was one of the Nazis' high-ranking officers. And his quote was, 'We did business during the Holocaust, we didn't profit off of the

Holocaust.' What we're finding now is that doing business with these maniacs was profiting, and you couldn't look the other way. Thank you."

Hausfeld had tuned out. He was searching the room for Neuborne. He wanted to tell him about his meeting with Fong. He spotted him during a break and rushed over to where he was standing.

"Fong's ready to do anything," he told him. "He's willing to hold a press conference and present our list of demands, and he's enthusiastic about the California suit." His voice was high-pitched and breathless.

Neuborne hadn't seen Hausfeld so hopeful and optimistic in a long time. He too became excited. Maybe momentum was behind them. Maybe, just maybe, the winds were shifting. Maybe they could make something happen. Maybe.

11

A Separate Peace

Honorable Court
Ladies and Gentlemen
My name is Polishchuk, Yakov. I was born in Kiev, Ukraine. I won't tell you much
about my biography. You can find it in Schindler's List. When fascists attacked Kiev,
walked into Kiev city, and it was September 29th, more than one hundred thousand
Jews were destroyed in Babyi Yar. In 1943, I found myself in concentration camp
Dachau. . . . That concentration camp . . . sent to different branches people to work
for industrial enterprises, at plants and factories, people who were basically slaves of
concentration camps and who worked at different types of horrible jobs. And one of
the teams—and I was a slave of that team. It was a very hard and exhausting work.
They fed us terribly. People—they were exhausted and . . . they died; they perished.

I ask you, your Honor, to pay special attention to the slavery conditions which fas-
cists or Nazi animals—the profits which they extract on our labor, and then they sent
it to different enterprises. And I ask you to distribute that amount of money in a fair,
reasonable way, adequate way. After the liberation, at the Stalinesque Regime, I
worked in mines of Ukraine. . . . I worked there for two years in the mines. If this
money would be distributed justfully . . . I will be very, very grateful to the judge and
to people who assisted him.

November 29, 1999, Swiss Banks Fairness Hearing

As soon as Hausfeld returned from California, his phone began to ring.

"Mr. Hausfeld, many people here are very offended by your statement that the Swiss banks were the root of Hitler's hatred of the Jews. Is
that what you really meant?" one Swiss journalist asked.

"In the context of the entire speech, I was using root as the financial
r-o-u-t-e as well as r-o-o-t. Hitler could not have carried out his atrocities for as long as he did with as much efficiency as he did unless he had
the money," Hausfeld explained.

Route or root. The Swiss heard only that they were part of Hitler's evil. Swiss lawyers and bankers were not surprised at his statement. After all, they hadn't nicknamed him Ayatollah for nothing.

During the first few calls, he tried to clarify his words, even defend himself. He went into long explanations. As incredulous callers kept asking the same questions, he got fed up.

"They're offended at what I say? Well I'm equally offended by what these banks did."

He stopped taking calls and turned his attention to Fong. He rewrote his five points and sent them to Fong's deputy treasurer, Natalya Smith de González. He got his reply on March 12.

NEWS RELEASE

MARCH 12, 1998

FONG SETS DEADLINES FOR SWISS BANKS TO COMMIT TO RESTITUTION

State Treasurer Matt Fong Thursday urged his colleagues on a national committee that monitors Swiss banks' restitution of Holocaust victims' assets to join him in issuing two demands to the banks as a condition of continuing the suspension of state and local investment restrictions.

In the letter, Fong asks the banks to accept the following two conditions: (1) "by March 31, 1998, the banks must reach written agreement with the parties in litigation and others that all monies to be paid in settlement of all claims asserted, or which could be asserted, and all claims for which releases are sought are to be paid to a Victims' Fund under appropriate jurisdictional authority; (2) by May 1, 1998, there must be a resolution of the amount of the Victims' Fund and a timetable for the transfer of those monies."

Fong said he developed the two goals after consulting Jewish community leaders, including officials from the Simon Wiesenthal Center (SWC) and World Jewish Congress (WJC). Both the SWC and the WJC endorse Fong's goals. . . .[1]

On Friday, March 13, Mendelsohn, Hausfeld, Swift, and Gallagher rode together in a cab to the State Department, where they were to meet with the defense.

"Why are you wearing that?" Mendelsohn asked Hausfeld, pointing

to his blue Save the Children tie. It had children in various colors float-
ing from big yellow and red parachutes.

"This is my bail-out tie," laughed Hausfeld. "This is it. We're going
into these meetings from now on, and we understand that we're dealing
with the busiest bankers in the world, and if they can't get to any schedule, then so be it."

They entered the small, crowded anteroom, which was unusually
noisy. State Department officials were not pleased that some people in
the room had urged Fong "to pop off." It was not necessary and was
nothing more than a "cheap shot."

The crux of the meeting centered around Volcker and whether he
would allow a nonvoting member onto ICEP. Volcker was not present.
He had sent Michael Bradfield, ICEP's attorney, to represent his position; a position that was becoming more and more set in stone. Volcker
did not want the plaintiffs involved. Bradfield explained that ICEP was
making great progress. It was compiling names from Yad Vashem and
seeing whether these names could be matched with open accounts. It
had been able to create a database beyond what it had initially expected. It was setting up a panel to study and determine retroactive
interest rates for owners of dormant accounts, since many of these accounts had not been credited with interest for years, though handling
fees had been debited from them. And it had retained an expert, Helen
Junz, to do a reconstruction of Jewish wealth in Europe. This last addition would allow ICEP to put parameters around the problem. If the
members found that the total deposits in Switzerland in 1945 equaled
$5 billion, then claims, such as $20 billion, would be baseless.[2]

Swift remained adamant. He wanted a nonvoting member on ICEP.
Most of his clients fell under the dormant and deposited-assets claims
and thus under Volcker's mandate. He knew how important it was to
become part of that process.

After hearing Bradfield, Hausfeld began rethinking Volcker. It was
obvious that the ICEP investigation was well under way. By the time
the plaintiffs got approval for a nonvoting member, that person would
be looked upon as a pariah. What access would that member really
have, and what information would he be able to share with the lawyers?
How would the plaintiffs be able to stand in front of a court and say
that they were satisfied with a process that they had had no part in?

Better to stay independent, he began to think, and not be bound by ICEP's final findings.

Discussion turned to the WJC leaders. The banks were concerned about Bronfman's latest quote in a Swiss journal. Responding to the bankers' denials of an approaching settlement, Bronfman had said: "It's coming to a point where it has to resolve itself or it has to be total war. I can't be sitting on my thumbs forever."[3]

Who would control him? Careless comments such as this could cause negotiations to tailspin. The Swiss were sensitive. After all, wasn't it a year ago that Ambassador Jagmetti had been forced to resign after using just that same analogy?

Hausfeld shook his head. Why should they get blamed and have to suffer the consequences of what everyone else said? It was similar to a teacher punishing all the children at recess because some of the kids were having an extra-good time. If that was the case, he thought, then he might as well enjoy himself, too, because the punishment was going to be the same. The issue had grown too large, and there were too many people involved.

He had no control over what others said, even within his own ranks; in fact, especially within his own ranks. A week earlier, the Swiss journal *Neue Zurcher Zeitung* had published an interview with Fagan in which he talked about what the article termed his fellow "crocodile lawyers."

> Fagan's barbed words make it clear that he regards Weiss and Hausfeld as his arch rivals. And then he warns that his own group of plaintiffs—allegedly more than 15,000—could "make or break" any legal settlement. Nor can Fagan hide his irritation at the fact that Weiss and Hausfeld have declared themselves willing to provide their services to Holocaust survivors free of charge. He sees this as a cheap marketing trick by rivals who have already pocketed a great deal of money. He practically accuses Hausfeld of discrimination, of being willing to work for Jewish plaintiffs gratis while having no compunction about earning millions in the discrimination suit which he conducted on behalf of African-Americans against the Texaco company, in which a settlement was recently reached for $170 million.[4]

Fagan was portrayed in the article as being equally unsympathetic to the WJC. "A rival for whom Fagan finds few good words is the World

Jewish Congress (WJC). He accuses that organization of deliberately dragging its feet in pursuing lost or dormant Holocaust assets, so that many more survivors will die off and leave a greater amount of compensation to be channeled through the WJC's own hands."[5]

Hausfeld now smiled at the thought of that article. The way he figured it, if Bronfman's comments had unsettled the bankers, then the article on Fagan should bring the bankers some comfort in knowing that all was not well among the plaintiffs.

On Thursday, March 19, 1998, Swift called Hausfeld. They had settled Sapir's case for $500,000. Swift and Witten were going to meet with the judge on Friday to announce the settlement and to get the court's approval.

Hausfeld had known this was coming, though he had not received a copy of the settlement. He certainly did not begrudge Sapir her money. He understood how immediate the need was. Still, he believed this was a dangerous precedent. The act was done, however, and now he was focused on the meeting with the judge.

He couldn't be at the meeting, and he was worried. Weiss was out-of-town, and Neuborne was unavailable. It was important that nothing be said that would make the judge believe that they were making progress in the negotiations before Eizenstat. He wanted Korman to understand that they were waiting for a decision. They wanted a decision.

Swift assured him that they were just going to announce the settlement. Nothing would be said about the negotiations. The next morning, Swift faxed Hausfeld a copy of the agreement and once again tried to allay his worries. Hausfeld would be added by telephone, and a court reporter would be present. If Korman were to ask about a settlement, Swift and Witten had agreed that they would simply tell him that they continued to meet but had nothing to report.

At four thirty, Swift and Fagan gathered in Korman's chambers with Witten and two of his New York colleagues. Hausfeld was connected by phone. Korman had brought his three law clerks.

"We have such a small group. We don't even have a minyan today," quipped Korman.[6]

Swift outlined the settlement and asked for court approval.

"Why do you need my approval? This is not a certified class," Korman asked in his usual low voice.

"I understand that," Swift answered, "but we want to exercise the utmost caution, I think, in telling you about this, because this is a fairly well-publicized case and we don't want to do anything that someone later on will accuse us of having engaged in improprieties.

"Mrs. Sapir gave her *de bene esse,* and she's seventy-two years old. Her stomach has been removed. She has eating disorders, sleeping disorders. She weighs under seventy pounds. Most recently, she's had very low blood pressure, which has caused her to have numerous falls. She should really be in a nursing home, but she does not have very much money. She lives in a one-bedroom apartment in Queens.

"Senator D'Amato intervened on her behalf and spoke to Mr. Witten's client, Credit Suisse. I think he was really the driving force in bringing us together and trying to reach an agreement on this. We're sensitive to our obligations, both as class counsel and also counsel for the individuals. We think that the circumstances here are such as to warrant a substitution of the class representative. I just wanted to tell you in general what the understanding is, without going into any detail. . . .

"There is confidentiality as to the amount and the terms but not the fact of the settlement. We understand Senator D'Amato intends to hold a press conference on Monday and mention the fact of the settlement."

"I have nothing to add," Witten said. "We're happy to work something out with Mrs. Sapir. We don't believe judicial approval is required as a matter of law, but we were happy to agree to a provision in the settlement agreement requiring it."

"If you want to settle with her, go ahead," Korman concluded. "I don't think you need my approval for any of this. If you need my approval, you have it."

"That was all we had this afternoon," Swift said. "Thank you very much."

Hausfeld said nothing. The court reporter turned off the tape. The meeting was officially over.

Korman paused for a moment and then turned to Witten and Swift. "What is the status of the talks with Undersecretary Eizenstat?"[7]

A few seconds passed. Hausfeld heard the faint shuffling of papers.

"I know everyone is going to try to talk about this, to be the first to speak, so let me begin." Witten shattered the silence. "Things are going along fine, there has been significant progress in the discussions—a lot of constructive dialogue. I am very optimistic about the process."

Hausfeld felt his throat tighten. Witten had promised he wouldn't say anything. Now he had emphasized the word *progress*. Exactly what progress was he talking about?

"Stay quiet," he told himself. "Let Swift talk."

"Discussions are occurring. I have nothing else to add," Swift finally replied.

Hausfeld needed to make a choice. He could let it slide or challenge Witten. It would be easier to let it slide. After all, nothing would be accomplished by arguing in front of the judge. For a moment he felt as if he were once again in that college psychology class, standing in front of the large lecture hall with people waiting for his answer.

"Your Honor," he ventured forth, "I disagree with the characterization of the status of the talks with Undersecretary Eizenstat. There will probably be a report that we will be making toward the end of the week which will disclose to the court whether or not there'd be any ongoing discussions with the undersecretary."

Swift was unaware of any such report.

Korman had had enough. This sounded like a replay from the early days. He ushered everyone out of his chambers.

At that moment, Neuborne came rushing down the hall.

"You're late," Korman needled him and walked with him down the corridor. "Listen," he whispered, "I'm just wondering what your views are on the progress of the discussions. I've heard two different reports."

"I really can't talk about them," Neuborne replied, not knowing what had just transpired in the judge's chambers. He then added teasingly, "But it looks like I'll be working on this case for the rest of my life. I'll get you for this."[8]

On March 25, 1998, members of the Plaintiffs' Executive Committee gathered in Hausfeld's conference room. Things were finally breaking. The banks were getting closer to accepting a structure that would call for a rough-justice amount that would be paid into a Victims' Fund under the jurisdiction of a U.S. court. The bankers would accept a nonvoting member on ICEP, provided Volcker could be convinced, and the plaintiffs would be allowed to nominate an historian to serve in an advisory capacity to the Bergier Commission. The bankers were moving toward an agreement just days before the ninety-day moratorium on sanctions was to expire. Tomorrow was the day Hevesi and his committee of financial officers were set to meet and decide what to do next. Hausfeld and the others knew it was no coincidence that the world's busiest bankers had finally found the time to agree to something.

"Let's get down to important aspects," Hausfeld declared after the Executive Committee had spent an hour discussing details of the structure. The table was filled with lawyers from all of the participating firms. A speaker phone was positioned in the center of the table. Every so often the voice of Weiss or Neuborne would emanate from it.[9]

Hausfeld glanced at Fagan, who was sitting across from him. Hausfeld had noticed that if Fagan wasn't getting up to make a phone call or go to the bathroom or get a soda, he was typing and scrolling on his laptop. He seemed to be always moving or doing something. His constant motion had become a pet peeve of Hausfeld's. Hausfeld recalled that just the other day he had watched Fagan arrive late to a meeting at the State Department and then leave the room for twenty minutes.

"The biggest breakthrough Eizenstat had was when he got Singer to commit to the Victims' Fund and let go of the Humanitarian Fund," Hausfeld reminded everyone.

"I'm really convinced he wants to be part of the team strategy," Weiss said.

"We need some guarantee he'll agree to a structure," a voice shot out from across the room.

"I agree with Mel," another lawyer joined in. "Early on, before any lawsuits, the WJC did a lot of work on this issue. They could file a separate suit."

"Here's my suggestion." Hausfeld wanted to keep the discussion on track. "I don't think we have much choice. It's the first time in two years that we're seeing a willingness. Can we come up with a structure to include them? First question is, do we accept their hand? They must adhere to the rules—no talking to the press."

"We have to formalize it and ensure confidentiality," Weiss added.

"Who's we?" Fagan looked up from his laptop. "Who's negotiating with the WJC?"

"What's the issue, Ed?" Hausfeld's knee began to bounce. *"Say it!"*

"You have people who want to negotiate. I walked out of the meeting last night and then find that the WJC meets with Mel and Michael. Who's going to negotiate money?"

"Eizenstat said that the WJC has to be part of the meeting. You were there," Weiss reminded Fagan.

"But you had a meeting with Singer and Burg," Fagan contested.

"I wouldn't call it exactly a meeting with Burg and Singer. I offered them a ride on my plane back to New York."

"I want to know who's negotiating with the WJC. They need to know the rules," Fagan said again.

"We're beyond that." Hausfeld's voice was rising in pitch. "We've agreed. What do you want to know?"

"Who's negotiating with the WJC. I'm uncomfortable with you, Mel, and Bob negotiating with the WJC."

Hausfeld closed his eyes and shook his head.

"I'm sorry you feel that way, Michael," said Fagan.

"So what is it you want?" challenged Hausfeld.

"I want to negotiate conditions with the WJC before meeting with them. Who is going to negotiate with the WJC?"

"Take a deep breath and count to three," Hausfeld whispered loud enough so that everyone could hear.

"What are your concerns?"

"Money," answered Fagan. "How much they want to take."

"We're not there yet."

"Meetings go on, things happen, not everyone is involved. This is a crucial point. I propose a group of people established to negotiate the money." Fagan was insistent.

"Is that different from the original group?" asked Hausfeld.

"That was for negotiating structure," answered Fagan.

"Is there a need to change the negotiating team?"

"Yep," a voice at the other end of the table mumbled.

"Okay, make your nominations." Weiss's voice emanated from the speaker.

For a moment, no one said a word. Then, one by one, around the table, they took turns.

"Satisfied."

"Like to change the composition but won't."

"Can't now. We need consistency."

Swift's turn came. Everyone waited.

"I'd like to add Ed. He adds credibility to clients."

Hausfeld placed both hands on the table. "Let me add one moment of emotion. *There's no fucking way I'm going to let a person who shows up a half hour late for Eizenstat and then leaves the room for twenty minutes. There's no fucking way!*"

"*You have no choice,*" Fagan shouted back. "That's my moment. My clients think lawyers are selling them out."

"Are you seconding yourself?" asked Hausfeld.

"Yes."

Hausfeld turned to the rest of the table. "Let's finish the vote."

"Keep the same team. Too delicate to change," Mendelsohn continued.

"Keep it."

"Keep it."

"Keep it."

Hausfeld counted the votes. "No consensus to change," he announced in a monotone. The negotiating team would remain Swift, Hausfeld, and Weiss.

"Now, moving on—what about the WJC meeting?" Hausfeld asked as if the near-coup had never taken place.

It was ten thirty in the morning, and Weiss and Hausfeld were supposed to meet Singer in fifteen minutes.

"We've got to go," Weiss told Hausfeld.

Hausfeld was on the phone in Weiss's office.

"A few more minutes," he whispered.

He was talking to Witten. They were just words away from agreeing to a final structure for negotiations. A few last-minute modifications, and they would be done. He had marks on every page of the six-page agreement.

"Unmatched assets" needed to be changed to "identified but not matched assets," "binding on" should be changed to "accepted by." The two of them hovered over every word and phrase. Neither one wanted to leave any possibility for misunderstanding. When they had finished, they agreed to exchange written copies at Hevesi's conference that afternoon.

Now, the banks wanted to know what the plaintiffs were going to say to Hevesi.

Hausfeld was clear. If the banks were prepared to begin discussing money on April 24, then the plaintiffs would recommend to Hevesi an indefinite moratorium on sanctions. Having watched the banks make all of their important moves just as sanctions were about to kick in, Hausfeld had become a firm believer in the power of the threat of sanctions.

Like a reluctant groom at the altar, Witten hesitated before finally agreeing to such discussions.

"We're done." Hausfeld grabbed his papers.

He and Weiss hurried out of the building, expecting to find a driver and car waiting for them. Instead, they were greeted by drums, tambourines, dancing clowns, jugglers, and a line of elephants. The circus had come to the city and was parading around Madison Square Garden. Traffic had stopped.

Hausfeld laughed. As unexpected as it was, there was something rather fitting about seeing the circus before they were scheduled to appear before Hevesi and his committee. The WJC, Eizenstat, Volcker, D'Amato, himself—they were all acts, performing simultaneously under the same tent.

When they arrived at Hevesi's office, they found Singer surrounded by dozens of reporters. He was waving a letter he had just received from Marcel Ospel, the president of Swiss Bank Corporation, in which he and the other CEOs formally welcomed the WJC into discussions with the plaintiffs over a global resolution of Holocaust-era resolutions. The WJC was vital. Singer was making it clear. He was now part of the settlement team. Like a ringmaster, he was cracking his whip. Let the negotiations begin.

Meanwhile, Hevesi and his committee were holding closed-door sessions. He had agreed to let everyone speak: the banks' CEOs, Eizenstat, Bradfield, D'Amato, Bloch, and the WJC and the plaintiffs' lawyers. If the latter two parties said that progress was being made, well, then, progress was being made.

Hevesi and his committee understood the full panoply of their powers. They could make small cuts or slash throats. Sanctions could start slowly or all at once or be a series of small steps that increased over time. Hevesi understood that the threat of sanctions can, at times, exert a greater influence than sanctions themselves.

When discussing the power of sanctions, Hevesi and others often referred to South Africa and the economic pressure brought against its apartheid government in the 1980s. The boycott of South Africa was a success story. It had helped force the white minority out of power and had led to the ascension of Nelson Mandela as South Africa's president.

Eizenstat was a staunch opponent of state-imposed sanctions, no matter where and for what cause.[10] As a representative of the U.S. federal government, he did not believe that state and local government officials should have the power or the means to affect foreign policy. What's more, there was the question of whether the states even had the legal right to impose such sanctions. The question of legality was being considered by the First Circuit in response to the Massachusetts Burma Law. That law restricted Massachusetts agencies from purchasing goods from individuals and corporations that conducted business in Burma (also known as Myanmar). The law had been passed to express Massachusetts legislators' disapproval of the dictatorial regime in Burma. If the First Circuit were to find that the Burma Law unconstitutionally infringed on the federal government's power over foreign affairs, the use of sanctions by state and local governments would be dealt a heavy blow.

But the First Circuit had not ruled. Besides, the Swiss banks' sanctions were different. They would be applied not against a foreign government but rather against private banks. The sanctions had a single purpose: to influence the outcome of a single lawsuit. This was a much narrower focus than in the other cases.

Eizenstat was adamant. Sanctions were an encroachment on the power of the federal government and, in this case, an obstacle to reaching a settlement. He would oppose them no matter what.

Weiss and Hausfeld made their recommendations. They wanted to give the banks another thirty to sixty, maybe even ninety, days to see what the process could yield. The banks wanted an indefinite moratorium, which was agreeable to the plaintiffs, given the fact that during that period, if they felt that the banks weren't following good faith, they could report back to the committee. Weiss and Hausfeld then left Hevesi's office. On their way out, they were asked whether they would please meet with several survivors who were there. When they walked into the room, they spotted Fagan. He was standing with the group.

"Who gave you the authority to speak on behalf of the gypsies?" one man shouted from across the room.

One of the lawyers began to answer when another man interrupted.

"You don't speak for me. Nobody speaks for me. I want to speak in front of this oversight committee, and I don't know why you took my spot in doing this."

An aide to Hevesi tried to explain the process, as did Hausfeld and Weiss.

"The purpose of these hearings is to get an update on the status of negotiations, not to hear individual claims," Hausfeld clarified.

The group didn't want to hear explanations. It had been over a year since the filing of the class action, and what did they have to show for themselves? They had read about secret meetings in Zurich, at the State Department, with Hevesi, and still they found themselves standing outside closed doors waiting for scraps of information.

"This conversation isn't going to go anywhere," Hausfeld whispered to Weiss. "We need to leave."

Hausfeld flew to Jacksonville, Florida, for another case. He was in court the entire day and didn't see the headlines in the *New York Times* until late in the afternoon: "Swiss Banks Plan Restitution Fund for the Nazis' Victims."[11]

He immediately called his office.

"People have been calling all day to congratulate us," Gallagher told him. "Survivors keep calling, wanting to know how they can apply to the fund. It's been crazy."

Twenty-four hours ago, the bankers could hardly agree to a structure, and now they were being pinned to a restitution fund and a global settlement. Somebody had done a great spin job.

He thought of Singer reading aloud his letter from the CEOs. The newspapers were speaking of a "rough-justice fund" and how the banks would have to pay for looted assets along with money deposited by German companies that had used slave labor.

Hausfeld smiled. They had gone from Volcker finding a couple of accounts to negotiating over the monetary equivalent of gold, art, real estate, and slave labor. The banks were caught in a cascade of events they couldn't stop. Only one answer would make it go away. How much?

12

Money Dance

Your Honor,
Special Master
. . . I have doubts about some of the claims I have seen that go to very religious organizations that would want to rebuild Yeshivas and synagogues and establish additional memorials which I myself and I'm only speaking for myself, have grave doubts . . . but I would like to point out and it might not be politically correct to say that here but the vast majority of these people that were herded in the gas chambers of Auschwitz Birkenau from 1941 through 1945, the end of '44 were undoubtedly Eastern Jews and probably most of them highly religious. And it is only in the last five minutes of their lives, herded naked into these gas chambers without knowing their fate and only after the Zyklon B had been administered through the roof and it took five minutes to die and we have this from the Auschwitz process in Frankfurt testimony both by the perpetrators and by the very few victims that it took five minutes to die. And only in those last five minutes, your Honor, do I think that the vast majority of these people . . . realized what their fate was when they died. And as they were gasping for air, and as they were suffocating and trampling over their weaker brethren and the children at the bottom, I myself believe, your Honor, that maybe they might have had some doubt about a God that had forsaken them. And I believe, your Honor, that these people probably would not want Yeshivas and other memorials in their name.
November 20, 2000, Swiss Banks Fairness Hearing

Like square dancers, the bankers took a few steps toward the center and then returned hastily to their original positions. Money was a long way off. This was only a working structure. There would be no apologies. No reparations. The main emphasis would be on dormant accounts. If they were to pay over and above those accounts, it would be because of business, not moral, considerations.

The Swiss government officials were more emphatic. They would have nothing to do with any global settlement. This past agreement was between the private banks and the plaintiffs and neither they nor the Swiss National Bank would participate. Some politicians and members of Parliament claimed that forcing Switzerland into a global settlement was just a way of prying more money out of them, a hark back to Defago's blackmail assertion. They warned that a global settlement would mark the end of the Solidarity Foundation.

The Swiss public weighed in. Many believed that the demands were unjustified and a form of extortion.

"There is a certain animosity, a certain resentment, a certain feeling against Jews in general and also against Swiss Jews," Rolf Bloch told the *New York Times*.[1]

Others accused the banks of acting rashly and of caring more about their balance sheets than their country's dignity.

"This 'global' solution for the partial interests of the big banks in America leaves the global interests of Switzerland out of the picture," the conservative newspaper *Neue Zurcher Zeitung* commented.[2]

Even some Jewish leaders were unhappy with the recent agreement. Avraham Burg, the Israeli chairman of the Jewish Agency, who had accompanied Singer and Bronfman to Switzerland on their first mission in 1996, dissented.

"So far it's a public relations campaign," he told Reuters.[3]

Unhappy that the SNB was not included, he wanted to know how the plaintiffs could claim a global settlement without the SNB.

You can't, Hausfeld asserted. There would be no global settlement until the SNB was included. After all, they took in close to 70 percent of the looted gold. But that didn't mean that one couldn't settle with the private banks and go after the SNB in a separate suit. In fact, this was exactly what he was preparing to do. He had been working on a SNB suit for quite some time and was getting ready to file.

Hold off, Eizenstat kept insisting. The SNB would willingly enter the negotiations. The bank's need for closure would be greater than its reluctance. As soon as negotiations progressed, the Swiss government would have no choice but to join.

Don't file against the SNB, he pleaded with Hausfeld.

When Hausfeld and his fellow negotiators—Swift, Weiss, and, now, Singer—met with Eizenstat and the defense again, they had only one issue that they wanted to discuss: money. Everything else could be worked out if they could agree on a monetary sum. Yet agreement was proving more elusive than ever.

Neither side wanted to be the first to reveal its number. The bankers were worried that their number would be leaked. The plaintiffs wanted an idea of where the negotiations would go. Everyone was cautious. Better not be the first one to speak. They circled the topic like moths.

Eizenstat met with each side separately. He tried to pry an opening offer from each, as well as a number that each side believed the other side would open with and a number that each believed its counterparts would ultimately move to. He skirted from one room to the other and heard numbers from both sides. He did not reveal them to either.

The plaintiffs referred to their Committee of Experts and its estimate of $10 billion. Ten billion dollars was not going to be their opening number, however. They were realistic. They would open at $5 billion. They would not credit the banks' contribution to the Humanitarian Fund. They would not pay for Volcker's expenses, estimated to be between $200 and $400 million, and they would not credit his matched and unmatched accounts. Those numbers were not included in the rough-justice sum. To achieve 1990s value, 1940s dollars would be multiplied by ten.

As for the defendants, they had a historian who said that, at most, the banks had made $4 million in profit and that the vast bulk of loot had remained in Germany and therefore the banks were not responsible for it. They had numbers showing that their deposits and assets hadn't increased during the war. And as for slave labor, the court clearly had said that this was the weakest of the claims. One couldn't blame the Swiss banks for the use of slave labor by German companies. The risk of litigation was minimal. The judge had shown no alacrity in dealing with the case. Hevesi, Fong, and D'Amato were greater threats. The potential terror was worth more than the actual terror.

The plaintiffs gave Eizenstat a litany of facts and figures to support their estimate. They appealed to his passion for the survivors. There were approximately four hundred thousand survivors. If every survivor were to get only $500, multiplied by ten for interest, the total amount would equal $2 billion. Giving $500 to every survivor could not be construed as justice. Besides, the suit was brought on behalf of all victims, not just survivors.

The plaintiffs soon decided that if by June 30 the process hadn't produced a result, they would be done talking. Instead, they would try to push the court to make its decision. June 30, 1998, became the arbitrary deadline. Eizenstat would need to work fast.

"God is the protector. God is savior. It is God's right hand that will protect you."

In the middle of Paradeplatz, a square in the center of Zurich, Fagan stood with three Holocaust survivors. He was reading a Hebrew psalm in commemoration of Holocaust Remembrance Day. It was April 23, 1998, and this was the first stop on his five-day tour of Europe. After Zurich, he planned to travel to the German insurers' headquarters in Munich, Germany; the Theresienstadt concentration camp, near Prague, in the Czech Republic; Auschwitz, in Poland; and finally the headquarters of Italian insurers in Trieste.

"It isn't just about money. It's not about justice. They'll be dead by the time we get justice, but it is about them," he declaimed, pointing to the three elderly survivors standing beside him.[4]

He was on a roll. Not only did he have suits pending against the Swiss banks and European insurers, but also he was getting ready to file against two German banks, the Dresdner Bank and the Deutsche Bank. He had yet to receive a penny from any of them, but that was about to change. The Swiss banks were coming round. A settlement was within reach. Money was near, very near.

With a settlement so close, the time had come to talk about distribution. And who better than he to head such talks? He sent a fax to the Executive Committee members in which he set forth a program for mobilizing all of the Jewish and non-Jewish NGOs for a meeting to discuss distribution of the Victims' Fund. He would be the leader.

Hausfeld threw Fagan's fax on his desk.

"He has spent the last two years essentially vilifying the very organizations he is now seeking to coordinate," he raged over the phone to Neuborne. "Now he thinks he can just step in and lead them? We set up an advisory committee of NGOs at the start of this whole case. We can't just marginalize them. Now is the time we need them. Why should we look for lists of survivors when these groups have been around for fifty years and already have lists? It's foolish."

"If anyone thinks that Korman is not going to listen to the traditional and respected and honored Jewish world organizations, they're nuts," Neuborne concurred.[5]

Fagan was determined not to lose control of this issue. Distribution decisions would have direct bearing on his clients. Until now, nobody had wanted to deal with distribution. There were too many claimants. There would be too little money. NGOs, survivors, communities, heirs—everyone claimed a right to the pot. The question of what proportion of money in the Victims' Fund should go to whom had been the elephant in the room that nobody had wanted to confront. Now that a settlement appeared imminent, everybody was talking about it.

Many of Fagan's clients believed that he was their one true and reliable representative. He was their voice in the media and in the courtroom, and now he would speak for them in decisions regarding money. He was their David, fighting against not only the beastly banks but the NGOs. He would confront them both. But he had a problem. Now that the WJC had been invited to join negotiations, he was joined at the hip with the very Goliath he was supposed to be fighting.

Gizella Weisshaus, for one, did not miss that point. Her white knight had linked himself with a major NGO. It didn't matter which NGO; she disliked them all. Not one of them deserved money in her eyes.

On April 26, she wrote Judge Korman. "At the beginning, Mr. Fagan assured me and the other claimants that this class action would be only for private claimants against private banks. I then realized that Mr. Fagan retained many attorneys and also joined other lawsuits with questionable claims from questionable organizations. Mr. Fagan permitted the other attorneys to take charge, prepare documents, accrue legal fees, *while our class action took a remotely back seat.*"[6]

She had read in the newspaper about the WJC entering the money negotiations. To her, Fagan was like all other lawyers. Even before the WJC connection came to light, she was reaching that conclusion. She was still embroiled in her old real estate case and was now haggling Fagan over money she claimed he owed her from that case. And then there was news of Sapir's private settlement. How could that have happened? How could one client have gotten money and no one else? Weren't they all in this together?

Fagan was representing twenty thousand individual clients. He would not be able to please them all. True, he had fallen out of grace with his star client, but Weisshaus was only one among twenty thousand. Although she was a leader among the small group in Williamsburg, his list had grown so much larger since that day she had appeared in his office, that day she had become his perfect plaintiff, his only plaintiff in his $20 billion lawsuit.

Hausfeld was not surprised by Weisshaus's letter to the court. To him, it was an inevitable result of Fagan's leading his clients to believe that he was representing them as individual claimants instead of as class members. Fagan was never going to be able to give individual treatment to twenty thousand individual clients. He was representing a class, yet he kept signing up individual clients. Hausfeld had predicted that the two roles would clash sometime. Weisshaus was just the first one to articulate the problem.

For two years the lawyers had put off the question of who should get money and how much. It lingered like a term paper that no one wanted to tackle.

"This is when things will really start to get ugly," Hausfeld had proclaimed. "I want nothing to do with it."

But he represented clients who were expecting a piece of the settlement money. For some of his claimants, the allocation would be straightforward. If they had deposited money in a Swiss bank and their accounts could be matched to ones on Volcker's list, then they would be repaid, with interest. But what about those like Lakner, who had deposited money but could not find a matched account? Those, like Salton, whose houses and possessions had been looted? Those, like Boruchowicz, who had worked as slave laborers? What about the refugees who had been turned away at the Swiss border? People like Charles Sonabend, living in England, who was one of Hausfeld's class representatives. What about Sonabend? He was blaming the Swiss for much more than the loss of his parents' money.

Sonabend grew up in Brussels, Belgium. His father, Simon, was a watch dealer who imported Swiss watches and was well known in Switzerland.

In the summer of 1942, the Nazis began rounding up Jews in Belgium. They issued papers for Charles's sister, Sabine, who was then fifteen years old. She was to report to the authorities.[7]

Fearing that his family would be captured and murdered, Simon made arrangements for his family, including Charles, who was eleven years old, to flee Belgium and move to Switzerland. Simon paid 125,000 French francs to smugglers who would transport them over the border.

On August 14, 1942, the family made it to Biel, Switzerland, where Simon had several business acquaintances. The family breathed a sigh of relief. They were unaware that, the previous day, Swiss authorities had issued an order to close the border to all Jewish refugees.

"We were in Switzerland," Charles recounted to the Swiss historian Stefan Mächler. "There was no thought of any danger. The Friday we arrived . . . we went for a walk in the area and along the stores. We all trusted that we had arrived in Switzerland and that we were safe."[8]

The only thing they had left to do was to make their arrival official by registering with the authorities. Neither they nor their hosts were aware of the new order against Jewish refugees. They just wanted to avoid any infraction of the rules.

A short time after they registered, the police showed up at their friend's apartment and arrested them. The officers took them by train to the small town of Pruntrut and handed them over to the military police. Simon was taken to prison, and his wife and two children were taken to a local convent to await deportation. Charles remembered watching the nuns through the bars of the convent as they prepared for festivities to celebrate Assumption. On one side of the convent stood St. Pierre, the largest Catholic church in the town; on the other was the priest's house.

They waited while the rest of the town celebrated. The police were not much interested in them. They did not ask why they had wanted to escape nor what they had hoped to do in Switzerland. The officials knew only that they were Jewish refugees. That was enough. They planned to take them back to the border at ten that night.

The district commander ordered a taxi so as to avoid public attention. The taxi arrived at the prison at nine P.M. Simon protested as the police shoved him into the car. The taxi then went to the convent to pick up the rest of the family. In a report to his superior, a military policeman described what happened: "We did everything possible to deport them, but despite the assistance from the cantonal police of Pruntrut it was impossible to take them away. Sonabend, as well as his wife and two children, were screaming. They did not want to move. They maintained that the Germans would shoot them, if they entered occupied France. Mrs. Sonabend even ripped up her clothes and lay down on the floor. It was pointless to insist, since about fifty passersby, alerted by the screams, were protesting and screaming that we were not allowed to act like this. Given the impossibility to take the refugees to the car and to deport them, we saw ourselves compelled to lock them up in the prison of Pruntrut."[9]

Charles, his mother, and his sister were taken back to the convent, where they were kept in the house alone with the nuns. Charles never forgot that experience.

He told Mächler,

> They were nuns . . . with a complete lack of compassion to comfort us, not my mother nor her children; to comfort us, to give us some hope that we would maybe not be deported. There was nothing like that; they were very cold. As if they were doing their job without thinking about it . . . but I did not understand why people could act like that. As if they were not realizing what was going on. Even though they had been told why we had left, why there were dangers, and that we would be sent into a certain death. It was as if they had completely detached themselves because they did not want to know what was going on. It is this impression of the Swiss that has stayed with me for fifty years, that they did not want to know, as if this had been a different world for them.[10]

Their deportation had been postponed but not canceled. On August 17, 1942, a taxi picked the family up again. This time they did not resist. They had resigned themselves, although Simon requested repeatedly to be taken to unoccupied France. His request was ignored. The police offered this report: "The border crossing took place under good conditions. After the German patrol had passed by, all members of the Sonabend family crossed the border with the intention of returning to their domicile in Brussels. The costs for the taxi and the escort were paid by the persons concerned. They did not offer any difficulties. The allegedly ailing woman finally agreed to follow her husband."[11]

The Sonabend family not only had to walk to their deaths; they had to pay for their journey. Once the family crossed the border, things happened quickly.

"We had no maps," Charles recalled, "and no indication as to where or to which side we should go. When we got to the path, we did not know whether we should go left or right. On one side, in the distance, there was a forest, on the other side there was a path. And in the meantime, while we were undecided about the direction in which to go, we heard a dog bark in the distance. . . . We hid behind a small bush. There was, in fact, a German patrol approaching. They had a dog which had tracked us down and was pulling on its leash. The Germans found us immediately."[12]

The parents were transported to Auschwitz on August 24 and gassed. Charles and his sister would have been sent, too, but the Nazis were overwhelmed at the time with prisoners, and so the children were left in the custody of a Jewish welfare organization in Paris.

After the war, Charles's sister tried to recover her father's assets in Swiss banks. One of Simon's business associates had told her that Simon had 200,000 Swiss francs in an account, but she was unable to uncover any information regarding her father or his assets.

She and her brother signed on to Hausfeld's suit. They hoped that it could do more than just recover their father's assets. They hoped that it could force the Swiss government to recognize the cruelty that they and other refugees had suffered at the hands of the Swiss bureaucracy. Like everything else in this case, that recognition could be achieved only through money.

At nine o'clock in the morning of Tuesday, May 26, Hausfeld hailed a taxi to the State Department. This was the first meeting in several weeks with the defendants, and he was feeling nervous. The plaintiffs had given Eizenstat an ultimatum: if he did not give them a money range to which he thought he could move the banks, the plaintiffs were through. All these intervening meetings had become futile. All they did was rehash the same facts and figures. The banks claimed that they had experienced a loss during the war; the plaintiffs claimed that their profits had soared. The banks said Volcker would find all that remained; the plaintiffs said all that remained was only 6 percent of what had once been there. On and on.

He walked briskly through the lobby.

"That's odd," he thought as he looked around. "Why do I not see anybody?"

He gave his name to the front desk and waited for his clearance pass.

"I don't see your name on the list," the woman said as she went through the list.

"Who are you supposed to meet?"

"Undersecretary Eizenstat."

"I don't have any passes available under that name. Does that person work in the building?"

Hausfeld nodded.

As he watched her run down the list of names, he looked around the lobby. Where was everyone?

"Nope, we don't have anybody by that name in the directory."

"Are you sure? E-I-Z-E-N-S-T-A-T," Hausfeld spelled the name out slowly.

"Here it is, but I still don't have your name on the list."

She called Eizenstat's office and sent him up.

When Hausfeld walked into the office, Eizenstat's secretary was laughing.

"You're two hours early. The meeting isn't scheduled until eleven o'clock."

As he started walking out, he turned to the secretary. "You might want to inform the desk downstairs that Eizenstat is spelled with an E, not an I."

He realized that he was more anxious than he had thought. During the actual meeting later that day, he understood why.

The banks were accusing the plaintiffs of trying to pressure Elizabeth McCaul, of the New York Banking Department, into postponing approval of the merger between the Union Bank of Switzerland and the Swiss Banking Corporation. McCaul had scheduled a meeting for June 4, 1998. Witten announced that the banks would be prepared to reveal their offer on June 5. In fact, he informed everyone that they had reserved three rooms at the Four Seasons Hotel in New York for just that purpose. When Weiss countered that his New York office had more than enough conference rooms, Witten insisted on the hotel.

"You're going to spend $15,000 a day for three conference rooms when Mel has rooms available?" one lawyer asked.

The banks would be more comfortable meeting elsewhere.

"This is ridiculous." Hausfeld turned to Weiss. "We're not going to not have a meeting because they can't come to your office because they feel that somehow or other it compromises, I don't know, their neutrality."

Everybody laughed at his word choice. Except him. He had been getting more and more frustrated at the banter. He had come to hear a monetary range. After lunch, Eizenstat met separately with the plaintiffs and, finally, Hausfeld heard what he had come to hear.[13]

"I've come up with a range that would produce, in my judgment, real justice for our clients and avoid protracted litigation and appeals," Eizenstat announced.

He explained that, in considering this range, the banks needed to take into account Hevesi and the merger and all the nonlitigation aspects. They needed to understand that it was impossible to reconstruct numbers from the bottom up. Yet, the plaintiffs had numerable litigation risks. They had evidence problems, discovery costs, linkage problems. They had weak claims and had misperceived Volcker's credibility.

So the range?

It came down to $1.35 to $1.85 billion to be paid out over seven years, deducting from that amount what the Volcker Committee would find as to matched funds and unmatched accounts, plus a $70 million credit to be paid by the banks to the Humanitarian Fund.

The plaintiffs needed to caucus.

Seven years was too long; $1.85 billion was too little. Five billion had been their opening offer. Two billion had been their walkaway number. Why credit the Humanitarian Fund? Why should Volcker determine the unmatched accounts' total? Still . . . $1.85 billion was more than they had ever heard uttered before. It was much higher than they expected Eizenstat to open with. It probably had surprised the defense, as well. It would be hard to let this opportunity pass.

Finally Gallagher ventured forth. "Why not tell the banks that

$1.85 billion is our drop-dead number? That's the final number." Either $1.85 billion or negotiations were over.

The plaintiffs put their offer on the table: $1.85 billion over three years for the three banks, deductions only for matched accounts and for the Humanitarian Fund. No Swiss government endorsement. That was it. Take it or leave it.

The plaintiffs had grabbed Eizenstat's high number. They had no idea that the banks had thrown out numbers closer to $400 to $600 million. The threat of the merger delay might push the banks higher, but to $1.85 billion? Eizenstat would need to convince Witten it was worth it. Surely having the merger approved would be worth paying extra.

The defense was adamant. The banks would not be pushed higher. The bankers would not be scared into doing so. The Swiss did not really believe that the New York Banking Department would hold up the merger.

Eizenstat wanted to avoid any problems with the merger. There was no way he wanted the U.S. government to be responsible for impeding the business of a European institution. Eizenstat was caught in a difficult predicament. He urgently desired to get money to the survivors quickly, yet he had to respect his role as a government official. Months later, his senior adviser, Bennet Freeman, would explain this particular challenge in a *Financial Times* interview.

"This is a man who cares in his bones about justice for survivors, but at the same time he had disciplined himself to balance the personal commitment with a rigorous sense of the U.S. government's interests. I don't think the plaintiffs' lawyers always appreciated what an extremely difficult balancing act that was."[14]

Witten also was not sympathetic. Eizenstat had opened too high. The banks were staying put with or without the merger. It was Eizenstat's problem now.

That afternoon, Eizenstat called Hausfeld. The banks would respond by the close of business on Friday, May 29.

Friday afternoon came and went. Had he meant the close of business Zurich time or Washington time? Hausfeld went home. Later that night, Eizenstat called. He tried to sound optimistic. He kept the conversation brief and vague. The banks had no written offer, but . . . if the plaintiffs remained silent and the merger went through, the bankers would be nice to them. Their number might come close to the lower end of his proposed range: $1.3 billion over seven years. They would give a definite number after the merger.

Hausfeld and Weiss talked throughout the weekend.

On Monday morning, Hausfeld sent a letter to Eizenstat.

> We thought we had made ourselves unmistakably clear. There is no negotiation from our communicated offer. We will not be placed in a position where we offer our bottom number and then are told to negotiate from that point downward. . . . Moreover, we will not engage in Pavlovian negotiations. It is both audacious and arrogant for the banks to condition communication of their reply upon our forced silence or assent on issues of "critical" importance to them. . . . Our offer remains. It is the banks' choice to accept it or not. . . . Although the process may remain in effect until June 30, 1998, there is no present need for a face to face meeting of all parties on June 5, 1998. Accordingly, neither Mel nor I will attend that meeting.[15]

The letter was signed by Hausfeld and Weiss only.

Fagan was angry. The letter had gone out without the approval of the others. When he read in the *Financial Times* that Hausfeld was planning to file against the SNB, Fagan confronted Hausfeld. He did not have the full endorsement of the Plaintiffs' Executive Committee. He was not a team player.

It was true. Hausfeld had decided that he did not want to wait any longer. He was moving ahead in spite of others who argued that, like sanctions, the threat of filing against the SNB could be more effective than the actually filing. They believed that the SNB suit would only complicate matters. But, for Hausfeld, negotiations were moving too slowly. When he got impatient, there were those who thought his obstinacy and arrogance took over.

UBS-SBC MERGER PLAN WINS NEW YORK BOARD'S BACKING
New York, June 4 (Bloomberg)—The planned $33 billion merger of Swiss Bank Corporation and Union Bank of Switzerland

to form the world's second-largest bank is likely to win U.S. clearance after New York State regulators said they won't oppose it.

"This board has withdrawn its opposition to the merger because we believe the message has been received," said Elizabeth McCaul.[16]

Twenty-four hours later, the *New York Times* journalist David Sanger wrote a report.

SWISS BANKS SAID TO OFFER HOLOCAUST PAYMENT
Switzerland's three major commercial banks have offered a settlement totaling more than $1 billion to end suits brought by Holocaust victims and their survivors who contend that the banks failed to return their assets after World War II, according to people familiar with the negotiations.[17]

On Friday, June 5, in the late afternoon, Hausfeld returned to his office after having spent the day in New York at the Four Seasons Hotel. He and Weiss had decided to go to the meeting after all. The merger had been approved. They had wanted the number.

"Eizenstat came into the meeting infuriated that someone had breached the confidentiality agreement and spoken to the *Times*," Hausfeld recounted to his colleagues back at the firm. "He made everyone agree to a ten-day moratorium from [*sic*] talking to the press."

Eizenstat had wanted to meet separately with the plaintiffs and with the defense. All day the two sides had shuttled from the board room to their separate conference rooms on the thirty-third floor. As Hausfeld, Weiss, Swift, Singer, and the others huddled in the lobby, the elevators doors would open and out would come Witten, Cohen, Cutler, and the Swiss lawyers. The whole scene had reminded Hausfeld of two groups of geese swimming to opposite shores.

Ranges were thrown out, rough estimates, but nothing concrete. "At one point we were told that the banks would pay for the looted and slave labor in the range of $450 to $750 million, net present value, over three years," Hausfeld continued, "plus they would consider guaranteeing some Volcker amount on the 'but for' accounts. That's when Mel and I got upset. We were not interested in guarantees anymore. We wanted to be able to resolve the whole claim. I lost it. I told Stu that we wanted the number now. I mean it was three o'clock, and I had figured that we'd get the number today so that we could leave and understand what number we were facing. Stu told me that I had to learn not to be impatient, that we had to give the banks a chance. I told him that if I were impatient I would have left a long time ago."

Hausfeld had been uneasy all day. Not only had he not gotten a concrete number, but also he had begun to feel that he was losing support. The Jewish leader Abraham Foxman had written a piece in which he urged an end to the Swiss banks conflict. Foxman claimed that all this talk about money was detracting from the memory of the Holocaust. There were others in the Jewish community who also felt that it was time to move on.

Hausfeld feared that they were right. People were beginning to lose heart. This had dragged on for too long. He and the others had to judge how much more they really thought they could get. No amount of money was ever going to restore the wealth of European Jewry before the war, and no individual was going to get wealthy. Should they lower their sights? To what level? What was a practical achievable number? They had already come down from $5 billion to $1.85. At what number would they be able to say yes, we did the best we could?

It was pouring rain as Hausfeld stood outside his firm and waited for a cab to take him home. The day had begun so differently. The sun had been out. The sky had been a deep, cloudless blue. He had arrived in New York almost hopeful. Holding his briefcase above his head, he was eager to get home. The rain had caught him off guard. His umbrella was in his closet at home. He remembered thinking it odd that Eizenstat had arrived that morning in a raincoat. Now he realized that he should have read that as a sign. He should have understood that the day would not end as clear as it had begun.

13

An Accounting

Honorable Judge Korman
Honorable Master Gribetz
Brethren survivors
I stand here before you as a Holocaust child survivor. The sole survivor of fifty some odd people. Then they killed my mother and brother . . . and it was a burning house and I was burning in it and I jumped out and they ran and chased me after that and I survived in spite of everything else. Since then, all survivors, especially child survivors, we have been a mental, miserable, physical mess in our bodies, in our souls, in our living. Go ask our wives, go ask our children, come to one of our meetings, you'll hear the stories. . . . This is fifty-five years later, after the war. We are a total mental mess.

And now in the dusk of our lives, we are asking not for goods, you are not going to change our life, you're not going to change our mode of living, what we ask is just for a little dignified respect of having . . . a dignified health plan for survivors. Two years ago, I was for a trip to Europe and I took sick all of a sudden . . . a heart attack. In a few days, ten thousand dollars cash I had to pay out and I've been in physical ill health since then. And we cannot cope with all this. Why couldn't we have for all those couple of dollars which will not change our lives, just for a plan that we should be able to live in dignity for the rest, for the couple of years that we've got left? Some kind of catastrophic plan. I don't want no goods, I don't want no nothing.

My father was a master mechanic and a machinist in motors and equipment. He was sending the checks to Germany and to Italy and Switzerland for parts and machine parts and motors. I don't have papers. I cannot show. I just know that he send it. And somehow we survived. . . . The other day, two days ago, a man found four survivors died in one day. We are dying. We are dying like flies. Our days are numbered. We are so much older. We were young when we started. Now we are old. We know where we are heading. So all we are asking some kind of dignified mode of health plan. We should not be as beggars and poor people that we cannot pay for our medicines and other things.

November 20, 2000, Swiss Banks Fairness Hearing

Hausfeld was working with Gallagher on finishing the Swiss National Bank and the California complaints. He was done with guarantees. He wanted to send a final version to members of the Executive Committee.

Everybody would get a copy. Although the Executive Committee would remain in place, Hausfeld had added firms to the two new complaints. Not only did he need help; he needed money. Several months earlier, he had asked the Executive Committee members to contribute an additional $20,000 to the case. Some had. Some hadn't.

Every time he turned around, he was paying for something else for the case. His Committee of Experts alone had cost his firm more than $100,000. Kleiman had been on his payroll for two years, and he had hired another paralegal. He, Gallagher, and the others had logged almost six thousand hours on the case. That was six thousand hours that would never be compensated. Hausfeld had established enough of a reputation that he could charge $435 an hour. People in his firm were beginning to grumble about the pro bono arrangement. The time he spent on the Swiss banks' case was lost revenue.

Lost attorney fees weren't the only complaint. Associates were growing frustrated. They had trouble getting their senior partner's attention. He was always on the phone, or at the State Department, or in New York. His mood swings were disconcerting. One day he would arrive jubilant and full of ideas, and the next day he would appear worn down and despondent. The case seemed to be sucking all of his energy—energy they and he needed for other cases. Every time the case appeared close to resolution, it broke down.

On Wednesday morning, June 10, 1998, Hausfeld called Eizenstat. The plaintiffs would not meet with him tomorrow unless the banks gave a firm number.

Eizenstat called him back. The banks had an offer: $630 million over three years. This would include the $70 million they had paid to the Humanitarian Fund and a $30 million floor for the "but for" accounts.

They would pay whatever additional amounts were found, and the Swiss government would not have to endorse the settlement. The banks were even willing to extend the payments for five years, which would generate an additional $100 million.

Hausfeld did not comment one way or another. He hung up, grabbed a piece of paper. and made some calculations. Take $70 of the Humanitarian Fund from $630 and you get $560 million. Then take away $30 million guaranteed for the "but for," which was money Volcker was supposed to include as part of his audit, and you were really talking about only $530 million in new money.

"They're not being rational," Neuborne asserted. "We need to show them why they're not being rational and ask how they can explain rationally how they came up with what they did."

"Burt, you have to realize that during this entire process, the banks have only said two things: one, that we can't prove our allegations in court, and two, that the banks lost money during the war. That's it, there's no further rationalization," Hausfeld responded.

The Plaintiffs' Executive Committee decided to tell Eizenstat that it would not come back to the negotiating table until there was a higher number, though they would allow the process to continue until June 30. In the interim, they would start to gather the support they would need to take a very proactive role if there was no response by the banks during that two-week period.

It was obvious that the banks were not interested in going higher. Too much money would send the wrong message. The lawyers recalled how, during one meeting, they had listened as the Swiss envoy, Thomas Borer, explained that the government of Switzerland would never admit guilt in any form, directly or indirectly. Anything more than one billion Swiss francs would be tantamount to an admission of guilt. He had made it clear that neither the government nor the banks would participate. Money wasn't the problem. It was the principle.

Ever since Ursula Erber had met Hausfeld in Zurich, she had been hooked on the case. She devoured all of the news articles on the subject and forwarded each one to him, complete with translations. She searched through books and documents, looking for anything she thought might help him. She included handwritten notes with her materials and told Hausfeld often how much she admired him. She even sent him a box of chocolates with an emblem of two figures embracing.

Hausfeld was appreciative of her efforts but uncomfortable with her personal overtures. He chose to let Kleiman handle the correspondence. She was asked to review Erber's materials; if something looked interesting, she was to leave it on his desk.

On June 17, Kleiman gave Hausfeld a cartoon that Erber had found in one of Switzerland's best-known satirical magazine. It had been partially covered by a "voluntarily censored" sticker. Someone had informed the Swiss Jewish Federation of its impending publication, and the federation had protested so vehemently that the editor had agreed to censor it. Erber spent two hours pulling the sticker off. When she saw what lay beneath, she was appalled. The cartoon pictured a man wearing wire-rimmed spectacles and a yarmulke, pressing a menorah-like vise down on a Swiss parliamentarian whose mouth was spewing gold coins. She couldn't help noticing that the Jewish man who was turning the vise bore a striking resemblance to Hausfeld. The caption read "Helvetia unter Druck" (Switzerland under pressure).

Kleiman was aghast. She didn't just see Nazi propaganda; she saw her boss. She kept staring at the glasses and the forehead. The resemblance was unmistakable. She quickly put it on his desk.

Hausfeld picked it up, examined it closely, then slipped it into his briefcase.

> SWISS BANKS MOVE TO SETTLE HOLOCAUST SUIT
> Credit Suisse, Swiss Bank Corp. and Union Banks of Switzerland Friday offered to pay $530 million into a "rough justice" fund to settle the class-action complaint. The offer came in a surprise public announcement—flouting a gag rule imposed by a New York judge when settlement negotiations began in early April. In a statement, the banks said they felt "obliged to set the record straight" in view of "misleading reports" and "repeated violations of the confidentiality order by plaintiffs' lawyers."[1]

Reporters called everyone. Was $530 million the final number? Would the plaintiffs accept it? What's the next move?

"We're not claiming that the banks are morally responsible for the Holocaust," Fagan told the *Journal* reporter.

Hausfeld was infuriated as much at the leaked number as at the comments Ranier Gut had made in regard to that number. The offer, he had told the *Wall Street Journal,* was "based on sheer economic facts, the banks' potential liability (excluding dormant accounts) is inconsequential."

"Borer was right," Hausfeld thought. "Neither the Swiss government nor the banks would ever apologize."

Gut had also claimed that the $530 million offer reflected "potential legal costs that the banks would avoid with an out-of-court deal."

"I knew Wilmer made money," Hausfeld reasoned, "but that's a lot by anyone's standards."

Reporters found out that Weiss and Singer were scheduled to meet with Hevesi, and they swarmed Manhattan's Municipal Building. Hevesi held an impromptu press conference. The Swiss were arrogant and obdurate. In a fit of anger, he held up a piece of paper. Reporters had grown accustomed to politicians waving 1940s documents in the air. But this was not a document. As they strained forward, they saw that he was holding a caricature of a Jew. It was the cartoon Erber had sent Hausfeld.

Against this background, the plaintiffs and Eizenstat met again. Again they sat in the undersecretary's office, and again they heard an offer. How about if the banks were to pay $1.05 billion dollars over three years, plus credit for the Humanitarian Fund? The net present value, if paid in one lump sum, would equal $911 million.

The plaintiffs took a long time to themselves. The banks were blinking. They could get them to move, but they would have to compromise. Weiss took the lead. How about $1.5 billion? This would include whatever Volcker would find. He could look to his heart's content, but the banks' liability would not go above $1.5 billion. In addition to this, they could sweeten the deal. The plaintiffs could give legal releases not only to the private banks but to the Swiss National Bank. What the banks wanted most was peace. Total peace. Throwing the Swiss National Bank into the deal would allow them that peace.

Hausfeld ruminated over this last addition. The SNB would virtually escape on the coattails of the private banks. How could they allow that? But Jewish leaders kept telling him that they wanted this over. Nobody had the will for a separate, long, drawn-out battle with the SNB. If he objected, he wasn't sure he had the strength to stand alone.

Several days later, Eizenstat approached them again.

Witten had gotten his clients to agree to the $911 million. If the plaintiffs would agree to something a little over a billion, they could negotiate the difference.

It was $1.5 billion, with or without the Swiss National Bank. Hausfeld and Weiss were adamant. They were giving them the Swiss National Bank. If they could get a division of that money among themselves that favored them, that was fine, but, as far as the plaintiffs were concerned, it was 1.5 to them plus the other banking institutions. They were holding firm to that. Not just the Executive Committee, not just the World Jewish Congress, but every other major Jewish organization, as well.

On June 3, 1998, Gizella Weisshaus sent a second letter to Judge Korman.

> Dr. Singer and Mr. Fagan are involved in the negotiations with the banks and the Holocaust survivors are *outraged to be left in the dark*. We will be in the dark for eternity. . . .
>
> There are many articles in the newspapers regarding humanitarian funds which raise the hopes of the Holocaust survivors only to have those hopes sink because nothing is happening on our behalf.
>
> We ask that you appoint a special counsel for the *first class claimants* to receive some measure of justice which we *are not* getting from Mr. Fagan and *"HIS TEAM."*
>
> We are also asking for depositions of witnesses to preserve their testimony as your Honor signed Order dated December 31, 1996—*which depositions were never taken and which depositions are most crucial to prove our claim that money was deposited before the war in the Swiss Banks.*[2]

Her letter was published on June 27 in the *New York Times*.

"I suspect she believes there's some deal between the World Jewish Congress and me over who gets the money—and nothing could be further from the truth," the paper quoted Fagan as saying.[3]

Weiss defended Fagan and his team in the Jewish newspaper *The Forward*.

"I have no idea what [Weisshaus] is talking about. . . . She couldn't be getting better representation in this matter from all of us as a group."[4]

Weisshaus also mentioned her other suit with Fagan and claimed he owed her $85,000. She was so angry that she wanted to break from him completely. She told the judge that she was looking for new representation.

Hausfeld shook his head as he read the reports.

A few days later, he grew enraged when he learned that neither Fagan nor Swift had informed him that the judge had referred Weisshaus to the magistrate who was going to set a hearing.

"They didn't tell the Executive Committee, the very people they're always blaming for not keeping them informed. Something happened in this case that could reflect adversely on all of us, and they didn't even tell us."

Swift was not apologetic. The same day that Hausfeld had yelled about Weisshaus, Hausfeld had kept him and other members of the Executive Committee waiting in a conference room while he and Weiss had carried on a private conference call with Jewish leaders and Eizenstat in Weiss's office. This was not the first time Swift had been excluded. He was growing suspicious. Maybe Weiss and Hausfeld were forging a secret deal that included compensation for the NGOs. He wouldn't put it past them.

On Thursday, June 25, the plaintiffs received an answer from the banks. They would not go up to $1.5 billion. In fact, they were now shying away from Eizenstat's $911 million figure.

The State Department called and asked whether Hausfeld and Weiss would come to meet with the bankers.

Weiss and Hausfeld were defiant. There was nothing to talk about anymore. There was a $1.5 billion figure on the table, and it would either be accepted or rejected. Beyond that, they just didn't care. They knew what they were going to do.

What they didn't know was that Eizenstat had called Swift and had asked him to come to the meeting. Swift had accepted the invitation. When Hausfeld found out that Swift had gone to the State Department and had met with Eizenstat, he was beside himself. He didn't know at whom he was more angry. He wrote a letter to Eizenstat.

"No one person, especially acting without knowledge of the rest of the group, had any authority or right to represent or speak on behalf of the group as a whole.

"This is not the first time that you and your office have attempted to exploit perceived differences within the group by segregating its members. It is one thing for the banks to try to divide our interests. It is a disgrace for you to do so."[5]

"Bob claims that he had no idea you weren't going to be there," Gallagher told him after speaking to Swift. "In fact, he says he was annoyed that he went to the meeting and none of you showed up."

"Even if he didn't call us to find out if we were going, when he got there and saw we weren't there, he was in Washington, why didn't he call me?" Hausfeld responded. "When he left, he never called anybody to say, hey, I came, nobody showed up, why not? That was on Friday. On Monday, he didn't even call to tell anybody. It's absolute malarkey."

"Swift didn't know the meeting was off. It was a miscommunication," Neuborne explained, trying to calm him down.

In the end, what did it matter? Negotiations were off. In fact, Neuborne had published an op-ed in the *New York Times* in which he called the banks' offer of $600 to $700 million "insulting." He used the public space to clarify the plaintiffs' position—their unified position. "A fair settlement must include the return of all Holocaust deposits, not merely those few for which records have survived. It must also require the banks to give up the unjust profits they earned by turning the looted assets into Swiss francs for the Nazis. Finally, it must require the banks to give up the profits they earned by financing the construction of slave labor camps. No settlement can possibly be defended if it allows the Holocaust to stand as a profit-making enterprise for the Swiss banks."[6]

Swift had grown more and more distrustful of his fellow negotiators. Not only had they gone ahead and filed both the SNB and California suits; they were clinging to a number that was unrealistic. The banks would never agree to $1.5 billion. Hausfeld's and Weiss's insistence was serving only to back his clients into a corner. He decided to take things into his own hands. On Wednesday, July 15, he and Fagan held a news conference.

Negotiations can be rekindled if two things happen. First, the banks need to reevaluate their final position and realize that unfettered access to U.S. financial markets will recoup whatever "excessive" amounts they believe are requested. Second, the Swiss National government on behalf of its banks [*sic*] SNB, needs to step up and help the monetary gap to bring closure to claims against it. While painful in the short term, it is the morally correct thing to do and will enhance the Swiss reputation worldwide.

If this happens, we as counsel for the Holocaust survivors pledge to be flexible at the bargaining table. We understand that "take-it-or-leave-it" positions rarely succeed and in this negotiation *cannot* succeed.[7]

"Flexible at the bargaining table." With those five words, the two attorneys had broken from the pack. Swift knew that his press statement would cause a rupture within the Executive Committee. He didn't care. The banks needed an opening, an excuse to return to the table. They needed someone with whom they could talk quietly, diplomatically. He had had it with the shouting and the high-strung emotions, the rhetoric and the name calling, the extremes and the polarization. The time had come to talk calmly and rationally.

Hausfeld and Weiss were horrified when they read the statement. This was not a calculated risk but a breach of loyalty. It was a public airing of the committee's dirty laundry. To them, this was the worst betrayal yet. Weiss sent a memo to committee members, calling the press conference an outrageous disregard of a court appointed Executive Committee and claiming that it showed weakness just at the time that the plaintiffs were "winning the fight hands down." He suggested removing both Swift and Fagan from the Executive Committee.

Swift was in no mood to cower. The others had made many a public statement without consulting him. And what about that conference call that they had conducted with the NGOs without him? Much of what they had done had been cloaked in secrecy. In fact, he wouldn't have been surprised if Hausfeld and Weiss had a secret deal going with Singer in which they planned to direct all of the rough-justice money to the Humanitarian Fund, thus giving the WJC authority over distribution. As for Weiss's threat to remove him as co-lead counsel, this too did not surprise him, since he claimed that Hausfeld had been trying to eliminate him as co-lead counsel from the beginning. Swift sent around a litmus test. Executive Committee members were asked to sign a statement declaring that they would not accept a settlement of less than $1.5 billion. How many would actually commit to that?

Both sides would have just as soon never spoken to each other again, but they were scheduled to meet with Korman on July 27 to urge him to lift the stay of discovery and to decide the motions. The banks had not moved from their $600-million-plus-Volcker offer, and the Swiss government was refusing to add to it. Eizenstat could not budge either of them. The plaintiffs gave notice to the court. The settlement talks under Eizenstat's guidance were over.

Pressure had begun building on the banks even before the dissolution of negotiations. On July 2 Hevesi had held a news conference in which he announced, with New York State Comptroller H. Carl McCall, that if no settlement was reached by September 1, 1998, they would bar short-term investments with Swiss banks, stop Swiss banks from selling state and city debt, and not allow Swiss banks to provide letters of credit. If the impasse continued, they would extend the sanctions to additional financial services on November 15, and to all Swiss companies on January 1. D'Amato had also held a hearing in which he had discussed reopening the 1945 Washington Accord. The vise was now tightening, not only against the Swiss banks but against the Swiss government, as well.

It was against this background that the attorneys gathered to strategize before their meeting with the judge. Swift's and Fagan's press conference remained at the forefront of everyone's thoughts, and it didn't take long before tempers flared. Each side leveled accusations against the other. Only an hour remained before the meeting with the judge. They needed a plan.

The last thing they wanted was to have the session with the court become an extension of the settlement discussions with Eizenstat so that they in effect would simply replace Eizenstat with Korman and start all over again. What they did want was a lifting of the stay of discovery and a trial date set for the issues that Korman would let move. Everyone agreed on those goals.

The session with the judge was to mark a new beginning. The Executive Committee members were returning to the judge with a renewed urgency. They were also returning after having fought among themselves for two years. This army of lawyers was reemerging from the trenches a battered battalion. Having hobbled through scores of decisions, they were going to stand before the court, still together, but barely.

When the lawyers arrived at the Brooklyn courthouse, Korman's clerk ushered them into the judge's chambers. Witten was there with Cohen and the rest of the defense team. Cutler was not present.

Korman sat at the head of his table in front of a window overlooking the Manhattan Bridge. Nobody engaged in small talk.[8]

Six hundred million dollars was a lot of money, Korman began. Had the plaintiffs really taken into account the uncertainty about whether they would really get $1.5 billion? Wasn't it better to give $10,000 now to a survivor than $15,000 at some much later time in the future, when that person might not even be alive? There were European Jews who were in desperate need, who hadn't received anything in terms of Holocaust recompense. Shouldn't the concern be about getting money to them? Before a settlement was reached in terms of an amount, wasn't it important to know how it was expected to be distributed?

A stunned hush fell over the plaintiffs' side. With each of Korman's questions, the lawyers sank into their chairs. Where to begin? His questions brought them back to old arguments, arguments they thought they had finished with long ago. How could they ever hope to convince Korman that $1.5 billion was not only reasonable but below what they believed the banks owed? They sank further when he revealed his desire to let Volcker finish his audit before making any final decision. There went their hopes of his lifting the stay of discovery.

The defense could not have been more relieved. The attorneys for the banks kept nodding their heads and seconding Korman. Yes, let Volcker finish. Whatever he found could be added to the $600 million. The plaintiffs' claims were serious moral claims, but they were dubious legal ones. The banks were offering an amount that was tied to reality. The defense had an historian who had gone back and looked at what they had made, and they were offering $600 million, ten times the largest amount. They were so encouraged that they proposed that they reenter settlement discussions, this time with Korman as the facilitator.

Hausfeld felt the ground slip out from under him. Another process, another chance for Witten to argue that they were engaging in good-faith negotiating and that everybody should hold off on sanctions.

He and the others asked for a break. The committee needed to decide. Did it want to restart negotiations?

"We should let natural forces take their effect," Weiss asserted. "If the judge doesn't want to decide, let him not decide, but if he wants to decide, let him decide, but let's just let things take their natural course and not agree to a process and not engage the judge and not allow them to go back to Hevesi or whomever and tell them that we're negotiating again."

In other words, why not meet and talk but commit to nothing, and, most important, let Hevesi and the other financial officers continue to do their thing?

"That's unacceptable," Witten proclaimed when he heard their plan. "You're basically saying that this is going on but we can't tell anybody it's going on?"

The plaintiffs nodded their heads.

"I won't agree to that," he insisted.

"If that's the position of Mr. Witten," said Neuborne, "we respectfully decline any position. We will not participate under those conditions."

"That's so unprincipled." Witten was losing his cool. He started haggling over their claims. He questioned the plaintiffs' numbers and estimates.

"Why don't you tell us where your numbers come from?" Cohen turned to Hausfeld.

"Well, we added certain things."

"Well, why don't you show us?" Cohen repeated.

"Wait a minute," Weiss jumped in. "Are you saying that if Mike shows you how we came up with these numbers, you'll pay them? So if we come over $1.5 billion you'll pay more if we can show you it was there and we don't have to settle for the $1.5?"

"Let me tell you what I think happened here," Witten began explaining to the judge. "I think what they did is that they floated so many numbers out there that they hung themselves. They put themselves in a box. They picked a number so high, they couldn't deliver to the Jewish community, and they're stuck with it, and we're not going to help them."

"No, you created the box," replied Neuborne. "You created your box by coming out with a public offer and saying, this is all we can justify because any more is blackmail."

"Let's say you're absolutely right," Korman turned to Witten later in the discussion. "That they put themselves in this box and they have no way out. Why can't you accept that?"

"I'll tell you why they can't accept it," Weiss jumped in. "Because they have a magic number." He recounted Borer's statement in which the Swiss diplomat declared that the Swiss would never go over one billion Swiss francs. "Borer has drawn this artificial line in the sand. . . ."

Singer, who had arrived late, joined in. He talked about the number of survivors and heirs and the challenge of getting enough money to make a difference. Throughout the discussion, Hausfeld noticed that Korman seemed particularly receptive to Singer.

The meeting soon became a free-for-all. Everyone jumped in, plaintiffs and defense alike.

"We gave you lists two years ago," Hausfeld threw out. "We said, search your accounts, we want to know. We gave you the names of S.S. people, Nazis, war criminals, people on the proclaimed list, and people on the enemies lists. We gave you the names of five hundred companies that used slave labor and we said, tell us their accounts. You never did. What were their accounts? How many of them had accounts, and what were in those accounts?"

"Roger, whatever money you took you're not telling us about, what value do you place on the fact that after the war you never gave it back? You never looked for it. You hid it. You concealed it. You lied about it. What value do you place on that?" Neuborne added.

"This is just foolishness," Witten said, shaking his head in exasperation. He turned to Korman. "We're not concentrating on what it is they can prove."

Weiss was now as focused as a snake waiting for its prey. He was completely absorbed in the fight. His enemy was in front of him. He heard "foolishness," and he sprang.

"I'll tell you what's foolishness. You think you're going to get this over with. This is a matter of money. You know it's a matter of money. You made it a matter of money and you have to pay for what you did, and if you think you're not going to pay it, you're wrong because *I tell you we're going to stay in here with this litigation until we kill you!*"

"This is completely inappropriate," Witten protested.

"You're going to kill us?" repeated a smiling Cohen.

"Now that's very constructive," one of the Swiss lawyers commented.

"Well, Mel," said Neuborne, "I have to tell you. I'm personally opposed to the death penalty."

Korman couldn't help but laugh.

Everybody was tired and ready to leave.

Hausfeld was more encouraged. In the second half of the meeting, they were no longer talking about Eastern European refugees or distribution or $600 million being a large sum.

"7:16 P.M., tide turned," one of the plaintiffs' attorneys had written on his sheet of paper. They had gotten across to the judge that they had numbers in excess of $1.5 billion.

"We want peace," Witten had declared in the meeting.

"Peace has a price," Korman had answered.

Both sides now had to decide. Just what price would be the right price for peace?

Weiss sent out a notice to everyone on the Executive Committee. The judge wanted to meet with the plaintiffs and the banks on Monday, August 10, at six in the evening. They would have dinner at Gage & Tollner, a famous steakhouse in Brooklyn, just blocks from the courthouse.

Korman had already held a series of separate meetings with the plaintiffs and the defense. He had listened to each side's arguments. Now, he wanted to bring them together.

Hausfeld was nervous. This was it—his last chance to persuade Korman. He prepared a settlement book filled with documents. Loaded with a stack of three-ring binders, he and Mendelsohn boarded a two-thirty plane to New York. No sooner had they seated themselves than the pilot announced that LaGuardia was closed due to thunderstorms. It was now three o'clock. The meeting was set for six. They frantically called the judge to push the meeting later. They took a cab to Union

Station and boarded a train. Every few minutes, Hausfeld got on his cell phone. He called Singer. He called Neuborne. He called Weiss.

They finally arrived at the restaurant at seven thirty. As they walked past the gas lights at the entrance, they were told to go upstairs to the private room. The carpeted stairwell was narrow and long. Hot and weary, they dragged their bags up the three flights of stairs. When they got to the top and turned to go into the room, they stopped.

Four large mahogany tables had been joined together in a giant rectangle. In the middle of the table, farthest from the door, sat the judge. Weiss was seated to his right, along with Fagan, Swift, and a long line of others. On the other side sat Witten and his team of Swiss and American lawyers. Singer and Steinberg entered several minutes later.[9]

"Do we have sufficient Haggadot for everyone?" Hausfeld joked, referring to the book used for Passover seders. He placed his papers on the table.

The room was not air-conditioned, and the temperature was in the high eighties. There were two narrow windows, each covered by a plant. Everyone was sweating. Their wrinkled shirts were wet, and they had already loosened their ties and unbuttoned their top buttons. Only Korman and Weiss kept their jackets on. After a few minutes, a waiter came and removed the plants from the windows. A slight breeze blew through. Everybody was fanning himself. To Hausfeld, the room looked like the trial scene from *To Kill a Mockingbird*.

They waited for a signal from Korman. When everyone was seated, he warned both sides that he would not force a settlement. He wanted an out-of-court deal. Then he turned to the plaintiffs. His nod was like a starting gun.

Hausfeld took off from the blocks. He did not wait for anyone. He did not pause. He did not get distracted by the heat. He just kept moving forward like a sprinter to the finish line. He went through the binder, document by document. Claim by claim. He wanted Korman to understand that he was giving an overview of what occurred. Individual documents alone would not be sufficient. Together, however, they told a story.

As he explained how the looted gold had made its way to Switzerland, he talked about documents they had that referred to trucks carrying looted gold to Degussa, where the gold was melted down, and then to the Reichsbank, where it was put into separate accounts that went directly to the Swiss commercial banks. He had U.S. intelligence documents listing inventories of dental gold.

"Where are those documents?" asked Cohen. "I haven't seen those documents."

"We're not going to show you all of our documents," Hausfeld answered. "This is not a one-way discovery."

To the defense, nothing he was showing or saying was new. Even to some of the plaintiffs' lawyers, his presentation was a repetition of past demonstrations. They had been through this before. They watched as Hausfeld carried on his one-man show.

Hausfeld didn't care what the others thought. Korman hadn't seen their story laid out in such a methodical and organized narrative. He was determined to convince him that $1.5 billion was the bare minimum. He flipped through his binder. Inside, he had a copy of a letter dated May 28, 1945, to a U.S. Treasury representative from Harold Glasser, the assistant director of monetary research. In the letter, Glasser tells the harrowing story of Henry Lowinger, a former Austrian who owned some of the largest laundries in Vienna. Lowinger was living in the United States at the time the letter was written: "With the invasion of Austria, Lowinger, *who is Jewish,* was arrested and after about two and one-half years of imprisonment and pressure against himself and his wife, he agreed to transfer to the Nazis all of the assets which he had, including the stock holdings of his *Swiss holding company,* and also to withdraw his Swiss franc deposits and to pay them over in cash in exchange for his freedom."[10]

The letter went on to describe how two Nazi lawyers and a dozen or more Gestapo agents brought Lowinger and his wife to the Swiss frontier, where he was met by his Swiss lawyer: "Lowinger signed the necessary documents and had his Swiss lawyer turn over the Swiss francs in cash to the Nazis, after which he walked across the Swiss border, penniless but alive."

What Glasser found particularly stunning came next: "Notwithstanding the Swiss secrecy law, *the Gestapo knew exactly how much Lowinger had on deposit and where it was held and told him so while shortly after he was imprisoned.*"

Hausfeld also had a telegram, dated November 24, 1942, from the

Foreign Service of the U.S. Department of State, detailing the German business of selling exit permits from occupied countries: "In practice, the Germans are attempting to obtain from relatives and friends of persons in these countries the payment of *ransom* payment being made in neutral currency useful to the German war effort. . . . Amounts as high as $75,000 for a single person have been quoted. These sums are required to be paid into an account in the name of some intermediary in a bank in a neutral country."[11]

To illustrate the plaintiffs' claims regarding looted assets, Hausfeld had in his binder a brief yet all-too-clear letter from a Mr. Frederick Weissmann to Paul Randolf, head of the delegation handling American-Swiss negotiations regarding German assets in Switzerland. It was dated March 21, 1946.

> I respectfully inform you that on December 28th 1938 after thirty years activity I was forced to sell at an immense sacrifice my establishment viz. Emil Jacoby, Limited, established 1872 at Berlin . . . because I am a Jew. Main purchaser of said establishment was Swiss Footwear Company Bally repeat Bally who from 1939 until 1945 were able to transfer by various methods proceeds from my Berlin establishment to Switzerland. In Germany Bally exclusively bought up businesses owned by Jews. As in my case Bally sometimes bought property for one repeat one Reichsmark. Unfortunately all these manipulations and considerable assets are not yet covered by Swiss legislation. Pray help us in our distress.[12]

Hausfeld stopped only when dinner was served. He wasn't hungry. While others ate, he sipped his iced tea. He went from deposited assets to looted assets to slave labor to gold. He even threw out the claim that Switzerland had helped prolong the war.

"Where does anyone say the commercial banks?" the defense side muttered.

He didn't care if he didn't have the proof. If this went to trial, who knew what a jury might decide?

"What value do you put on the hundreds of thousands of lives that were lost in 1944 and '45 if this statement were believed by a jury?" he countered. After all, these were settlement talks, and one could put a price on every release.

More than two hours passed.

"This is a case that needs to be settled, and it needs to be settled now," Korman finally concluded. He had listened carefully. He had asked questions. Now, both sides needed to understand their predicaments.

Although he hadn't ruled on any of the motions, he had hinted more than once that the slave labor and looted-assets claims were headed for dismissal. He had also made it clear that, although some issues might be dismissed, he could certify the question of others for the circuit court to allow the plaintiffs the right to appeal. Did the defense really want to be embroiled in this conflict for years? Did the plaintiffs really want to litigate for years? And what about the deposited-assets claims? Did the defense want to risk discovery? Did the plaintiffs want to wait and deal with Volcker? Unlike Eizenstat, he was not under any pressure to please. His power came from tapping into everyone's fears. His two-year silence had spoken louder than his words. Now, it was time for his words.

Many of the attorneys would later come to praise Korman's quiet patience. Even Neuborne and Hausfeld admitted, when they were completely honest with themselves, that a trial would have presented tremendous obstacles. Their best hope was for a settlement. Korman's silence was the necessary tailwind that pushed them forward.

"I have two formulas," he announced.

Everyone waited.

The first, he explained, would be for the banks to pay $1.25 billion for everything. The second would be payment of $1.05 billion plus whatever Volcker found. He explained his rationale. In the end, he confessed, there was no magic in either.

It was almost eleven o'clock. The stifling heat and the late hour were making it hard to stay focused. Korman instructed those present to discuss his proposals among themselves and their clients and to meet at noon the next day at the courthouse.

Hausfeld hung around the room. He was exhausted but exhilarated. Weiss and Neuborne were equally buoyant. The judge's number was double the sum the banks had offered them.

Hausfeld shook hands with Witten. All evening, he had noticed something different about his counterpart. He seemed quieter, less combative. He had not started off the discussions with a joke or complaint. Maybe, just maybe . . . Hausfeld stopped himself. He had gotten his hopes up before. No use reading tea leaves. One and a quarter billion was more than the banks had ever wanted to pay. No reason to think that they would accept it now.

14

The Reckoning

Your Honor
First I want to thank you for giving me the opportunity to stand before a high
tribunal. . . . I was persecuted since I was a child and I never had opportunity in a
court of justice. And hearing all this spectacles, I have never heard anybody mention
anything about those which they lay on the ground dying and they asked us don't for-
get that you survived. Don't forget us. . . . Everybody's talking about money. I'm not
here to ask for more or less. I just want a little bit justice, justice for the survivors and
for those which they died . . . there was no Holocaust for no other nationality but for
the Jews. There was no Final Solution for nobody but the Jews. We couldn't even in
the concentration camps and I was in the last camp, I was in a cage behind barbed
wires in a barrack because I was Jewish and they know that this is what we had to
have plus the number, the yellow stripe. We didn't have enough room to sleep. We slept
like the chickens, sitting down. So give us a little bit of justice. . . .
                    November 20, 2000, Swiss Banks Fairness Hearing

At noon the next day, everybody was milling around the courthouse. No
one wanted to make the first move. Witten wanted the plaintiffs to meet
the judge first so that he could see whether they had come down from
their $1.5 number. Hausfeld wanted Witten to go first so that he could
find out whether the banks had come up from their $600 million. They
were assigned to separate jury rooms, but they kept darting into and out
of the hallway. Finally, Witten agreed to make the first presentation.[1]

Singer arrived at the courthouse energized. He had good and bad
news. The good news was that the banks had been shaken by Korman's
numbers. The bad news was that they were going to demand releases for
the Swiss-owned insurance companies. These companies were named
in Fagan's and Swift's suit against European insurance companies.

The plaintiffs were called into Korman's chambers an hour after

Witten. More than twenty attorneys filed in. Korman was prepared. Not only had he set up his usual conference table with its ten chairs, but also he had arranged two rows of six big, heavy armchairs each. Everybody would want to get in on the final act, if indeed a deal was close.

Weiss took the lead. The plaintiffs had nothing to report other than to hear what the defendants had to say.

Korman was irritated at their reticence but went ahead and divulged the banks' position. They had chosen his first formula of $1.25 billion. But . . . the devil was in the details, and they had details. Lots of them.

Among their demands was precisely the one that Singer had announced. The banks wanted total peace. They wanted a release for Winterthur, an insurance company that Credit Suisse had just recently purchased. They wanted commitments from Hevesi and Burg that they would support the settlement. They wanted to include the Meili lawsuit, as well as all legal fees and costs, in the $1.25 billion. They wanted to credit the Humanitarian Fund. And they wanted to pay out the $1.25 billion in six years with no interest.

The plaintiffs returned to their jury room.

"We need to separate the garbage from the details," Hausfeld remarked.

They also needed to be realistic. There was no way that they were going to get the banks up to $1.5 billion. Considering where they had started, $1.25 billion was pretty damn good. But . . . they didn't have to give them everything. They would not credit the Humanitarian Fund, and they would not include a release for Winterthur. Credit Suisse knew when it bought the company that the insurance lawsuit was pending. Although they would not give the banks a release on the insurance companies, they would give them as near total peace as they could. As angered as they were that the Swiss government was not participating in the settlement, they would stick to the concession that they had made with Eizenstat. They would give the SNB a release from all present and future lawsuits. They also would include Meili in the $1.25 billion.

Along with the insurance release, there was another detail the plaintiffs would not concede: interest. The banks owed money, and they mustn't be allowed to pay it out over time without interest. The plaintiffs had always spoken about net present value. Anything else they would not accept.

They gave their final proposal to Korman and left for the night. They would return the next morning to hear the banks' response. The attorneys began to speak optimistically. The banks wouldn't let this opportunity slip by. After all, they were getting the SNB in the deal. Surely that kind of peace was worth $1.25 billion.

Hausfeld felt a heightened tension in the air, as if the inevitable was coming. He had experienced this in other cases. Settlements often brought a certain energy, a momentum, when the negotiations began nearing the end. One detail builds upon another and another, until suddenly, like a wave, the force of closure begins to sweep everyone along, push them in the same direction. Everyone heads toward the same goal, the same shore.

Of course, he had been fooled many times before, as well. Settlements could just as quickly disintegrate. They could change courses without warning. They could implode over a specific word or particular, over a personality. He knew one should never get complacent. Negotiations were delicate. Like milkweed, they could be blown apart in a single breath.

Hausfeld and Mendelsohn arrived at the courthouse at ten the next morning. Several of the plaintiffs' attorneys were already in the jury room, waiting. Witten had called. He was going to be late. He had just gotten in touch with his clients.

Singer entered, all excited. This is what was going to happen. The banks were going to mention the insurance companies and interest. He was chatting to everyone, talking about all the conversations he had had during the night.

Everybody was nervous. Weiss was pacing the room. He had to leave by noon. It was his wife's birthday, and they were going on a cruise. He had promised her that he'd be back in the early afternoon. Neuborne was also on edge. He, too, was supposed to leave on vacation with his wife. Hausfeld had his own worries. Having missed out on a recent family outing, he wanted to make sure that he was home to celebrate his thirtieth anniversary. He had only one day to go.

Ten thirty passed. Eleven o'clock. Eleven thirty. Weiss would need to leave soon.

People were bustling in the corridor. Reporters had heard of the discussions and were now vying for information. They congregated by the doorway. Hausfeld remembered watching Fagan earlier in the morning, standing in the hallway, answering questions from reporters.

At eleven thirty, Korman called them in. He wanted only the negotiating team.

There was one hang-up. The banks didn't want to pay interest.

Weiss and Hausfeld did not hesitate.

No deal.

It could fall apart, the judge warned.

"There's going to come a time that you're going to want to have every dollar available for distribution purposes," Hausfeld explained, "and if you spread the payment over time without interest it's diminishing the net present value of the settlement by approximately $50 to $75 million. They're banks. Nobody gives out money interest free, particularly banks."

Korman was quiet for a moment. What should he tell them?

Convey to them that that's the way it is, the two answered.

The judge called the defense back in, and the negotiating team returned to the jury room. Another hour passed. Weiss kept circling the room. He had to leave. As he and Hausfeld walked down the corridor, the judge's clerk announced that Senator D'Amato had arrived.

"What's D'Amato doing here?" wondered Hausfeld. "This is beginning to look bizarre. Fagan has Sapir and Meili here. There are tons of reporters, and now D'Amato is showing up."

Weiss pulled D'Amato aside. "Senator, stand firm. They want an extension of time, and they can have it, but they have to pay interest. Stand firm."

D'Amato nodded and headed to Korman's chambers.

At one thirty, Korman called for the plaintiffs. Once again, the judge wanted only the negotiating team. The marshals had to clear the hallway. The swell of reporters had grown. Word had gotten out that D'Amato had come. What was going on? Who was saying what? Was there a deal?

D'Amato was sitting next to Korman.

The banks don't want to move, the judge declared.

Sometimes there are opportunities, and this is an opportunity, D'Amato explained. The banks want a four-year payout with no interest. He outlined the reasons behind their insistence, then turned to the negotiators.

No deal. The plaintiffs need every dollar.

What kind of interest are you talking about? D'Amato could see that they weren't going to budge. He wanted a number. Two point three percent?

Treasury rates, Weiss insisted. Three and a quarter, three and a half.

Last month they were three and seven eighths, Hausfeld corrected him.

Okay, three and seven eighths, D'Amato concurred.

No, that's just what they were last month. Eight is prime.

Not prime. Three and seven eighths, D'Amato insisted. He would take it back and see what he could do.

D'Amato returned to Witten, Cohen, and the Swiss lawyers in the jury room. He did not bother with decorum. He wanted to clinch a deal, and if he needed to do it with Weiss, who was giving money to his opponent for the Senate, then so be it. Let's get this deal done. They want interest.

"In terms of pulling together all of these forces, D'Amato was the only one who could do it," a Swiss bank official later commented. "He had the credibility, was pragmatic and very smart even though he was a political animal."[2]

At two o'clock, Weiss could not wait any longer. He had to leave. He went to say goodbye to Korman and D'Amato. He explained that he had to go pack. Witten heard this and couldn't resist commenting.

"Mel, I remember what you did in Zurich. You just bought everything fresh, right from there. Do it again."

Everyone laughed. They all remembered his Zurich buying spree.

"I can't do that. I promised my wife." Weiss smiled. He then gave his phone number to Hausfeld and told him to call him when he found something out.

Three o'clock. Hausfeld was in the hallway with Mendelsohn when he saw Cohen.

"Marc, how long is this going to continue? Are we going to negotiate? Are we going to continue?"

"You know what you have to do," Cohen answered. "It's in your hands."

Hausfeld marched to Korman's office. He had had enough. "We're not going to sit here if they have no idea how long this is going to take," he told Korman's secretary.

Just a little longer, she coaxed, just give them a little more time.

Hausfeld called Weiss. He told him about Cohen and said they were still waiting.

At four thirty, Hausfeld was beside himself. "If anyone in this case ever accuses me again of being impatient," he thought to himself, remembering Eizenstat's comment, "I will remind them of how I sat all day waiting for a simple yes or no." He returned to Korman's office.

As he entered the anteroom with Mendelsohn, Swift, and Neuborne, he saw that the judge's door was open. He caught Korman's eye.

"Why don't we just quit for the evening? If the banks have something to report, you can call us tonight and tell us what it is."

As he was talking, Korman stood and motioned them to come in.

Hausfeld froze. Around the table, seated alongside the judge, were D'Amato and Singer.

Singer?

The three sat down. D'Amato walked over and shut the door and explained that the banks had conducted parallel negotiations with Singer and himself the night before.

"You have put back on the table a deal we had rejected. We had already reached a different agreement with the banks on Tuesday night," D'Amato stated. And that deal was $1.25 billion for total peace, not to include the insurance companies, paid out over four years with no interest.

Hausfeld suddenly remembered Weiss's warning him that the banks were going to try to put them in the position of being the money grubbers, of hanging in there for every penny of interest. How could Hausfeld have been so naive? He suddenly understood how Singer had known the "news" before everyone else.

"That's not the deal. We don't agree," he answered defiantly.

Neuborne was equally enraged. How could this have happened?

The deal had to get done, D'Amato insisted. Were the plaintiffs really going to jeopardize the entire deal over something less than 2 to 3 percent of the total settlement? It's minuscule.

Hausfeld's mind raced. It might be minuscule, but that wasn't the point. He was furious with Witten. Once again, it appeared that he had tried to capitalize on the plaintiffs' differences by settling with individuals. And, once again, he felt deeply betrayed by members of his own group. This was as outrageous as Swift's and Fagan's press release. He got up to leave. He needed to get his thoughts together.

D'Amato followed him out. They spoke for a few minutes. Then Hausfeld went to the anteroom. Mendelsohn joined him.

"He told me that I can't afford to blow the whole deal," Hausfeld said to Mendelsohn of his conversation with D'Amato. "He said, 'Aren't these the worst sons of bitches you've ever seen? They can make life real tough for you, and you know that they will. Their word is no good. You know that they'll do anything possible to string this out as long as they can and make sure that the victims get nothing. You can't go. You can't let this deal go by. You only have a certain amount of time to do this.' I told him that I needed some time to myself."

He took a deep breath. "We have to find a way of saving face and finishing this off." He and Mendelsohn talked it through. After two and a half years, after having been laughed at, after having been told that the banks would never pay a dime for the claims for slave labor and looted assets, after the banks had said that anything over $530 million was blackmail, after they had been forced to pay tens of millions of dollars in legal fees, the plaintiffs *had gotten* $1.25 billion from them, and everyone was referring to it as rough justice. In insisting on another 2 or 3 percent, what would they gain if they really did blow this whole deal? If they walked out at this point over interest, would Swift and Fagan collapse their side? Would Hevesi and McCall think that they were being too petty? Would the judge think that they were throwing away a once-in-a-lifetime opportunity?

He stood quietly for several minutes and then had an idea.

There was $130 million left in the Humanitarian Fund that had not been allocated, and it would take another year or two to be distributed.

"We can split the interest. There could be four installments of the Victims' Fund. Two would be interest free, and two would have interest at three and seven eighths. The Humanitarian Fund could then be rolled into the Victims' Fund."

He figured that if they could invest the remaining $130 million in the

Humanitarian Fund and earn interest on it, that interest would replace some of the interest lost on the interest-free payments. It was a way of saving face and not giving in completely.

They went back to the judge and D'Amato. They called in Witten.

Witten was insulted. The plaintiffs had turned down their request to credit the Humanitarian Fund, and now they were saying that they wanted to blend it into the Victims' Fund and earn interest on it?

"Yesterday was yesterday, and today is today," explained Hausfeld. "Just like at one time you only wanted to negotiate on behalf of the defendant banks, and now you want total peace."

It was five o'clock. If Witten was going to agree, he would need approval from his bankers in Switzerland. It was eleven at night their time. He wasn't sure he would be able to get hold of them. Korman was in no mood for excuses. Witten could use his private office line if he needed to.

As Witten walked out, he turned to Hausfeld.

"Are there any other new conditions that you want?"

Hausfeld laid down his pen.

"*No.* There are no other new conditions unless you're conducting some more private negotiations outside of us where you're going to try to conclude deals and force them on us."

Nobody said a word.

Witten disappeared.

D'Amato tried to make small talk.

Hausfeld stayed quiet.

At five forty-five, Witten returned.

We have a deal, he announced.

Hausfeld looked up from his legal pad. "A deal." He should have been ecstatic. They were finished. The case was settled. Two and a half years, and the banks were finally going to pay. But . . . he was still smarting from the ending. The betrayal. The banks maneuvering for every penny. There were no apologies. No grace. This was a business deal. Yet . . . the banks were finally going to pay.

"Okay, let's get this on record." Korman jumped up. He called for a court reporter.

The banks would pay $1,250,000,000 in four payments over the course of three years. Two would be interest-free, and two would pay interest at three and seven eighths. (The Humanitarian Fund would be rolled in to collect extra interest.) The banks would receive credit against the payments they made directly on dormant account claims; they (including the SNB) would receive releases, with the exception of the three Swiss insurers, who were defendants in another lawsuit; they would not be responsible for legal fees and costs, nor would they have to pay any costs associated with giving notice to class members. Volcker's ICEP would continue its investigation into identifiable accounts, and all economic sanctions would be lifted. The agreement regarding Meili would be under seal.

They were done. They had recorded their agreement. D'Amato began to prepare a press statement.

"Material justice."

"Moral justice."

"Heal the wounds."

Hausfeld felt numb. Words sounded hollow. He left to tell the rest of the Executive Committee members waiting in the hallway about the deal. He watched as everyone congratulated one another. They shook hands and hugged. By the time Hausfeld stepped outside, D'Amato had already taken center stage.

Standing on the courthouse steps, flanked by Sapir and Meili, D'Amato was surrounded by microphones. He motioned to Hausfeld.

As Hausfeld made his way over, he heard Fagan whispering from behind.

"Senator, you've got to get Swift up here. It's not fair. Bob Swift has got to be up here."

D'Amato acknowledged Swift.

Hausfeld looked at Mendelsohn, who was standing off to the side. He nodded to him, left D'Amato's side, and pushed past the crowd. The two headed down the steps just as reporters began asking questions.

"When will the survivors get their money?"

"Is the SNB participating?"

"How much of this is rough justice?"

Looking back at the scene in front of the courthouse, he paused for a moment and thought of his father, then crossed the street and walked away.

Epilogue

"I'm the rough without the justice," sobbed Greta Beer into the phone. "I haven't received a penny. Nothing. I have a broken heart. The money would give me comfort."[1]

It was May 30, 2002, nearly four years after Senator D'Amato, Jewish leaders, and the attorneys stood outside the Brooklyn courthouse and announced their historic settlement with the Swiss banks. For Greta Beer, the tallying went back further. It had been seven years since the *Wall Street Journal* had publicized her story, forty-two years since she and her mother had approached the Swiss banks, and more than sixty years since her father had deposited money in a Swiss bank. "My father's account can never be found," she asserted. "They destroyed it."

Tired and recovering from a mild stroke, Beer was as adamant as ever. She remembered speaking at Senator D'Amato's first congressional hearing. Nothing had changed for her. She was frustrated and disappointed. Many other plaintiffs in the class action were also expressing sentiments that echoed those beginning days when they were asked to recount their stories, the days before the banks had committed to pay $1.25 billion.

But the banks had agreed to pay. The settlement marked the end, not the beginning. So why the frustration and disappointment? Part of the answer lies in the fact that so much time had transpired since the Holocaust. Many of the records that could have proved ownership to accounts no longer existed. Volcker's audit had taken three years to complete.

Another part of the answer, however, lies with the mechanics of a class action. As powerful as a class action is, its unwieldiness can present its own set of problems. It may be as commanding as a tank, but it can also be as slow. Its mass and strength can help clear a path to a settlement, but these very characteristics can also leave disappointed individuals in the wake of a victorious action. As stated in the summary of the plan for allocation and distribution:

> The settlement is not a treaty, nor is it legislation (as is the German agreement). It is, instead a contract between the plaintiff class members and the two defendant Swiss banks, governed by contract law but also subject to the stringent due process requirements of a procedural device apparently unique to the United States: the class action lawsuit. These requirements are intended to protect the interests of all class members, but may have the unfortunate effect of delaying distribution of the Settlement Fund to those who, by now, have been waiting for more than two years—and in the case of the claimants to Swiss bank accounts, more than fifty years—to receive payments.[2]

As soon as the plaintiffs and the banks reached agreement on the amount the banks should pay, the questions that everyone had dreaded took center stage. To whom should the money go? How should it be distributed? What groups should be included in the settlement? Was the settlement fund meant for just Jewish victims? What about the Romani Gypsies who had signed on at the beginning? There were no easy answers. The amount in question, $1.25 billion, sounded like a lot, but it would run out quickly if every victims' group was included. After much discussion, the attorneys decided to open the fund to Jewish victims, the Romani, Jehovah's Witnesses, homosexuals, and the disabled. The fund excluded, among others, political prisoners.

On March 31, 1999, Judge Korman appointed Judah Gribetz to be the Special Master of the Swiss banks settlement fund. Gribetz was a highly respected attorney who had served as counsel to the governor of the State of New York and as deputy mayor of the City of New York. He was also a member of the board of the Museum of Jewish Heritage in New York. Uncharacteristically, nobody objected. Gribetz was the perfect choice.

Gribetz had the overwhelming task of coming up with a fair and equitable plan for the allocation and distribution of the settlement fund. For months, he listened as survivors, heads of organizations, Jewish leaders, and attorneys presented their perspectives and their passions.

Some survivors wanted all the money to go only to survivors. Others argued that it should be used to set up a survivors' health care plan. There were Jewish leaders and attorneys who argued that the money was meant for all of the victims of the Holocaust and that therefore some funds should go into education and research. The issues were delicate. If Gribetz were to lean too heavily one way or another, he could face the wrath of those who would feel that they had been marginalized. He could also create discord within and among the victims and victim groups themselves.

This last danger, according to Neuborne, who had been appointed lead settlement counsel, was to be avoided at all costs. "The members of the plaintiff classes are elderly victims of an unparalleled human catastrophe. At the close of their lives, it would be socially and psychologically irresponsible to pit one group of Holocaust victims against another in an unseemly battle for a larger share of a limited settlement fund that cannot do real justice to all."[3]

On March 30, 1999, Korman approved the proposed settlement and certified five settlement classes. Approval of a settlement and certification of the class are required in a class action. This class was divided into five categories. There was the Deposited Assets Class, which included victims who asserted claims against the banks for unreturned bank accounts and deposited assets; the Looted Assets Class, which was broader and included those with claims against the banks for looted and cloaked assets; the Slave Labor Class I, which included victims who had performed slave labor for companies that deposited revenues or cloaked assets through the Swiss banks; the Slave Labor Class II, which consisted of individuals who had performed slave labor for Swiss-owned or -controlled companies; and the Refugee Class, which consisted of victims who were denied entry to or who were expelled from Switzerland or who, after having gained entry, were abused or mistreated there.

Once Korman granted preliminary approval and class certification, he needed to make sure that the information was conveyed to the class members. This, too, was not an easy task. In a class action, class membership can include hundreds of thousands of individuals who are dispersed across the globe. Several attorneys were responsible for implementing this stage. Not only did they have to utilize press coverage and community outreach programs, but they had to send out more than 1.4 million notice packages to class members in at least forty-eight countries.[4]

The final preliminary step in a class-action settlement is to hold fairness hearings. Class members are invited to write letters or to come to voice their agreements or objections. Korman held two fairness hearings: one in New York, on November 29, 1999, and a second by electronic hookup in Israel, on December 14, 1999. Although some members objected to having a fairness hearing before they knew how much money each class was going to be allotted, Korman asserted that it would be impossible to provide that information prior to the completion of Gribetz's process. He did allow, however, that once the Special Master issued his plan, which would happen shortly, the plan would be disseminated to all class members just as the settlement agreement had been.

In reality, it wasn't only the legal machinations of a class action, or the task of figuring out who should get the money and how much, that slowed distribution. As in the past, the defendants bore some of the blame for the slow pace.

On December 6, 1999, the Volcker Committee issued its final report. In the report, the committee revealed that it had identified 54,000 accounts that were "probably" or "possibly" related to Holocaust victims. Of those 54,000 accounts, 25,187 accounts were identified as "probably" related to Holocaust victims (this was a far cry from the 775 accounts that the banks had originally reported to Bronfman). The committee recommended immediate publication of those 25,187 accounts so that claimants could match names and accounts. Volcker also called for the creation of a centralized database of the 4.1 million accounts that the committee had determined had been opened in Switzerland between the years 1933–1945.

The Swiss Federal Banking Commission hesitated. Many of the accounts would have no documentation other than names. As the bankers and auditors had discovered from previous published lists, it would be hard to prove matches, especially if accounts had several claimants. After four months and much complaining by Volcker and his attorney, Michael Bradfield, the Banking Commission authorized publication of information relating to the approximately 26,000 "probable" accounts.

It did not authorize publication of the remaining 28,000. Nor did the commission mandate the creation of a central database for the 4.1 million accounts. Nor did it require the small cantonal or private banks to publish information relating to any of the accounts.

This last refusal particularly irked Korman. "The unwillingness of the SFBC to mandate compliance with the recommendations of the Volcker Committee is inexplicable, and the failure of the private and cantonal banks to voluntarily comply is inconsistent with the spirit of the Settlement Agreement. . . . It also amounts to nothing less than a replay of the conduct that created the problems addressed in this case."[5]

Korman repeated what Volcker had asserted in his committee's report. While the auditors had found "no evidence of systematic destruction of records of victims' accounts, organized discrimination against the accounts of victims of Nazi persecution, or concerted efforts to divert the funds of victims of Nazi persecution to improper purposes," they had found "evidence of questionable and deceitful actions by some individual banks in the handling of accounts of victims." Those actions included the withholding of information from Holocaust victims or their heirs, the inappropriate closing of accounts, and the failure to keep adequate records.[6]

On July 26, 2000, Judge Korman granted final approval to the settlement agreement, and on September 11, 2000, Special Master Gribetz filed his proposed plan. The class action was now lumbering into its final phase.

Using the Volcker report as his guide and recognizing that the deposited-assets claim had the most legal weight, Gribetz allotted $800 million of the $1.25 billion to the Deposited Assets Class. He recommended that the Claims Resolution Tribunal, which had been established by the Swiss Bankers Association, the Swiss Federal Banking Commission, and the Volcker Committee in 1997 to deal with the first list of names, continue as the mechanism to arbitrate the deposited-assets claims. That left $450 million in the settlement fund.

Gribetz allotted $100 million to the Looted Assets Class, 90 percent of which would go to the Jewish class members and 10 percent to the Romani, Jehovah's Witness, disabled, and homosexual members. Because of the widespread membership in this class and the impossibility of retracing the path of looted assets, Gribetz recommended that the court make two *cy pres* payments. *Cy Pres* means "next best"; in this case, money would go to programs that serve the neediest survivors. He identified the elderly survivors living in Central and Eastern Europe and the former Soviet Union as among the neediest. Distribution to the needy Jewish class members would be handled by the American Jewish Joint Distribution Committee and the Conference on Jewish Material Claims Against Germany (the Claims Conference). The International Organization for Migration (IOM) would distribute the allocated $10 million to the non-Jewish victims.

For the Slave Labor Class I, Gribetz and Korman both believed, on the basis of lists of frozen German assets in Switzerland, that the hundreds of companies that had used slaves had had financial relationships with Swiss entities. Nevertheless, it would be very difficult for former slave laborers to produce a link between the companies for which they had labored and the defendants. Many survivors did not even know the names of the companies. For these reasons, Gribetz decided that "all persons who performed slave labor for private entities, entities owned or controlled by the state or by Nazi authorities, or by the concentration camp or ghetto authorities, are members of 'Slave Labor Class I.'"[7]

These members would receive two payments. One payment of up to $7,500 would be paid to slave laborers by the German foundation. This foundation, established as a result of contentious negotiations in the two years following the Swiss banks affair, was a response to charges, both political and legal, that German companies had never accepted historical or financial responsibility for their use of slave and forced laborers; in the end, an agreement was forged between the U.S. and German governments. A second payment of up to $1,000 for slave laborers would come from the Swiss banks settlement fund. The Claims Conference and the IOM would be in charge of distributing payment to these class members.

Slave Labor Class II would affect persons who had performed slave labor for a Swiss entity. In an attempt to identify these companies and those who had performed slave labor for them, Korman ordered all Swiss companies who sought releases to identify themselves, as well as their wartime subsidiaries. He also asked them to provide lists of names of those who might have performed slave labor. Nestlé was among the companies that responded. The names of several thousand former slave laborers were provided to Gribetz. The payment to these claimants would be an amount up to $1,000.

For the Refugee Class, Gribetz determined that those who had sought refuge in Switzerland but had been mistreated there generally fared better than those who had been denied entry or expelled. As a result of that determination, he designated a payment of up to $500 to those who stayed in Switzerland and a payment of up to $2,500 to those who had been denied entry or expelled.

Gribetz also designated $10 million to fund a Victim List Foundation. This list would compile the names of all victims or targets of Nazi persecution, Jews and non-Jews. He also added a category to help victims who had claims against specific Swiss insurance companies that were included in the settlement.

Greta Beer was not the only one who was still waiting for her money. Armand Lakner had yet to receive a penny. Lewis Salton had died in 1999, a year before the settlement had been officially approved. And Gizella Weisshaus had opted out altogether, distraught by the entire plan. By January 2002 the Claims Resolution Tribunal had paid out only $10 million of the allotted $800 million for the deposited-assets class. It had received more than 32,000 claims and had matched 59. The awards had averaged $165,000, with the largest being $3.5 million to an heir in Australia.[8] The slow pace of matching claims prompted Korman to change the rules. There would now be a "higher degree of plausibility," as Volcker put it.[9] For the many accounts that were missing documentation, a name and an address might be all that would be needed to make a match. When the amount was not known, the tribunal auditors would estimate the average value of Nazi-era bank accounts and multiply by 11.5 for appreciation. Korman authorized payments in full instead of waiting until all the claims had been processed, and he approved distribution of money to daughters- and sons-in-law, instead of just to blood relatives.

"I regret to say that first of all, the way they treated the people without any heart, without any explanation. They sent the money without compassion, without explanation." Charles Sonabend was not referring to the Swiss.[10] In this instance, Sonabend was directing his anger towards the Claims Conference. "They sent the money without compassion, without any explanation. I was shocked."

As disenchanted as Sonabend was, he had received a portion from the Swiss banks settlement, unlike many others. When asked how much, he paused. "Are you sitting down? Don't fall off your seat. I got $2,500 from the class action."

Twenty-five hundred dollars out of $1.25 billion. Twenty-five hundred dollars as a member of the Refugee Class. Twenty-five hundred dollars.

For many of the survivors, the amount did not begin to address the wrongs that had been committed against them and their families. How could it? How could $2,500 or $3,500 or $7,500 express the grief or the pain or the anger that they had endured during their lives? It couldn't.

To Sonabend, the payment felt like a slap in the face. Others couldn't help feeling regret over the passage of time—even those who had received a much larger sum than Sonabend. Charles Roman, of Teaneck, New Jersey, had received a check for $32,101, 35 percent of the $90,000 that he was slated to get from his deceased aunt's dormant account. As surprised as he and his wife were, they "lamented the fact that they didn't have the money when they married in 1955 and were barely able to afford an apartment. 'You know the pathetic thing is how much was taken. . . . This is the horrible thing. And they got away with it for as long as they did.'"[11]

Some of the survivors had hoped that this case would provide them the opportunity to expose history's injustices through a legal forum. "My only regret," Sonabend asserted, "was that this case did not go to court. In court, every day more evidence comes out. I wanted to go to court and tell the world how Switzerland supplied Germany and enabled her to continue the war for five long years."[12] Had the case proceeded to a courtroom, survivors would have had the chance to articulate their deepest desires for justice and retribution.

Other survivors had hoped that the settlement would improve their lifestyles. Maybe they would receive enough money to live out their lives more comfortably. Still others had hoped that a payment would provide a link to their lost pasts. Like a photo, an account could take them back, reconnect them to their dead mothers, fathers, aunts, uncles.

The Swiss banks case was a journey back for many of the plaintiffs. The journey proved painful, but the plaintiffs had hoped that they would arrive at a clear destination, one that would provide a swift and direct remedy, that would embrace simple justice.

But large class actions that address human rights are rarely simple. And the gap between the journey and the final destination can be immense. In many class actions, this gap is never more apparent than in the discrepancy between attorney fees and plaintiffs' payments. Even though, in class actions, the judge determines and limits legal fees, often there remains a large discrepancy. Critics never cease to seize upon this fact. In the Swiss banks case, this issue was less significant. Many of the lawyers provided their services pro bono. Some asked that their fees be donated to charitable causes. Others, like Hausfeld and Weiss, waived their fees completely. Those who were seeking fees agreed to limit their applications.

For many of the plaintiffs' attorneys and representatives, the lawsuit was a journey forward. This was their chance not only to expose the past but to pose questions for the future. What does it mean to be neutral? Who is accountable for crimes against humanity? Should one blame only those who perpetuate human rights crimes, or does guilt fall on those who aid and abet them? How interrelated are financial and human-rights crimes? Would the secrecy that characterizes Swiss banking ever be thought of in the same way? Should it be? The class action against the banks did not answer these questions. It raised them. The legal forum allowed attorneys to pose these questions in complaints, briefs, motions, and arguments to the court. With pressure from government and from Jewish leaders, the Swiss and the general public were also forced to ask them. Publication of reports from the Volcker Committee, the Bergier Commission, the State Department, the National Archives, and numerous independent historians did the best they could to offer some answers.

In addition to raising questions, a class action can achieve something else, something more tangible than discussions and questions. In the case of the Swiss banks, that something was $1.25 billion. The banks were forced to pay $1.25 billion. Broken into individual payments, the figure loses its impact (most large settlements do), but, as an aggregate sum, $1.25 billion serves as an important symbol. It is a statement that proclaims to the world that a great wrong was committed. In the western world, money can achieve an impact that words, with their many interpretations and permutations, often fail to convey. The higher the sum, the stronger the declaration.

The case against the Swiss banks involved a host of different players and a multitude of different viewpoints and expectations. There were the plaintiffs, the attorneys, the organizations, the Jewish leaders, the politicians, the state financial officers, the U.S. government officials, the judge, and the Special Master. While it was "a miracle," as one attorney described it, that anything got accomplished, it was also inevitable that there would be those who would feel disillusioned at the outcome. That is the nature of a large class action. One might better understand its dynamics by borrowing a metaphor from the quantum world. A class action is like a wave. Composed of a multitude of separate particles, its energy derives from its cohesive and unified movement. Through one lens, one might see all of the individual entities colliding and rebounding off one another, but, through another lens, one might see a single confluence of forces moving toward an elusive notion called justice. The view one sees depends upon the lens through which one looks.

Postscript

On September 11, 2002, the plaintiffs' law firm of Lieff, Cabraser, Heimann & Bernstein sent a letter to Judge Korman informing him of the firm's decision to donate $100,000 of its legal fee to the survivor Greta Beer, in recognition of her services to the Settlement Class members. The $100,00 exceeds the $1.5 million fee that Lieff, Cabraser is donating to endow a human rights chair at Columbia University Law School. The payment is to be distributed directly to Beer by the court in appreciation of all of her efforts before, during, and after the Swiss banks settlement. In its letter, the firm states that "Ms. Beer has drawn upon increasingly limited emotional reserves in order to recount for the Court and a worldwide audience, through numerous interviews with newspapers, television reporters and other media outlets, her harrowing personal experiences during and after the Nazi era. Ms. Beer remains vitally interested in the rapid and equitable distribution of the Settlement Fund that her efforts helped to create, particularly in connection with Swiss bank accounts that were the foundation of the litigation."

In addition to Lieff, Cabraser's donation to Greta Beer, Ed Fagan donated $400,000 of his fees to five plaintiffs, including $100,000 to Gizella Weisshaus.

NOTES

FOR FURTHER READING

INDEX

Notes

Chapter 1. Winds of Truth

1. Peter Gumbel, "Secret Legacies," *Wall Street Journal,* June 21, 1995, p. 7.

2. Bank Julius Baer, "Clarification," June 29, 1995.

3. Friedman Complaint, Civil Action no. 96-5161, p. 89.

4. Interview with Rolf Bloch, July 30, 1999.

5. The account of Bronfman's meeting is based upon: interview with Hans Baer, July 29, 1999; Itamar Levin, *The Last Deposit,* pp. 112–15; John Tagliabue, "A Human Face for Swiss Banks," *New York Times,* January 1, 1998.

6. Interview with Baer, July 29, 1999.

7. Jean Ziegler, *The Swiss, the Gold, and the Dead,* p. 261.

8. Marcus Kabel, "Swiss Bank Denies Holding Huge Sums from Holocaust Victims," Reuters, February 23, 1996.

9. Johanna McGeary, "Echoes of the Holocaust," *Time,* February 24, 1997, p. 21.

10. Independent Committee of Eminent Persons Memorandum, May 2, 1996.

11. Interview with Baer; interview with unnamed source, January 1999.

12. Transcript, hearing of the United States Senate Committee on Banking, Housing, and Urban Affairs, Washington, D.C., April 23, 1996, p. 3.

13. Interview with Greta Beer, September 8, 1998; Greta Beer, "Interview by Survivors of the Shoah Visual History Foundation," Jackson Heights, N.Y., October 10, 1996, tapes 1–5.

14. *Wall Street Journal,* June 21, 1995.

15. Transcript, hearing of the United States Senate Committee on Banking, Housing, and Urban Affairs, p. 17.

16. Ibid., p. 22.

17. Ibid., p. 73.

18. Interview with Beer.

19. Levin, *The Last Deposit,* p. 139.

Chapter 2. Looking Back

1. Allanna Sullivan, "The Attorney Behind Texaco's Big Settlement," *Wall Street Journal*, November 26, 1996, p. B1.
2. Susan Konig, "Blazing the Way in Class-Action Law," *New York Times*, November 16, 1997.
3. Dean Starkman, "Milberg Weiss Still Reigns in Holder Suits," *Wall Street Journal*, December 30, 1997, p. B6.
4. Interview with Mel Weiss, September 16, 1998.
5. Stuart E. Eizenstat, "U.S. and Allied Efforts to Recover and Restore Gold and Other Assets Stolen or Hidden by Germany during World War II," p. 16.
6. Ibid., p. 33.
7. Transcript, hearing of the United States Senate Committee on Banking, Housing, and Urban Affairs, April 23 1996, p. 5.
8. Interview with unnamed source, 1999; Gregg J. Rickman, *Swiss Banks and Jewish Souls*, p. 48.
9. Interview with Miriam Kleiman, February 25, 1997.
10. Tom Curley, "Faded Papers May Clarify Swiss Moves," *USA Today*, November 11, 1996.
11. Interview with Kleiman.

Chapter 3. Plaintiffs Speak

1. The Whittier Tapes, "The Fifteenth Annual International Law Symposium: Nazi Gold and Other Assets of the Holocaust," panel 5, "The Lawyers Speak," Whittier Law School, March 1, 1998.
2. Barry Meier, "Lawyer in Holocaust Case Faces Litany of Complaints," *New York Times*, September 8, 2000.
3. Henry Gottlieb, "Inviting Disaster," *New Jersey Law Journal*, January 22, 1996; Michael Booth, "Senator Renews Call for 31-Day Solicitation Ban," *New Jersey Law Journal*, January 29, 1996.
4. Susan Orenstein, "Gold Warriors," *American Lawyer*, September 1998, p. 62; Meier, "Lawyer in Holocaust Case Faces Litany of Complaints"; interview with Gizella Weisshaus, September 3, 1998.
5. Weisshaus Complaint, Civil Action no. 96-4849, pp. 1, 18.
6. Elaine S. Povich, "Hunt Renewed for Swiss-Held Funds of Jews, Nazis," *Newsday*, February 23, 1997, p. 5.
7. Lewis Salton's history is based on Sidney C. Schaer, "Holocaust Survivors Seek Fate of Families Assets," *Newsday*, February 24, 1997; transcript, hearing of the United States Senate Committee on Banking, Housing, and Urban Affairs, October 16, 1996, pp. 47–51; Friedman Complaint; telephone interview with Lewis Salton, October 6, 1998.
8. Telephone interview with Salton.

9. "Swiss Banks Accused of Making Money off Marcos Billions," *Agence France-Presse,* September 25, 1997; Henry Weinstein, "Swiss Bank Accounts Frozen in Marcos Case," *Los Angeles Times,* September 30, 1997.

10. Interview with Burt Neuborne, October 22, 1998.

11. Memories of D'Amato told to author by Burt Neuborne.

12. Hearing of the United States Senate Committee on Banking, Housing, and Urban Affairs, p. 8.

13. Ibid., p. 21.

14. Ibid., p. 55.

15. Phone interview with Estelle Sapir, October, 1998.

Chapter 4. The Devil's Bridge

1. Friedman Complaint, p. 76.

2. David Boruchowicz, "Interview by the Survivors of the Shoah Visual History Foundation," Toronto, Ontario, Canada, December 1, 1994, tapes 1–4; Friedman Complaint, p. 14.

3. Trials of War Criminals before the Nuernberg Military Tribunals, vol. 14 (October 1946–April 1949), p. 611, cited in Plaintiffs' Opposition to Defendant's Motions to Dismiss for Failure to State a Claim under International Law, master docket no. CV 96–4849, p. 32.

4. Treasury Report, 1942, cited in Friedman Complaint, p. 65.

5. Censorship intercept from a letter dated October 24, 1943, from the War Department Military Intelligence regional files on Switzerland, section no. 5970, "War Morale of the Civil Population," SB #2277, cited in Friedman Complaint, p. 21.

6. Based upon Declaration of Christoph Meili, February 3, 1997. Included in Declaration of Michael Witti in Support of Plaintiffs' Motion for Expedited Discovery, February 13, 1997.

7. Michele Chabin, "Jews Angered by Swiss President's Remarks," *St. Louis Jewish Light,* January 8, 1997, p. 2.

8. Alan Cowell, "How Swiss Strategy on Holocaust Fund Unraveled," *New York Times,* January 26, 1997.

9. Anne Swardson, "Swiss Regrets Remarks on Jewish Demands," *Washington Post,* January 16, 1997.

10. "What Ambassador Carlo Jagmetti Wrote to his Colleague Thomas Borer on the Jewish Holocaust Assets in Switzerland," *Tages Anzeiger,* January 27, 1997.

11. Jim McGee, "Outgoing Swiss Ambassador Releases Secret Cable," *Washington Post,* February 1, 1997; William Drozdiak, "Swiss Envoy Resigns over Strategy Paper," *Washington Post,* January 27, 1997.

12. Based upon author's interview with two Swiss attorneys who wished to remain unnamed, June 28, 1999.

Chapter 5. An Uneasy Alliance

1. Michael Hirsh, "The Holocaust in the Dock," *Newsweek*, February 17, 1997, p. 43.

2. Ibid.

3. Ibid.

4. The account of the meeting is based upon author's notes, February 19, 1997.

5. John Authers and Richard Wolffe, *The Victim's Fortune*, p. 13.

6. Interview with a Swiss journalist who wished to remain unnamed, November 27, 1998.

7. Friedman's history is based upon Ann Louise Bardach, "Edgar's List," *Vanity Fair*, March 1997, p. 262.

8. Blaine Harden and Saundra Torry, "N.Y. Law Firm to Advise Swiss Bank Accused of Laundering Nazi Loot," *Washington Post*, February 28, 1997.

9. The account of the meeting is based upon conversations with several participants at the meeting, February 28, 1997.

10. The courtroom discussion is excerpted from the Transcript of Civil Cause for Conference before Judge Edward R. Korman, Brooklyn, New York, February 28, 1997.

11. Based upon the observations of author and several people present.

12. Alan Cowell, "Swiss Use Gold to Set Up Holocaust Fund," *New York Times*, March 6, 1997.

13. Letter to the Honorable Edward R. Korman from Robert A. Swift, Re: Weisshaus v. Union Bank of Switzerland, no. 96–4849, March 5, 1997.

14. Based upon Hausfeld's and Neuborne's recollections.

Chapter 6. A Rough Calculation

1. The account of the meeting is based upon observations of and conversations with several participants, March 12, 1997.

2. The account of the meeting is based upon Hausfeld's recollections and other participants' observations, March 19, 1997.

3. The account of the meeting is based upon author's notes, April 2, 1997.

4. "Interim Report of Committee of Experts in Holocaust Victim Assets Litigation," April, 29, 1997.

5. Letter to the Honorable Edward R. Korman from Roger M. Witten, Re: Holocaust Victim Assets, CV 96–4849, April 28, 1997.

6. Oral history of Aaron Lakner, June 28, 1992, U.S. Holocaust Memorial Museum Archives.

7. Interview with Armand Lakner, June 11, 1998; Michael Shapiro, "A Son Seeks His Father's Savings, Justice," *Washington Jewish Week*, August 21, 1997, p. 25.

8. Letter to the Honorable Edward R. Korman from Roger M. Witten.

9. Letter to the Honorable Edward R. Korman from Burt Neuborne, Re: Holocaust Victim Assets, CV 96–4849, May 1, 1997.

10. The discussion is excerpted from the Transcript of Civil Cause for Conference before Judge Edward R. Korman, Brooklyn, New York, May 1, 1997.

Chapter 7. Arguments and Motions

1. Stuart E. Eizenstat, "U.S. and Allied Efforts to Recover and Restore Gold and Other Assets Stolen or Hidden by Germany during World War II," May 1997, pp. iii, v.

2. "Declaration of the Federal Council on the Eizenstat Report," Bern, May 22, 1997.

3. Based upon a phone conversation with Bennett Freeman, December 2, 1999.

4. Interview with Greg Bradsher, August 26, 1998.

5. Transcript, hearing of the United States Senate Committee on Banking, Housing, and Urban Affairs, Washington, D.C., May 15, 1997, p. 48.

6. Ibid., p. 94.

7. Ibid., p. 81.

8. Interview with Eric Wollman, January 26, 1999.

9. Jane Kramer, "Manna from Hell," *New Yorker,* April 25 and May 5, 1997, p. 89.

10. The account of the meeting is based upon statements made at the meeting, May 19, 1997.

11. Alan Cowell, "Swiss Bank Reports Finding More in Wartime Accounts," *New York Times,* July 24, 1997.

12. James Barron, "War-Era Swiss Bank List Produces Mostly Rancor," *New York Times,* July 24, 1997.

13. Letter to the Honorable Edward Korman from Paul Volcker, July 24, 1997, p. 7.

14. Ibid., p. 8.

15. The account of the meeting is based upon observations of and conversations with several participants, July 25, 1997.

16. Letter to the Honorable Edward R. Korman from Burt Neuborne, Re: Holocaust Victim Assets, CV 96–4849, July 28, 1997, pp. 1, 2.

Chapter 8. The Hearing

1. The court discussion is based upon the Transcript of Civil Cause for Oral Argument before Judge Edward R. Korman, Brooklyn, New York, July 31, 1997.

2. This meeting is based upon the recollections of Neuborne, Hausfeld, and an unnamed source.

3. Memo to Plaintiffs' Executive Committee from Burt Neuborne, August 3, 1997.

Chapter 9. Stucki's Ghost

1. David Cay Johnston, "U.S. Aides Urge Easing of Holocaust Sanctions on Swiss Banks," *New York Times*, December 9, 1997.

2. "Eizenstat Asks States Not to Interfere with Nazi Gold," *Jerusalem Post*, December 9, 1997.

3. Based on author's interview with two Swiss attorneys who wished to remain unnamed, June 28, 1999.

4. The Zurich meeting is based upon Hausfeld's notes and interviews with a State Department official and two attorneys who wished to remain unnamed.

5. Based on author's interview with the two Swiss attorneys, June 28, 1999.

6. Anne Swardson, "Chastened Swiss Banks Search for Key to New Prosperity—and Respect," *Washington Post*, December 12, 1997.

7. Peter Nielsen, "UBS Chairman Has No Plans to Resign," Reuters, October 17, 1997.

8. Consent Order Section 39 in the Matter of Swiss Bank Corporation, Basle, Switzerland, and Swiss Bank Corporation, New York Branch, New York, New York, December 5, 1997.

9. News release, Fagan & Associates, October 25, 1997.

10. Marilyn Henry, "Holocaust Fund Becomes 'Franc Follies,'" *Jerusalem Post*, September 17, 1997.

11. Ibid.; Marcus Kabel, "Swiss Say Jewish Groups Hinder Holocaust Aid," Reuters, September 15, 1997.

12. Ed Stoddard, "Swiss Holocaust Fund Pays First Money to Latvian," Reuters, November 18, 1997.

13. Eric Jansson, "Holocaust Survivors Receive Checks," Associated Press, November 18, 1997.

14. Eric Jansson, "Swiss Banks Pay Jewish Survivors." Associated Press, November 17, 1997.

15. Jansson, "Holocaust Survivors Receive Checks."

Chapter 10. A Victims' Fund

1. Press release, Fagan & Associates, January 13, 1998.

2. Alan Morris Schom, "The Unwanted Guests: Swiss Forced Labor Camps 1940–1944," prepared for the Simon Wiesenthal Center, January 1998.

3. "Swiss Urge Jewish Critics to Renounce Camp Report," Reuters, March 4, 1998; "Jewish Group Rejects Swiss Request on Camp Report," Reuters, March 5, 1998.

4. Memo to Plaintiffs' Executive Committee from Hausfeld, January 23, 1998.

5. Press statement by Ambassador Stuart E. Eizenstat, Davos, Switzerland, January 30, 1998.

6. Letter to Eizenstat from Hausfeld, February 3, 1998.

7. Memo to Plaintiffs' Executive Committee from Hausfeld, February 10, 1998.

8. Letter to Eizenstat from Plaintiffs' Executive Committee, February 12, 1998.

9. This meeting is based on Hausfeld's notes and the recollections of two unnamed sources.

10. The Whittier Tapes, "The Fifteenth Annual International Law Symposium: Nazi Gold and Other Assets of the Holocaust," panel 3, "American Government Officials Speak," Whittier Law School, March 1, 1998.

11. Ibid., panel 5, "The Lawyers Speak."

12. Ibid.

Chapter 11. A Separate Peace

1. News release, California State Treasurer Matt Fong, March 12, 1998.

2. Interview with Michael Bradfield, November 25, 1998.

3. *Jewish Telegraphic Agency*, March 10, 1998.

4. Nikos Tzermias, "The Sensation Hunter," *Neue Zurcher Zeitung*, February 12, 1998.

5. Ibid.

6. Transcript of Civil Cause for Status Conference before Judge Edward R. Korman, Brooklyn, New York, March 20, 1998.

7. Based upon a memo from an observer at the meeting and Hausfeld's notes.

8. Telephone conversation with Burt Neuborne, March 5, 2001.

9. This meeting is based on observations of and conversations with several participants, March 25, 1998.

10. "U.S. Official Warns against Sanctions," Reuters, March 24, 1998.

11. David E. Sanger, "Swiss Banks Plan Restitution Fund for the Nazis' Victims," *New York Times*, March 27, 1998.

Chapter 12. Money Dance

1. Alan Cowell, "Swiss Seek to Narrow List of Holocaust Funds to Be Recovered," *New York Times*, March 31, 1998.

2. Ibid.

3. "Israeli Leader Rejects Holocaust Settlement Bid," Reuters, March 27, 1998.

4. "Holocaust Survivors Mark Remembrance Day in Zurich," Reuters, April 23, 1998.

5. Based on recollections of Hausfeld and Neuborne

6. Letter to the Honorable Edward R. Korman from Gizella Weisshaus, Re: Weisshaus vs. Union Bank of Switzerland, no. CV 96-4849, April 26, 1998.

7. Stefan Mächler, "Ein Abgrund zwischen zwei Welten. Zwei Rückweisungen jüdischer Flüchtlinge im Jahre 1942" (A Chasm between two worlds.

Two deportations of Jewish refugees in the year 1942), in *Die Schweiz und die Flüchtlinge, 1933–1945* (Switzerland and the refugees, 1933–1945), *Studien und Quellen 22,* edited by Schweizerisches Bundesarchiv (Bern, Stuttgart, Wien: Haupt, 1996), pp.137–232.

8. Ibid., p. 147.

9. Ibid., p. 153.

10. Ibid., p. 158.

11. Ibid., p. 161.

12. Ibid., p. 163.

13. Description of meeting based on Hausfeld's notes and the observations of two unnamed sources.

14. John Authers, William Hall, and Richard Wolffe, "Banks Pay a High Price for Putting the Past Behind Them," *Financial Times,* September 9, 1998.

15. Letter to Eizenstat from Hausfeld, June 1, 1998.

16. "UBS-SBC Merger Plan Wins New York Board's Backing," *Bloomberg Financial News,* June 4, 1998.

17. David E. Sanger, "Swiss Banks Said to Offer Holocaust Payment," *New York Times,* June 5, 1998.

Chapter 13. An Accounting

1. Stephen D. Moore, "Swiss Banks Move to Settle Holocaust Suit," *Wall Street Journal,* June 22, 1998.

2. Letter to the Honorable Edward R. Korman from Gizella Weisshaus, Re: Weisshaus vs. Union Bank of Switzerland, no. CV 96–4849, June 3, 1998.

3. "Swiss Bank Plaintiff Accuses Lawyer," *New York Times,* June 27, 1998.

4. "City Desk," *Forward,* June 26, 1998.

5. Letter to Eizenstat from Hausfeld, Weiss, and Singer, June 29, 1998.

6. Burt Neuborne, "Totaling the Sum of Swiss Guilt," *New York Times,* June 24, 1998.

7. Press conference at the office of Fagan & Associates, Wednesday, July 15, 1998.

8. Meeting based upon Hausfeld's notes and Neuborne's recollections and the observations of four unnamed sources.

9. Meeting based upon Hausfeld's notes, Neuborne's recollections, and the observations of three unnamed sources; Susan Orenstein, "Gold Warriors," p. 67; John Authers, William Hall, and Richard Wolffe, "Banks Pay a High Price for Putting the Past Behind Them."

10. Harold Glasser, Assistant Director of Monetary Research, to James Mann, U.S. Treasury Representative, American Consulate General, Zurich, Switzerland, May 28, 1945; Records of the Office of Alien Property; Foreign Funds Control Files, General Correspondence, Safehaven Project, Omgus, Record Group 131, Entry NN3-131-94-001, Box 389, National Archives at College Park, Maryland.

11. Department telegram, November 24, 1942; American Legation, Bern, Conf., 1940–1949; 1942: 840–892.43; Foreign Service Posts of the Department of State, Record Group 84, Box 7, National Archives at College Park, Maryland.

12. Frederick Weissmann to Randolf Paul, Head of Delegation for American-Swiss Negotiations, State Department, Washington, D.C., March 21, 1946; American Legation, Bern; Economic Section, Safehaven Name Files, 1942–1949; Foreign Service Posts of the Department of State, Record Group 84, Box 6, National Archives at College Park, Maryland.

Chapter 14. The Reckoning

1. Final negotiations based upon Hausfeld's notes, Neuborne's recollections, and the observations of several participants; Orenstein, "Gold Warriors," p. 67; Authers, Hall, and Wolffe, "Banks Pay a High Price for Putting the Past Behind Them."

2. Interview with a Swiss bank official, March 3, 1999.

Epilogue

1. Telephone interview with Greta Beer, May 30, 2002.

2. Summary of Special Master's Proposed Plan of Allocation and Distribution of Settlement Fund: In Re: Holocaust Victim Assets Litigation, no. CV 96–4849, September 11, 2000, p. 6 (hereafter Gribetz Summary).

3. Ibid., p. 20, citing Declaration of Burt Neuborne, November 5, 1999.

4. Memorandum & Order: In Re: Holocaust Victim Assets Litigation, no. CV 96–4849, Judge Edward R. Korman, July 26, 2000, pp. 6–7.

5. Ibid., p. 30.

6. Ibid.

7. Gribetz Summary, p. 29.

8. Stewart Ain, "At Last, Heirs Get Swiss Money," *Jewish Week*, February 1, 2001.

9. "Tribunal to Speed Swiss Bank Holocaust Claims," Reuters, June 10, 2002.

10. Telephone interview with Charles Sonabend, May 30, 2002.

11. Ain, "At Last, Heirs Get Swiss Money."

12. Sonabend interview.

For Further Reading

Articles and Documents

Bazyler, Michael J. "Nuremberg in America: Litigating the Holocaust in United States Courts." *University of Richmond Law Review,* March 2000.

Bilenker, Stephanie A. "In Re Holocaust Victims' Assets Litigation: Do the U.S. Courts Have Jurisdiction Over the Lawsuits Filed by Holocaust Survivors against the Swiss Banks?" *Maryland Journal of International Law and Trade,* fall 1997.

Eizenstat, Stuart E., "U.S. and Allied Efforts to Recover and Restore Gold and Other Assets Stolen or Hidden by Germany during World War II." May 1997.

Friedman Complaint: United States District Court for the Eastern District of New York. Civil action no. 96-5161.

Independent Committee of Eminent Persons: Chairman Paul A. Volcker. *Report on Dormant Accounts of Victims of Nazi Persecution in Swiss Banks.* December 1999.

Independent Commission of Experts: Chairman Jean-Francois Bergier. *Switzerland and Gold Transactions in the Second World War: Interim Report.* Bern, May 1998.

"Nazi Gold and Other Assets of the Holocaust: The Search for Justice." *Whittier Law Review,* fall 1998. Also the tapes from that conference, March 1, 1998.

Picard, Jacques. "Switzerland and the Assets of the Missing Victims of the Nazis." January 1993.

Slaughter, Anne-Marie, and David Bosco. "Plaintiff's Diplomacy." *Foreign Affairs,* September-October 2000.

Transcript of Civil Cause for Conference before Judge Edward R. Korman, Brooklyn, New York, February 28, 1997; May 1, 1997; July 31, 1997; March 20, 1998; August 12, 1998; November 29, 1999; November 20, 2000.

United States Senate Committee on Banking, Housing, and Urban Affairs, "Hearing on the Status of Assets Held in Swiss Banks by Jews and Others before and during World War II and the Holocaust." Washington, D.C., April 23, 1996; October 16, 1996; May 15, 1997.

Vagts, Detlev F. "Switzerland, International Law, and World War II." *American Journal of International Law,* July 1997.

Weisshaus Complaint: United States District Court for the Eastern District of New York. Civil action no. 96–4849.

Books

Aalders, Gerard, and Cees Wiebes. *The Art of Cloaking Ownership*. Amsterdam: Amsterdam University Press, 1996.

Authers, John, and Richard Wolffe. *The Victim's Fortune*. New York: HarperCollins, 2002.

Barkan, Elazar. *The Guilt Of Nations*. New York: W. W. Norton & Company, 2000.

Bower, Tom. *Nazi Gold*. New York: HarperCollins, 1997.

Halbrook, Stephen P. *Target Switzerland*. Rockville Centre, N.Y.: Sarpedon, 1998.

Higham, Charles. *Trading with the Enemy*. New York: Barnes & Noble Books, 1983.

Levin, Itamar. *The Last Deposit*. Westport, Conn.: Praeger, 1999.

Rickman, Gregg J. *Swiss Banks and Jewish Souls*. New Brunswick, N.J.: Transaction, 1999.

Schuck, Peter H. *Agent Orange on Trial*. Cambridge, Mass.: Belknap Press of Harvard University Press, 1986.

Simpson, Christopher. *The Splendid Blond Beast*. Monroe, Mont.: Common Courage Press, 1995.

Vincent, Isabel. *Hitler's Silent Partners*. New York: William Morrow, 1997.

Ziegler, Jean. *The Swiss, the Gold, and the Dead*. New York: Harcourt Brace, 1997.

Index

287